THE END OF THE COLD WAR

THE END
OF THE COLD
WAR

Edited by

David Armstrong and Erik Goldstein

FRANK CASS

First published in 1990 in Great Britain by
FRANK CASS & CO. LTD
Gainsborough House, Gainsborough Road,
London E11 1RS, England

and in the United States of America by
FRANK CASS
c/o International Specialized Book Services, Inc.
5602 N.E Hassalo Street, Portland, Oregon 97213

Copyright © 1990

British Library Cataloguing in Publication Data
The End of the Cold War.
1. Western bloc countries. Foreign relations with
communist countries, history
I. Armstrong, David *1945*– II. Goldstein, Erik
327.091713

ISBN 0–7146–3419–0

Printed in Great Britain by Antony Rowe Ltd, Chippenham

CONTENTS

A World Transformed?

DAVID ARMSTRONG
and ERIK GOLDSTEIN

Great historical turning points are seldom all they seem. The Peace of Westphalia in 1648 did not so much establish a new state system as confirm that the principles by which one part of Europe had long conducted its international relations were applicable to another part. Several events between 1783 and 1793 could advance at least a plausible claim to be considered the 'true' origin of the French Revolution. 1917 did not mark the beginning of the end for capitalism (indeed, viewed from 1990, it may simply have marked the end of the beginning). And the enunciation of the Truman Doctrine in 1947 did not 'begin' the cold war but rather it took to a new stage a confrontation that had been in the making since the October Revolution (or even earlier, as Richard Langhorne and Geoffrey Warner suggest here).

Similarly, historians, who will be granted hitherto undreamt of access to the archives of Eastern Europe, may well come to see the events of 1989–90 as less sudden and dramatic than they seemed to those watching them with awe from the secure sidelines of Western Europe. Yet it is difficult to resist the conclusion that Europe was fundamentally transformed – and transformed irreversibly – during those stirring months, and in the process the whole structure of East-West relations was profoundly altered. It is true, as Gerry Segal reminds us, that the two superpowers retain the capacity to destroy themselves and the rest of us several times over and although the atmosphere between them is more relaxed in some respects than it was even when they were wartime allies, their weapons are still pointed primarily at each other. It is also true that political instability and perceived power vacuums have seldom in the past proved conducive to international order, whereas the balance of terror was, at least in Europe. In addition, as Bennett Kovrig argues, the states of Eastern Europe may have won freedom but they have a long road to travel before they can hope to achieve the prosperity of their neighbours in the European Community, which, as Pierre Laurent suggests here, was one of the sources of inspiration for Eastern Europeans who could see with increasing clarity the failings of their own system. In particular, a great many animosities and national rivalries which had been kept on ice during the Soviet imperium have begun to re-emerge. Finally, the Soviet Union itself remains somewhat unpredictable. Beset by economic crises, breakaway nationalism and mounting popular discontent and with rumblings of disquiet from its powerful military establishment, it is still far from certain that it will make the steady, uninterrupted progress towards full membership of the Western political and economic order that many believe to be President Gorbachev's aim – indeed Gorbachev himself has assumed even greater powers in recent years and has yet to prove himself immune from Acton's *dictum* about the corrupting qualities of power. Moreover, as Uri Ra'anan reminds us, previous experience of the Soviet Union might lead us to expect merely another swing of the pendulum rather than movement in a single direction.

Hence, it may still all end in tears. Yet, even if Moscow decides that the process of perestroika should stop short of the point where the Soviet Union begins to disintegrate and in the course of implementing this decision begins to adopt a tougher negotiating stance with the West, even the most cautious – or cynical – observer is unlikely to conclude that nothing has changed. There are four principal grounds for arguing that those aspects of the structure of post-1945 international relations that are encapsulated in the phrase 'cold war' have definitively come to an end and that we are not simply in the midst of yet another false dawn. First, the ideological dimension of the superpower relationship, which distinguished it from most previous great power confrontations, has been reduced to insignificance. It was the perception on both sides that they were engaged in a struggle to the death between two fundamentally opposed politico-economic systems which made their conflict so all-embracing and so much of a zero-sum game, in which compromise was acceptable only as a temporary tactical expedient. Lenin depicted the relationship between Soviet cold war imparted to the Soviet-American relationship, there was little in international history to lead one to expect that two great powers were ever likely to be other than competitors and rivals. The underlying assumption of sovereign states was that since no superior authority existed to protect their interests, they had to do so themselves, primarily by accumulating sufficient military power to safeguard their security. Inevitably one state's additional security, if obtained by such means, was seen as an increase in its rivals' insecurity, with mutual suspicion, arms races and a continual struggle for advantage the predictable outcome. Well before Gorbachev's accession the destructive potential of nuclear weapons had forced upon the superpowers an obligation to find ways of preventing this traditional pattern of international relations from ending in its traditional result: war. In the process they had already developed numerous rules and conventions that added up to a unique 'adverse partnership'.[3] But recent years have seen the prospect emerge of more than this marginal modification of the rules of the game, which was limited to imposing such constraints upon superpower competition as were neccessary to avoid Armageddon.

Soviet 'new thinking' on international relations has continually reiterated certain key themes which amount to a call for the game to be played by new rules – and ultimately to be replaced by a different game altogether. While there is doubtless a purely rhetorical aspect to all this, as when any statesmen wax lyrical about the prospects for peace and harmony in the world, in most cases the Soviets have accompanied their words with constructive actions. Moreover, their new approach conincides with an acceleration of the integration process inside the European Community, with Washington anxious to encourage and be associated with both developments.

Six aspects of Soviet 'new thinking' are particularly significant in the context of the possible emergence of a restructured international system based upon new premises and assumptions. The first is an attempt to shift away from an essentially competitive conception of 'national security', which constantly sought a margin of military strength over the US towards a notion of military 'sufficiency' for the Soviet Union within an overall context of the pursuit of 'international security' in collaboration with the United States and others. As Gorbachev put it in 1986:

Security, if we are talking about relations between the USSR and the US, can only be mutual, and, if we take international relations as a whole, it can only be universal. The highest wisdom is not to be concerned exclusively for oneself, especially when this is to the detriment of the other side. It is necessary that everyone feels equally secure, since the fears and anxieties of the nuclear age give rise to unpredictability in policies and concrete actions.[4]

Secondly, Gorbachev has placed very strong emphasis upon the necessity of seeking political solutions to East – West problems (and internal Soviet difficulties) rather than attempting to resolve them through the use of force. His adherence to this principle has been severely tested, first in the Soviet withdrawal from Afganistan (which was not followed by the widely predicted collapse of the Soviet backed regime in Kabul), then in Moscow's response to the Eastern European revolutions and breakaway nationalism amongst the Soviet republics. Even in the last case there had only been marginal deviations from this principle by mid-1990.

Thirdly, Gorbachev in particular has moved a considerable distance from orthodox Soviet analysis of international relations in terms of 'class struggle' and 'contradictions' to depicting the world as an interdependent 'single organism' in which 'universal human interests' are discernible which require 'fundamentally new machinery', especially in respect of environmental and economic problems.[5] Global problems which endanger 'the very foundations of the existence of civilization' needed 'cooperation on a worldwide scale – the close constructive interaction of the majority of countries'.[6]

A fourth aspect of 'new thinking' concerned the proper relationship between foreign and domestic policy. In the aristocratic Europe of the eighteenth century it was generally assumed that foreign policy requirements had primacy over domestic policy. Indeed, opposition to this doctrine was one element in the revolutionary ideologies of both France and America.[7] Similarly, the absence of any genuinely democratic constraints on Soviet policy making had led to heavy financial and economic sacrifices being made in pursuit of foreign policy objectives that were designed to sustain the Soviet Union's superpower status. However, under Gorbachev a different set of priorities began to emerge. Nowhere was this more clearly stated than by foreign minister Edward Shevardnadze in 1987. After criticising previous commitments of 'enormous material investment in hopeless foreign policy projects' he argued that:

> The main thing is that the country not incur additional expenses in connection with the need to maintain defensive capability and protect its lawful foreign policy interests. This means that we must seek ways to limit and reduce military rivalry, eliminate confrontational features in relation with other states and suppress conflict and crisis situations.[8]

On another occasion he explicitly stated that '. . . the most important function of our foreign policy is to create the optimal conditions for the economic and social development of our country'.[9]

Two additional facets of 'new thinking' are interrelated: Gorbachev's image of a 'common European home' and his call for an enhanced role for the United Nations. In both cases Gorbachev is implying that the Soviet Union should pursue its foreign policy goals within the context of and under the constraints imposed by its relationship to the region of which it is part and its membership of the United Nations. This is a considerable step away from the orthodox Soviet position, reiterated in different forms since Lenin, that only relations based on peaceful coexistence rather than any true community of interest were possible between the socialist and capitalist worlds. In a 1988 speech to the UN, Gorbachev stated:

> Our ideal is a world community of States which are based on the rule of law and which subordinate their foreign policy activities to law. The achievement of that goal would be facilitated by an agreement within the United Nations on a uniform understanding of the principles and norms of international law, their codification with due regard to new conditions and the development of legal norms for new areas of cooperation.[10]

Alan James in this volume provides some detail of how the Soviets have accompanied their words by actions in the UN, and also urges caution, if not scepticism in appraising prospects for far-reaching changes in international society, as against a more limited shift from the ideological rooted antagonisms of the cold war. Indeed, the possibility that the world may return to more 'traditional' rivalries and alignments is also suggested by the re-emergence of long buried animosities among the states of Eastern Europe and the Balkans.

It was Bismark who once said that if the European equilibrium was to be disrupted it would be over some damn fool question concerning the Balkans. Yet another World War over the Balkans seems unlikely but this region still has the potential to disturb European stability. The frontiers of Eastern Europe are mostly the result of a frenetic effort by overworked technocrats at the 1919 Paris Peace Conference to establish some sort of framework with which to fill the vacuum created by the fall of the great dynastic empires. Modifications to these frontiers were later imposed by the Soviet Union in the aftermath of the Second World War, and it was the lid imposed by the Soviet Union which forcibly contained the ethno-territorial claims and counter-claims of a region once rightly nicknamed the power-keg of Europe. The sudden removal of this Soviet constraint has again raised the possibility of upheaval, and the imposed concept of fraternal alliance through the Warsaw Pact and Comecon can now be replaced by more familiar historical animosities.

Yugoslavia, no longer united by a possible Soviet threat, seems even more than usual on the verge of disintegration, yet it was only in 1914 that the world went to war over an event caused by the desire for Yugoslav unification. Both Romania and Hungary have both publicly thrown off their communist pasts, but neither has discarded their long ethnic struggle. After all the Romanian revolution began at Timosara (or Temesvar, a traditional diplomatic flashpoint in previous centuries) over the oppression of the Hungarian population by the Romanian authorities. The question of Transylvania and the rights of the ethnic Hungarians will continue to doom Romania and Hungary to decades of fraught relations. Likewise, the future of the Moldavian SSR, better known as Bessarabia, will eventually pose problems for Soviet–Romanian relations. Bessarabia is a traditional geographic ping-pong ball, and in this century has only switched sovereignty four times. Admittedly there is no rush in the Moldavian SSR to join post-Ceausescu Romania, but the clear desire for ethnic reunification is there.

The growing nationalist discontent within the Soviet Union itself not only poses problems for the future of that country, but also raises questions about regional stability. The conflict between Armenia and

Azerbaijan over Nagorno-Karabakh has already shown the potential for national strife between the components of the Soviet Union. The demands of several of the union republics for full independence cast up the probability of even greater regional instability. The testing ground for independence seems to lie in the old Baltic republics, with Lithuania leading the way. These states' claims enjoy general sympathy in the West, which has never acknowledged *de jure* their annexation, but the practicalities of independence are full of danger. The frontiers in this area are quite different from when Baltic independence was snuffed out in 1939. Lithuanian independence would cut off the Kaliningrad (Konigsberg) area from the remainder of the Soviet Union. This little colonial outlyer, ethnically Russian in composition, would therefore be isolated. Historical experience has frequently shown that such separated territories lead to conflict. Indeed, only one such very obscure territorial pocket has survived in Europe without causing crisis (the Belgian Baarle-Hertog enclave inside the Netherlands).

Any changes to the Soviet Union's western frontiers therefore involve an almost endless variety of complexities. Poland could reassert claims to at least some of the territory lost in 1939 under the Molotov-Ribbenthrop pact, which has been condemned by the Soviet Congress of People's Deputies. Russo-Polish antagonism is after all very much the historic norm. Poland and Lithuania, who enjoy a long interwoven history, could also clash. The young Lithuania Republic in 1919 established its capital at Wilno, (Vilnius, Vilna, Wilna), only to have the area snatched by the Polish army in 1920, and returned again to Lithuania by the Soviet Union in 1939. The growing Ukranian independence movement not only threatens the breadbasket of the Soviet Union but its success would mark the collapse of the Soviet imperium. This would throw all the frontiers of eastern Europe into flux. All this indicates that the frontiers of the common European home envisaged by Mikhail Gorbachev are far from stable, and it should not be forgotten that Europe in the 20th Century has seen more frontier changes than any other part of the world. It was the American secretary of state, Henry Kissinger, who early on identified the critical nature of Europe's frontiers. He recognised, perhaps from his early studies on the Congress of Vienna, that stable frontiers were the best guarantor of a stable polity. The result of such thinking was the 1975 Helsinki Final Act, but it must not be forgotten that this only accepted the *de facto* face of Europe and left open the future *de jure* political shape of the continent.

The question of what sort of world is likely to emerge from the end of the cold war is one that perplexes the policymakers. Such upheavals usually do. The danger in this period of transition from the cold war and the retreat from empire of the Soviet Union is that the Eastern European territorial framework is tenuous at best. There is the risk that a situation similar to 1919 could again arise, and that a hurried solution would have to be concocted, with all the dangers inherent in that. Politicians and diplomats will certainly try to play for time to create the space needed to work through a settlement, but events often outpace the designs of governments – particularly where long suppressed national aspirations are at work.

Germany is also a concept which retains dramatic possibilities in the post-*perestroika* world. The idea of Germany has more often than not been divorced from the political reality. For over a century the German question has dominated Europe, and it was the Soviet acquisition of a European buffer zone to protect itself from a recurrent German threat that marked the period known as the cold war. The ending of the cold war has however not resolved the German problem. Mrs Thatcher has drawn attention to the difference between German unification and reunification, and this mirrors the old *kleindeutscher* and *grossdeutscher* solution for Germany. Any moves towards a Great Germany solution have serious implications for Germany's neighbours, and in particular Poland. The Western powers have never accepted *de jure* the territorial changes in eastern Europe after the Second World War, although it was understood that Polish gains were in compensation for Soviet acquisitions in eastern Poland.

The future alignment of Europe will be very much determined by the shape of German unification. European states have always configured themselves in relation to the single most powerful country, be that the empire of Charles V, the France of Louis XIV and Napoleon, of post-1871 Germany. Those European states with a free choice after the Second World War, having identified the Soviet Union as the single most powerful and threatening European country, grouped themselves into a defensive alliance and strengthened it by bringing the United States into the European system (through the euphemism of 'atlanticism'). The reduction of the Soviet threat, occurring simultaneously with a significant upsurge in German power is also certain to generate some form of realignment of states. Europe is certainly not immune to diplomatic revolutions, when previously unbelievable combinations become reality. Nevertheless, Europe is still fundamentally dominated by the same Great Powers as it has been for 200 years or more. France, Germany, Great Britain, Italy, and Russia, with the United States now added as a sort of honorary European power. There is some suggestion that what the international system is reverting to is a state of multipolarity after the somewhat forced bipolarity engendered by the Second World War. This suggests the ghost of the Concert of Europe, though the concert did not have to consider the existence of many smaller nation-states. It should be noted however that the United States has no experience of the concert method of diplomacy, having moved directly from the hemispheric isolation of the Monroe Doctrine to its post-war role as the dominant member of the international system. One reason for the failure of *détente* was the American decision to maintain a clear superiority of power over Moscow, implicitly treating Moscow not as an equal but rather as a junior superpower.

What is certain is that the geopolitics of Europe have changed irreversibly. The Second World War created a situation whereby within a bi-polar world lay a divided Europe, within which in turn was a divided Germany, at the centre of which was a divided Berlin. Nothing more powerfully symbolised the ending of the cold war than the breaching of the Berlin Wall on 9–10 November 1989. This symbolic reunification of Berlin has sent vibrations through the entire divisive post-war structure of international relations. In a sort of reverse polarity the key word is now 'unification' and not 'division'. A unified Berlin will lead to a unified Germany, while in turn momentum gathers for a united Europe. The only safe conclusion between the optimistic scenario of Gorbachev's 'new thinking' and the pessimism induced by any cold consideration of Europe's past is that the future is far from clear. The lessons of the past provide at least a key to some of the potential problems to be faced by the post-cold war world, but in a world transformed there can be no certainties.

Graduate School of International Studies,
University of Birmingham

NOTES

1. F. Fukuyama, 'The End of History', *The National Interest*, Summer 1989, pp. 3–18.
2. *The Guardian*, 8 May 1990, p. 1.
3. A term coined by Coral Bell. See her *Conventions of Crisis*, London 1971.
4. Cited in Paul Marantz, *From Lenin to Gorbachev: Changing Soviet Perspectives on East-West Relations*, Occasional Papers of the Canadian Institute for International Peace and Security, May 1988, p. 63. I have benefitted from several discussions with Professor Marantz on Soviet 'new thinking'.
5. See in particular Gorbachev's speech to the UN General Assembly, 7 December 1988, UNGA, A/43/PV.72.
6. Cited in P. Marantz op. cit. p. 64.
7. See David Armstrong, *Revolution and World Order: the Revolutionary State in International Society*, (to be published by Oxford University Press).
8. Cited in Paul Marantz, *The Gorbachev Revolution: Emerging Trends in Soviet Foreign Policy*, Paper for Annual Meeting of the International Society of Political Psychology, Tel Aviv, 20 June 1988, p. 8.
9. Ibid.
10. Speech to the General Assembly, op. cit., pp. 22–3.

The Study of Cold War Origins

GEOFFREY WARNER

The cold war may be over, but the contents of publishers' catalogues and academic journals show no sign of any diminution in scholarly concern with its origins and history. The purpose of this article is to examine cold war origins in the light of some recent work and to suggest some guidelines for future study.

An obvious question with which to start is: when did the cold war begin? There is no simple answer. When members of the Open University's course team preparing course U235 ('Nuclear weapons: inquiry, analysis and debate') visited the Soviet Union in 1984, they found that the Russian historians and analysts to whom they spoke were unanimous in maintaining that the cold war began with the Bolshevik Revolution in November 1917, for this was when the capitalist world began its systematic opposition to and effort to undermine the world's first socialist state and society. Indeed, for them, the cold war became 'hot' between 1918 and 1922, the period of allied intervention in the Russian civil war.

The ideological component of the cold war is of course highlighted by dating its commencement from 1917. Others have adopted an even longer geopolitical perspective. The late Geoffrey Barraclough, for example, suggested in a brilliant essay published in 1964 that one has to go back to events in the Far East at the turn of the century in order to locate the origins of the cold war. During the previous hundred years, he argued, Russia and the United States had tended to support each other against England; but 'now, as England's power passed its zenith, they came face to face across the Pacific. Thus began a conflict of interests which was eventually to spread to Europe, to south-east Asia and to the Middle East, until in the end it divided the world into two hostile camps. What today we too easily simplify as an ideological conflict – the so-called 'cold war' – had its origins in the new power constellation which began to take shape at the beginning of the twentieth century.'[1]

Donald Cameron Watt is impatient with those who would date the cold war from 1917. '. . . To apply the term "Cold War" to the whole history of Soviet relations with the capitalist powers since 1917', he wrote in an important article in 1978, 'is to destroy any value that may lie in the concept and render it urgently necessary to devise another to cover the period since 1945.'[2] Watt thereby identified himself with the general consensus among western historians: viz., that the cold war is a post-World War II phenomenon, beginning at some point between 1945 and 1947. Watt, it should be noted, was not denying that the *origins* of the cold war might be sought in 1917, or even earlier for that matter, but merely that it was unhelpful to pretend that it *began* before 1945. Moreover, he warned, 'origin hunting is a pastime which carries its own set of inherent vices and losing a sense of historical proportion is notoriously one of them'. He suggested that historians should 'draw a distinction between more distant and more immediate origins', offering as his own assessment of the latter 'the events of the summer of 1943, the Soviet breach with the London Poles, the Soviet exclusion from the Italian armistice, the Soviet establishment of a Free German movement, the German–Soviet peace feelers, [and] the failure of the British venture in the Aegean . . .'.[3]

Nevertheless, it would be a great mistake to try and write a history of the cold war which began in 1945, or even in the summer of 1943. As far as its 'more immediate origins' are concerned, the recent study of Steven Merritt Miner has rightly emphasised the importance of the negotiations leading up to the signature of the Anglo–Soviet treaty of May 1942 as a foretaste of the difficulties which the anti-German alliance was to encounter later in the war,[4] and since these negotiations were so difficult in part because of the Russians' determination to hang on to the gains they had achieved as a result of the Nazi–Soviet Pact of August 1939,[5] perhaps one should begin the story there.

At the same time, it would be equally misleading to ignore the longer perspective. The fact that American–Russian rivalry in Manchuria at the turn of the century – and Anglo–Russian rivalry in Persia for that matter – was to recur in the aftermath of the second world war is surely not without significance. Similarly, the mutual hostility and suspicion which characterized relations between the Soviet Union and the capitalist world between 1917 and 1941 need to be stressed, if only because an awareness of them will guard against any tendency on the part of readers to regard the 'grand alliance' of World War II as a norm from which post-1945 developments were to deviate. Even if we accept that the cold war itself began between 1945 and 1947, any proper history of it must begin much earlier.

The answer to the question of where the cold war began is no more obvious than that to the question of when. At a seminar run by the Institute of Contemporary British History on 'The Origins of the Cold War' held in the summer of 1989, the panel adopted an entirely Eurocentric view: as far as they were concerned, the cold war began in Eastern Europe and Germany. There is, of course, much to be said for this point of view. The fate of Poland, in particular, was a matter of keen dispute between the Soviet Union and its western allies from the outset of their joint involvement in World War II, while the future of Germany was seen by everyone as crucial to post-war stability. Nevertheless, despite rhetorical flourishes to the contrary, Soviet hegemony in Eastern Europe was in effect conceded by the western powers during the course of 1945, and, as we shall see, the conflict over Germany did not crystallize until the middle of 1946.

On the other hand, one might well obtain the impression from the work of Bruce Kuniholm that the cold war began in the eastern Mediterranean and the middle east, or, to quote from the subtitle of his book, 'in Iran, Turkey, and Greece'.[6] Whether one adopts the view that the great shift in American policy towards the Soviet Union took place at the beginning of 1946[7] or one year later[8], there is no doubt that conflicts over the eastern Mediterranean and the middle east (Turkey and Iran and Greece respectively) played a crucial part. Kuniholm, too, is one of the few scholars who draws attention to the influence that the captured German foreign office documents, with their revelation of Soviet attempts as early as November 1940 to gain control of the Turkish Straits and to secure a sphere of influence in 'the area south of Batum and Baku in the general direction of the Persian Gulf', may have had upon American perceptions of post-war Russian objectives.[9]

At the same time, Marc Gallichio rightly draws our attention in a recent study to the importance of far eastern issues in the origins of the cold war.[10] The struggle for the control of China between Mao Tse-tung's Chinese communist party and Chiang Kai-shek's *Kuomintang*, which broke out anew as soon as the war in the Pacific was over, was a proxy conflict between the Soviet Union and the United States as well as a civil war,[11] while Russia's resentment at its exclusion from any effective role in the control of defeated Japan may have been the principal cause of the first open breakdown of the wartime alliance at the London conference of foreign ministers in September 1945.[12]

If any one lesson is to be drawn from these various studies, it is that any study of cold war origins which confines itself to a particular region is bound to be incomplete. The cold war was a global phenomenon. Thanks to the destruction of German and Japanese power as a result of World War II, 1945 saw the emergence of an essentially bipolar world, in which the United States and the Soviet Union confronted one another more or less right around the Eurasian land mass, from the Bering and La Pérouse Straits in the northern Pacific, through the Korean peninsula (arbitrarily divided at the 38th parallel), across China, in Iran, Turkey and the mountains of northern Greece, and across the middle of Europe, from Trieste in the south to Lübeck, or even Kirkenes, in the north. It follows that any history of the cold war must take this reality into account.

Both Kuniholm's and Gallichio's books deal essentially with American policy and are based upon research in American archives. The article by Donald Cameron Watt cited above was couched in the form of a plea to British historians to plunder the newly available British archives in order to break what Watt saw as the hitherto almost complete American monopoly of the study of cold war origins. Apart from the fresh perspectives he felt sure they would discover in the Public Record Office, Watt hoped that the historians he was addressing would break away from what he called the 'essentially unhistorical' nature of the American debate about who was responsible for the cold war.[13]

Watt's plea has undoubtedly been heeded. There has been a proliferation of work, both published and unpublished, examining the origins of the cold war on the basis of the British documents. However, one cannot help wondering whether it has not merely replaced the Americanocentrism he so strongly criticised by an Anglocentrism which is even less justified given the relative power of the two countries in 1945.

The strengths and weaknesses of what may be called the new British school of cold war historians are highlighted in the recently published proceedings of a conference held at King's College, London, in the spring of 1988. The contributors are, for the most part, young teachers and graduate students in institutions of higher education in this country and their essays are based on recent research into the British archives.[14] A principal theme of the book, in the words of its editor Anne Deighton, is that 'a drive to sustain Britain's own world role and to contain Soviet power underscored British policy even before the declaration and implementation of containment by successive United States' governments. In short, the protection of a favourable balance of power and the containment of the Soviet Union were initially British phenomena.'[15]

Deighton herself is a specialist on the German problem and her full-length book on the division of that country is eagerly awaited by all students of the period.[16] In her essay in this book, she maintains that while 'it has often been argued that, for two years after the war ended, Britain genuinely sought to achieve agreement to control Germany within the framework of the 1945 Potsdam Protocol, and that only by the end of 1947 . . . did Foreign Secretary Ernest Bevin and his senior officials regretfully conclude that four-power cooperation would not be possible because of Soviet intransigeance', the documentation in the archives suggests that, on the contrary, 'by mid 1946, a consensus was reached that effective cooperation with the Soviet Union over Germany would only be possible on British terms, and further, that such cooperation was unlikely, and maybe even unwanted, because of Britain's own strategic interests in Europe'.[17]

No one will fault Deighton's analysis of the way in which the British government and bureaucracy reached the consensus to which she refers – her account of the interplay between Bevin and his officials is particularly useful – but is her contention, both here and elsewhere,[18] that Britain took the lead in promoting the division of Germany, correct? Granted that American policy often seemed confused and contradictory, it was nevertheless the case that a consensus in favour of consolidating the western zones of occupation was developing independently inside the United States administration at much the same time and for much the same reasons as that in Britain.

Deighton cites a cabinet paper of 3 May 1946 to the effect that the Americans were 'not yet ready for a "western" [German] policy', which would certainly be bitterly opposed by their military commander in Germany, General Lucius D. Clay.[19] While the British may have been right about Clay, things were perceived rather differently in the State Department. Thus, James Riddleberger, the head of the central European division of the State Department, which was responsible for German affairs, was arguing as early as 28 March 1946 that, while it was 'both necessary and urgent' to set up central German agencies, he was convinced that the Russians would only allow them to function in their zone of occupation to the extent that they believed they could be used for their own purposes, and that any central government machinery must therefore be constructed in such a way that it could 'eventually be utilized in the western zones alone if it becomes apparent that four-power cooperation in the occupation of Germany has broken down'.[20]

By 10 June Riddleberger was proposing to Secretary of State, James Byrnes, that the United States should in effect table an ultimatum at the Paris meeting of the council of foreign ministers (then in temporary recess) calling for the establishment of a provisional central government based upon the principle of decentralization consistently favoured by the United States. 'Should we fail', wrote Riddleberger, 'we shall perhaps have no practical choice other than giving up, at least temporarily, any serious hope of restoring the unity of Germany', in which case 'the least bad program . . . would be an attempt to organize the three western zones into some kind of economic, and later some kind of political, entity.'[21]

Byrnes did not table Riddleberger's proposal for a central government, but since he had already disclosed to a journalist 'that he had almost given up hope for a united Germany' and had begun to think that the three western zones could become a viable unit, it is not surprising that when he became exasperated in Paris by what he saw as Russian obstructionism, he adopted Riddleberger's *pis aller* and told the council of foreign ministers on 11 July that, pending four-power agreement on the treatment of Germany as an economic unit, 'the United States will join with any other occupying government or governments in Germany for the treatment of our respective zones as an economic unit'[22], an invitation which, as Riddleberger had predicted, was welcomed by the British and eventually led to the formation of the 'Bizone', the nucleus of the future Federal Republic of (West) Germany. In the circumstances, it is misleading to suggest, as John Gimbel has done for example, that Byrnes' 11 July proposal was prompted in anything other than a tactical sense by Bevin's announcement on the previous day that, since there was no agreement under the terms of the Potsdam Protocol on the treatment of Germany as an economic unit, Britain would be compelled to go it alone in its zone in order to protect the British taxpayer.[23]

Interestingly enough, at least one eminent Soviet figure had reached the conclusion that the division of Germany was inevitable at about the same time as the British and the Americans. This was the former people's Commissar for Foreign Affairs, Maxim Litvinov. He told the CBS correspondent, Richard Hottelet, on 18 June 1946 that the country 'would obviously be broken up into two parts', since neither the Soviet Union nor the west would be prepared to accept a united Germany which was not under its control.[24] His assessment of Russian policy was not dissimilar to that of Byrnes, Riddleberger, Bevin, or the British Foreign Office.

In another recent symposium John Kent developed a challenging thesis to the effect that it is a gross distortion to view British foreign policy in the immediate post-war period as dominated by cold war considerations and, in particular, by an attempt to enlist American support to dam the Soviet tide in Europe. Rather than giving up its world role to act as a 'brilliant second' to the United States, Kent argued, Bevin sought to build Britain up as an independent 'third force' in the world based upon its leadership of a bloc of colonial powers.[25] In the present volume, however, Kent shifts his focus in an attempt to assess the extent to which this policy influenced the development of the cold war. In her introduction, his editor claims that 'the effect of this policy was in fact to draw the superpowers into conflict' – another example of Britain precipitating the cold war.[26] Kent's own conclusion, however, is more nuanced. He does not affirm, he writes, that Britain's efforts to preserve its power position in the Mediterranean and the middle east 'were solely responsible for the breakdown of Allied cooperation, or that they were a major influence on American policy; but a study of Bevin's imperialism does suggest that his policies could only lead to cold war confrontation and were therefore more a cause of Allied disagreements than a response to them'.[27] Certainly, no one reading either Kuniholm or the work of other American historians like Melvyn Leffler could possibly argue that the United States was in any way manoeuvered into an anti-Soviet stance in the middle east by the British.[28] It is, of course, undeniable that the British government's note of 21 February 1947 led to the formulation of the Truman Doctrine, but Robert Frazier has shown conclusively that the British government had no such grandiose hopes in mind. Moreover, we also know that President Truman had been looking for an excuse to take such a stand since the beginning of the year.[29] As in the case of Byrnes' initiative on Germany, British actions were the occasion rather than the cause of American pronouncements.

If Anne Deighton argues in her essay on Germany that Britain took a tougher line towards the Soviet Union in advance of the United States and drew the latter along in its wake, Louise L'Estrange Fawcett, in her essay on the equally significant country of Iran, takes the view that the United States confrontation with the Soviet Union was in large part the consequence of growing American concern with British incompetence and pusillanimity in dealing with the threat posed by the Russians. If moves towards the partition of Germany were the mark of a strong British line there, they were the sign of a weak British policy in Iran. Britain's 'repeated willingness to sacrifice its [Iran's] independence', concludes Fawcett, 'had been a major factor in drawing the United States into conflict with the USSR'.[30]

It is true that in Iran, as later in Indochina, successive US administrations regarded European imperialism as an ineffective barrier against communism and were convinced that their 'disinterested' help would achieve much greater success. But the important thing to remember is that the anti-communism was not the result of the anti-imperialism; it was an independent variable. Where is the evidence to suggest that, if the British had not been involved in Iran, the United States would have been any the less concerned about its possible absorbtion into the Soviet sphere of influence? American anxieties about post-war oil supplies and Russia's secular tendency to expand into Iran would almost certainly have led to a clash of interests between the two superpowers in that country after 1945, regardless of any British presence in the area, let alone the existence of ideological rivalry and Russo–American tension in other parts of the world.

These comments should not be construed in such a way as to undermine the value of the research contained in this book. All the essays are absorbing and the collection as a whole adds a great deal to our knowledge of the subject. Apart from those already cited, Alan Foster's on 'The British Press and the Coming of the Cold War' and Sheila Kerr's on 'The Secret Hotline to Moscow: Donald Maclean and the Berlin Crisis of 1948' are particularly interesting.[31] Foster shows how both *The Times* and the *Daily Express*, much to the irritation of the Foreign Office, were as inclined to appease the Soviet Union in the immediate post-war period as they had been to appease Nazi Germany before 1939, and basically for the same reason; viz, that Eastern Europe was not of vital importance to Britain. Kerr provides a fascinating preview of her forthcoming study of Donald Maclean. Her painstaking identification of the documents which passed through Maclean's hands and the contents of which he could therefore presumably have passed on to his masters in the Kremlin is in sharp contrast to the overblown and often undocumented assertions contained in much of the literature on this subject. As Kerr concedes, however, the problem remains that 'little is known about how the Soviets used the information they collected from their secret sources or what role their intelligence agencies played in the formulation of foreign policy . . .'.[32]

Nevertheless, while the contributors to this symposium would no doubt deny that their aim, individually or collectively, was to shift the responsibility for the cold war from the United States (or the Soviet Union) on to Britain, that is the impression with which the reader is often left. As long as the latter remembers to treat it as a contribution to an eventual synthesis and not as anything approaching the synthesis itself, no harm will be done and much profit gained. Indeed, all students of the period should endeavour to read it, and it is only to be regretted that the publisher has put it out of the reach of undergraduates by not issuing it in paperback and by pricing the hardback on the assumption that Croesus is in charge of university library budgets.

If work on the British role in the origins of the cold war is flourishing, the same, alas, cannot be said of the Russian role. In large part, of course, this is due to the non-availability of the relevant archives. Indeed, we are still waiting for the publication of the final volume (XXII) of the inter-war series of *Dokumenty Vneshnei Politiki SSSR*, 13 years after the appearance of Volume XXI. The fact that it will have to deal, among other things, with the Nazi–Soviet Pact probably has something to do with the delay. Still, it is encouraging to see the recent Russian acknowledgement of the existence of the notorious secret protocols to the said pact as well as of MVD responsibility for the equally notorious Katyn massacre of Polish officers.[33] Progressive and piecemeal revelations of this kind are probably more likely over the next few years than any large-scale opening or publication of the archives themselves, although more may be forthcoming from the ex-communist states of Eastern Europe.

In the meantime, the scholar has to make do with existing Russian material. This is perhaps more useful than many people realise. Thus, in addition to the two volumes of correspondence between Stalin, Attlee, Roosevelt and Truman, which was recently reprinted,[34] the Russians have published a collection of their records of the wartime conferences at Moscow, Teheran, Dumbarton Oaks, Yalta, San Francisco and Potsdam[35] as well as two volumes each on Soviet–American, Soviet–British and Soviet–French relations between 1941 and 1945.[36] It would be misleading to suggest that these publications are without blemish. The Teheran Conference volume, for example, carefully omits Stalin's statements in favour of the dismemberment of Germany, while the reader will search the appropriate volume on Soviet–British relations in vain for the Russian records of the conversations which produced the so-called 'percentages agreement' in October 1944.

At the same time, it would be equally mistaken to sell them short. If the documentation published by the Russians is incomplete, there is no evidence to suggest that what has been made available is falsified. In some cases it provides the only record of a conversation we have, for example that between Litvinov and President Roosevelt on March 12 1942 and between Stalin and President Truman on July 17 1945.[37]

Soviet secondary sources also provide useful information, although western historians all too frequently ignore them. It is odd, for example, to find a former British Foreign Office official and Asian specialist writing in a recent book on Soviet policy towards south-east Asia that the Vietnamese communist leader, Ho Chi Minh, did not visit the Soviet Union until the mid-1950's, when a Russian history of Soviet–Vietnamese relations published as long ago as 1975 revealed that Ho 'found himself' in Moscow in December 1949 'where there took place an exchange of views on many questions relating to the revolution in Indochina and the international situation'.[38] What is particularly significant about the timing of this visit is, of course, that it coincided with that of the Chines communist leader, Mao Tse-tung. Since the emergence of the Sino–Soviet rift in the 1960s, it has become customary to dwell on the tensions between China and the Soviet Union which were no doubt present during the Stalin–Mao conversations. But the two communist states also had interests in common and these included support for Ho Chi Minh's war in Indochina. It was certainly true that both the Chinese People's Republic and the Soviet Union recognised Ho's Democratic Republic of Vietnam early in 1950 and that the latter's army, with Chinese backing, launched a major assault upon the French later in the same year.

'Kremlinological' studies of Soviet foreign policy can also yield some positive results, although it is disconcerting when two accounts of the power struggle between Zhdanov and Malenkov in the post-war years reach diametrically opposed conclusion about the position of the former: one labelling him a 'moderate' in foreign affairs and the other a 'hardliner'.[39] In the circumstances, it is not hard to see why wading through page after tedious page of *Pravda*, *Izvestia*, etc, has so little attraction for western scholars in comparison with the lure of once 'top secret' documents in their countries' archives.

These archives themselves, of course, often contain valuable information on Soviet foreign policy. Given the importance of Italy in the early stages of the cold war – the country was, after all, the subject of the first policy papers of the newly formed US National Security Council in 1947/48 – it is strange that so little attention has been paid by historians to the pathbreaking study of Italo–Soviet relations between 1944 and 1948 by Roberto Morozzo della Rocca.[40] On the basis of the Italian archives, Morozzo della Rocca shows how early and how completely the Soviet Union abandoned Italy, despite its powerful communist party, to the American sphere of influence. An important Italian communist party source confirms Soviet reluctance to countenance any insurrectionist tendency on the part of the former at precisely the moment when the Americans were becoming increasingly exercised by the possibility.[41]

Whatever the problems of studying and explaining Soviet foreign policy, there can be no justification for the comparative neglect of the Soviet perspective in most literature on the origins of the cold war. If, like Donald Cameron Watt twelve years ago, I were to offer advice to the British scholar interested in the cold war, it would be quite simple: learn Russian and help to fill the gap.

Graduate School of International Studies,
University of Birmingham

NOTES

1. Geoffrey Barraclough, *An Introduction to Contemporary History*, London, C.A. Watts, 1964, pp. 102–05.
2. Donald Cameron Watt, 'Rethinking the Cold War: A Letter to a British Historian', *Political Quarterly*, Volume 49, No. 4, Oct.–Dec. 1978, p. 451.
3. Ibid., p. 452.
4. Steven Merritt Miner, *Between Churchill and Stalin: The Soviet Union Great Britain, and the Origins of the Grand Alliance*, Chapel Hill, University of North Carolina Press, 1988.
5. Another important factor, of course, was the timing of the 'second front'.
6. Bruce Kuniholm, *The Origins of the Cold War in the Near East: Great Power Conflict and Diplomacy in Iran, Turkey, and Greece*, Princeton, Princeton University Press, 1980.
7. See John Lewis Gaddis, *The United States and the Origins of the Cold War, 1941–1947*, New York, Columbia University Press, 1972.
8. See Deborah Larson, *Origins of Containment: A Psychological Interpretation*, Princeton, Princeton University Press, 1985.
9. Kuniholm, *The Origins of the Cold War in the Near East*, pp. 293–94; Schulenberg telegram, 26 Nov. 1940, in Raymond J. Sonntag and James S. Beddie (eds.), *Nazi–Soviet Relations 1939–1941: Documents from the Archives of the German Foreign Office*, Washington, US Department of State, 1948, pp. 258–59.
10. Marc S. Gallichio, *The Cold War Begins in Asia: American East Asian Policy and the Fall of the Japanese Empire*, New York, Columbia University Press, 1988.
11. See Steven I. Levine, *Anvil of Victory: The Communist Revolution in Manchuria. 1945–1948*, New York, Columbia University Press, 1987.
12. See Herbert Feis, *Contest Over Japan*, New York, Norton, 1967, Chapter IV.
13. Watt, 'Rethinking the Cold War . . .' p. 448.
14. Anne Deighton (ed.), *Britain and the First Cold War*, London, Macmillan, 1990.
15. Ibid., p. 4.
16. *The Impossible Peace: Britain, the Division of Germany and the Origins of the Cold War*, to be published by Oxford University Press later in 1990.

17. Deighton, *Britain and the First Cold War*, p. 53.
18. See Anne Deighton, 'The Frozen Front: The Labour Government and the Origins of the Cold War, 1945–7', *International Affairs*, Volume 63, No. 3, Summer 1987, pp. 449–65.
19. Deighton, *Britain and the First Cold War*, p. 66.
20. Riddleberger memo., 28 March 1946, US National Archives, Record Group 59, State Department Central European Division Records, Box 1.
21. Riddleberger memo., 10 June 1946, US National Archives, Matthews Papers, M1244, Reel 15.
22. Mowrer letter, 4 June 1946, cited in Daniel Yergin, *Shattered Peace: The Origins of the Cold War and the National Security State*, Boston, Houghton Mifflin, 1977, pp. 226, 457; US Delegation Record, Council of Foreign Ministers, Second Session, 40th Meeting, 11 July 1946, in US Department of State, *Foreign Relations of the United States, 1946*, Volume II, *Council of Foreign Ministers*, Washington, US Government Printing Office, 1970, p. 897; Riddleberger memo., 10 June 1946, cited in note 21.
23. John Gimbel, 'Cold War Historians and the Occupation of Germany', in Hans A. Schmitt (ed.), US *Occupation in Europe after World War II*, Lawrence, The Regents Press of Kansas, 1978, pp. 91–92.
24. Unsigned memorandum of conversation between Hottelet and Litvinov on 18 June [1946], George Elsey Papers, Box 63, Harry S. Truman Library, Independence, Missouri. The memorandum carried a 'top secret' classification and its contents were not published until after Litvinov's death in 1951. It should be noted, however, that there is no record of Stalin talking in these terms until the begining of 1948. See Milovan Djilas, *Conversations with Stalin*, San Diego, Harcourt Brace Jovanovich, 1962, p. 153,
25. John Kent, 'Bevin's Imperialism and the Idea of Euro–Africa', in Michael Dockrill and John W. Young (eds.), *British Foreign Policy, 1945–56*, London Macmillan, 1989, pp. 47–76.
26. Deighton, *Britain and the First Cold War*, p. 6.
27. Ibid., p. 81.
28. Bruce Kuniholm, *The Origins of the Cold War in the Near East, passim*; Melvyn P. Leffler, 'Strategy, Diplomacy, and the Cold War: The United States, Turkey, and NATO, 1945–1952', *The Journal of American History*, Volume 71, No. 4, March 1985, pp. 807–25.
29. Robert Frazier, 'Did Britain Start the Cold War? Bevin and the Truman Doctrine', *The Historical Journal*, Volume 27, No. 3, Sept. 1984, pp. 715–27; and Truman's letter to his wife on 14 March 1947, printed in Monte M. Poen, *Letters Home by Harry Truman*, New York, G.P. Putnam's Sons, 1984, p. 231. This letter does not appear in the better known collection of Truman's letters to his wife edited by Robert H. Ferrell.
30. Deighton, *Britain and the First Cold War*, p. 198.
31. Ibid., pp. 11–31; 71–87.
32. Ibid., p. 71.
33. Dimitri Volkogonov, *Triumf i Tragediya: I.V. Stalin. Politicheskii Portret*, Book II, Part 1, Moscow, Novosti, 1989, p. 31; Tass statement, 12 April 1990, reported in *The Independent*, 14 April 1990, p. 1.
34. Ministerstvo Inostrannykh del SSSR, *Perepiska Predsedatelya Soveta Ministrov SSSR s Prezidentami SShA i Prem'er-Ministrami Velikobritanii vo Vremya Velikoi Otechestvennoi Voiny, 1941–1945 gg.*, 2 Volumes, Moscow, Izdatel'stvo Politicheskoi Literaturi, 1986. The original edition appeared in 1957.
35. Ministerstvo Inostrannykh del SSSR, *Sovetskii Soyuz na Mezhdunarodnyk Konferentsyakh Perioda Velikoi Otechestvennoi Voiny, 1941–1945 gg.*, Volume I, *Moskovskaya Konferentsiya Ministrov Inostrannykh del SSSR, SShA i Velikobritanii (19–20 Oktyabrya 1943 g.)*, Volume II, *Tegeranskaya Konferentsiya Rukovoditelei Trekh*

Soyuznykh Derzhav – SSSR, SShA i Velikobritanii (28 Noyabrya-1 Dekabrya 1943 g.), Volume III, *Konferentsiya Predstavitelei SSSR, SShA i Velikobritanii v Dumbarton-Okse (21 Avgusta-28 Sentyabrya 1944 g.)*, Volume IV, *Krimskaya Konferentsiya Rukovoditelei Trekh Soyuznikh Derzhav – SSSR, SShA i Velikobritanii (4–11 Fevralya 1945 g.)*, Volume V, *Konferentsiya Obedineniykh Natsii v San-Frantsisko (25 Aprelya-26 Iyunya 1945 g,)*, Volume VI, *Berlinskaya (Potsdamskaya) Konferentsiya Pukovoditelei Trekh Soyuznikh Derzhav – SSSR, SShA i Velikobritanii (17 Yulya-2 Avgusta 1945g.)*, Moscow, Izdatel'stvo Politicheskoi Literaturi, 1978, 1978, 1984, 1984, 1984, 1980.

36. Ministerstvo Inostrannykh del SSSR, *Sovetsko-Amerikanskie Otnosheniya vo Vremya Velikoi Otechestvennoi Voiny, 1941–1945*, 2 Volumes; *Sovetsko-Angliiskie Otnosheniya vo Vremya Velikoi Otechestvennoi Voiny, 1941–1945*, 2 Volumes; *Sovetsko-Frantsuzkie Otnosheniya vo Vremya Velikoi Otechestvennoi Voiny, 1941–1945*, 2 volumes; Moscow, Izdatel'stvo Politicheskoi Literaturi, 1984, 1983, 1983.

37. Litivinov telegram, 12 March 1942, *Sovetsko-Amerikanskie Otnosheniya*, Volume 1, No. 77; unsigned memorandum of Truman-Stalin conversation, 17 July 1945, *Berlinskaya (Potsdamskaya) Konferentsiya*, Nos. 3. There are some rough and somewhat cryptic notes of the latter conversation in the published American records of the Potsdam conference, but no full record.

38. R.A. Longmire, *Soviet Relations with Southeast Asia: an Historical Survey*, London, Kegan Paul, 1989, pp.37–8; M.P. Isaev and A.S. Chernyshev, *Sovetsko-V'etnamskie Otnosheniya*, Moscow, Izdatel'stvo 'Mysl', 1975, p. 89.

39. Werner G. Hahn, *Postwar Soviet Politics: The Fall of Zhdanov and the Defeat of Moderation, 1945–53*, Ithaca, Cornell University Press, 1982; Gavriel D. Ra'anan, *International Policy Formation in the USSR: Factional 'Debates' during the Zhdanovschina*, Hamden, Archon Books, 1983.

40. Roberto Morozza della Rocca, *La Politica Estera Italiana e l'Unione Sovietica (1944–1948)*, Rome, La Goliardica, 1985.

41. Enzo Collotti (ed.), *Archivo Pietro Secchia 1945–1973*, Milan, Feltrinelli, 1979, pp. 211, 426.

The Cold War:
The Historical Context

RICHARD LANGHORNE

To read the existing literature on the cold war, even ignoring the purely polemical, might certainly lead an interested but inexpert reader to suppose that there was a vast confusion both about when and why it began, and when and why it ended – indeed even as to whether it did not abate and then recur. Naturally, certain lines of thought predominate. The idea that the cold war was essentially a result of the immediate post-second world war situation is fairly common ground. That it either ended or slowed in Khruschev's time is at least as acceptable a view as that it has ended, or is ending, now, in response to Gorbachev's reformist policies, or their consequences for the USSR.

The recent changes in Eastern Europe have not only had the effect of proposing yet another end to the cold war era, but also of pointing up the long period during which Russian predominance lasted. This can lead to an oversimplification by which the cold war period is simply equated with that of superpower dominance – a simplification all too easily espoused by particular political groupings and their public supporters. Difficult as they can be to disentangle, there remains the risk of confusing cause with consequence. The state of affairs in Eastern Europe was primarily caused by the preponderance of Russian power in the region at the end of the war. The precise form that preponderance took was the consequence of the American response to it. It is not certain, and cannot be until Russian motives can be satisfactorily established, how far the gradual installation of communist dictatorships in Eastern European countries was related to American policy, but there certainly appears to have been a temporal relationship between events there and the build up of anti-Soviet sentiment in the US, following the failure to alter Russian policy in Poland and subsequently achieve a settlement in Germany.

Thus the political forms overturned by the recent revolutions were not so much caused by the cold war as they were its consequence. Their removal has signified the end of the stable, if still *de facto*, conditions which registered the result of the cold war proper: Russo-American management of the international system, effectively since 1954. This overwhelming shift has been caused by changes in the very nature of power, one of whose results has been a reduction in the relative importance of the military expression of power. For Russia, who had always had to rely on military superiority to match American economic power, this development was particularly serious, and its effects within and without the Russian empire have been and remain correspondingly dramatic.

Looked at in this way, it is now easier to see the half-century since 1941 in its historical perspective, and less as a vehicle for domestic and contemporary political invective. Doing so will also enable some discussion of the legacies left by the cold war to the post-1954 international environment. First might be considered the differences between 1945 and other great pacifications. Since a system of states developed in Europe, there have been three such episodes, in 1814/5, 1919 and 1945. The treaties of Utrecht and Westphalia do not offer much useful comparative information, though the latter, of course, brought to an end a previous period in which post Reformation ideological differences had provided much of the vocabulary of international exchanges and conflict. 1945 was by contrast near the beginning rather than the end of such a period.

It is immediately clear that the importance of the content, even the existence, of a peace treaty has had little effect on the quality of subsequent international politics. At Vienna, the powers were certain that with differing emphasis they wanted to suppress the ideas let loose by the French Revolution, whether in terms of liberal constitutions or the legitimacy of the principle of national self-determination. Both none the less came to dominate the political scene but neither was able to destroy the basic stability of the international system. In 1919, great care was taken to try to ride with rather than against the tide of public opinion, and an attempt was made to reform the system in a positive and institutionalized way. For the first time, an effort was made actually to render warfare obsolete. In less than 12 years decay became evident, and in 20 years it was complete. In 1945, no treaty was made at all, and while some of the results of the *de facto* settlement which perforce emerged have been recently changed, major wars have not occurred, and none seem to be in view. Those conflicts which have broken through from time to time have either been too small to engage any general interest or been rapidly enfolded within the limiting arms of the system, much as the Concert of Europe dealt with the insoluble Eastern Question during the nineteenth century. This comparison suggests in itself, and there is other evidence also, that while 1919 offers little useful information, 1815 and 1945 may have things in common, despite the apparently total contradiction between the broad scope of the Vienna treaty and the total absence of a settlement in 1945.

One of the most important factors affecting the character of international politics after the conclusion of a serious conflict concerns the degree to which the circumstances at the end of the war accurately reflected the existing distribution of power, particularly in the likely event that the war itself had been caused by a shift in the previous distribution. It seems immediately clear that in 1815 and 1945, a new distribution had been registered or confirmed by the result of the war, but that in 1918 this was not so. The events which prevented the First World War from bringing in a new phase of international relations were those which prolonged the European predominance of Germany: the Russian revolution, which allowed the US to be secure while enjoying the privilege of isolation, the damage that was done to Britain and France, the implosion of the Hapsburg Empire and the substitution of a congerie of weaker and less stable states, of whom several had German minorities and one, Austria, was wholly German. On the other side of the world the contrasting futures of victor and vanquished were absent because the Japanese had been easy winners, but none the less there remained unfinished business in respect of Japan's implicit claim to a future as an Asian empire and a global power. In these circumstances, a settlement which treated Germany as defeated – a position only sustainable in the event of the continued involvement of the US in European affairs – would not long survive American withdrawal. It was American power which gave colour to the Allied claim of victory when what had occurred was a truce, and the absence of American power rapidly drained all colour from a settlement which was only enforceable with American support.

In 1945, the position was to be wholly different, once the US had fully grasped the significance of the Russian victory over Germany. Before that point there were some signs that the US would have preferred a repeat of 1919/20, even in circumstances where conditions in Europe were infinitely worse than they had been in 1918, but Stalin's determination over Poland, Persia and Germany brought any such tendencies to a swift end. This reaction of the US gave notice that the new distribution of global power predicted since the mid-nineteenth century and in train since its last quarter had at last come to fruition. With all the reservations which the actual and potential disequilibrium between the two new superpowers imposed, their triumph over all rivals had been complete. Where Britain and France had been gravely weakened by the 1914 war, the war of 1939 ruined the former as an economic global force and led to the elimination of the state itself for a period between 1940 and 1944 in the case of the latter. Germany and Japan, whatever their future economic might was to be, lay in ruins, militarily devastated. In the face of such change, the differences between Russia and the US, however real, paled into insignificance compared with the gap between them and any other conceivable centre of power. And for as long as power came in the forms which had emerged during the nineteenth century, gradually pushing the great continental states into prominence and their rivals into essentially pre-emptive wars, it would remain so.

If the result of the Second World War is clear enough now that its basic conditions are beginning to pass away, it was altogether less clear in its immediate aftermath. There were numerous reasons for this. The most commonly believed was probably that ideological difference had come to play a crucial role in international affairs, and thus both prevented a rational assessment of the distribution of power and propelled the two superpowers into a moral, but physically expressed, struggle à l'outrance, a struggle which any rational assessment, had it been available, would have suggested neither could actually win.

Looked at from a distance, this point of view seems more than ever symptomatic rather than causal – which is not to deny its importance as the determinant of some of the forms of conflict which were to affect the international system for fifty years – suggesting that other factors might be involved. One of these was the sheer speed with which one set of assumptions about the condition of international relations was exchanged for another. No one could have doubted the significance of the powers who entered conflicts between 1937 and 1939. Neither in the case of Japan nor the European powers was it, or could it have been, supposed that the crises in which they were involved – Shanghai, Tientsin, the *Anschluss*, Munich and Poland, were not of the first significance; or that the agreements they might make, the Nazi–Soviet Pact, the British guarantee to Romania and Poland, for example, were not part of the innermost stuff of international politics. The Congress of Berlin of 1878 and the conference of Munich of 1938 were divided by many things, but they were not divided in the rating which they were given on the scale of international importance. Only six years separated the opening of a war in Europe which was indisputably the work of great powers from the meeting between Russian and American troops at a point near the centre of the greatest of the former European great powers. Never before had the formal structure of the international system been so swiftly altered. This was mostly caused by past postponement, principally arising from the internal consequences of the Russian Revolution; but, whatever the cause, its effect was inevitably confusing, and it was worsened by the sheer physical disruption brought about by the scale of the conflict. An accurate diagnosis of what the distribution of power now had become, let alone the equally vital assessment of how stable it would be, was hardly likely to be available or widely believed.

The contrast with the events of 1814/5 is very clear. Napoleon's imperium in Europe represented not so much a postponement of the movement of power more or less evenly towards the five greater European powers, as a deliberate attempt to reverse it. It was an attempt only made possible by the international benefits accruing to the ruler of France from the ideology of the revolution, and did not rest on any permanent change in the realities of the distribution of power. The emergence of a community of states in Europe in the course of the eighteenth century had been accompanied by much tension and warfare, and the consequential stress was still the predominant factor in international relations when the revolutionary wars broke out. This stress did not indicate that the new distribution of power was uncertain, so much as that states had not yet fully accepted its stability. The effect of Napoleon's claims and his military successes was first to highlight the disarray of the other states, but eventually their persistent opposition and Napoleon's inability to establish a secure and legitimate rule, convinced them of the stability of the basically even distribution of power and of their determination to defend it.

The result was that even before the war ended, despite many fears and disagreements, there was a common assumption about how the international system was arranged. A grand settlement was arrived at on that basis, and the first ever attempt was made to arrange for the defence of the system on an institutionalized basis. The remarkable effectiveness of the nineteenth-century states system was not a consequence of the fact or the content of the settlement itself, so much as a tribute to the convergence between reality and perception which underlay what had been done. Plainly the contrast between this situation and that of 1945 could not have been greater, and the implication was that until a similar recognition of what the *status quo* actually was, and that it was stable, could be arrived at, no settlement, *de facto* or *de jure*, would emerge. The period between 1945 and 1955 seen from this point of view certainly looks like a period of adjustment to the new realities, a time of testing, such as the Napoleonic wars had provided of themselves, without which the superpowers would not accept the validity of a more or less equal relationship.

The consequences of this period of intense stress were serious. The precise forms that the testing took arose from the particularities of the period, and two of them became long lived. The first to occur was the eruption of ideological conflict conducted in terms of extreme abuse, with the consequence that the political colour of a particular government was held to be an exact guide to its loyalties in foreign affairs. This then had the further consequence that subversion and all the associated paraphernalia of undercover operations at many levels and heavy propaganda at all levels, became for the first time since the reformation a significant part of international relations. It was rejected in several quarters, particularly by the new states of the 1947–49 vintage, and by Yugoslavia, but its weight was none the less overwhelmingly oppressive, and nowhere more so than in the Russian dominated states of Eastern Europe. For practical purposes ideological abuse began to disappear from private – but not public – inter-bloc exchanges after 1954 and significantly in 1955; but it has only been very recently that the habits of the past fifty years have begun to decay, taking with them other imitators, whose abuse was based upon ideological objections to imperialism as well as capitalism so that it seems almost as if theologies have now replaced ideologies as the principal motive power in some foreign policies.

The second persistent consequence of the post-war period of adjustment was the militarization of the new distribution of power, particularly expressed in the form of alliances – one of which, NATO, emerged in a hitherto unknown guise giving it some of the characteristics of an international organization. This was the consequence of such close integration of its members' defence systems that the loss of sovereignty was only rendered tolerable by regarding the alliance as a political structure and giving it the appropriate forms. On the other side, the essentially imperial stance of the Soviet Union made such a structure unnecessary in the Warsaw Pact. The emergence of grand military coalitions is characteristic of periods where a reasonably even distribution of power is giving way to the construction of a deliberate balance of power. The classical example of this process can be seen in the evolution of the pre-1914 groupings. The rise of Germany and the general globalization of international politics which resulted from the new Pacific arena created by the decline of China, the increasing power of Japan and the interventions of the US and Russia created unbearable tensions. The most obvious consequence was the acceptance by Germany of an obligation to defend the Austrian Empire, and the setting up of the Anglo-Franco-Russian combination after 1907 to balance the weight of the Triple Alliance in central Europe. After 1945, however, the movement of power was creating a more rather than less balanced condition and its militarization seems an unexpected development. The explanation lies in a particular aspect of the emerging distribution of power. The precise relativity has varied over time, but there has always been an imbalance between the US and Russia in favour of the US. This has generally been obscured by the enormous gap between them both and all other states, but has until very recent times always been regarded by Russia as a gap which had to be filled – and the filling agent was military power. From the moment that the Red Army was clearly being maintained and not stood down after the war, Russo-American tension was forced into a military expression, and in the uncertain perception of the natural distribution of power, a felt need developed to create a balance, as if the situation were fluid, in the manner of the late nineteenth century, whereas in practice it was not. The striking power and weight of the alliance systems in Europe, and the ever present and apparently insoluble question mark over the future of Germany which served to given them their purpose, combined to give them a longer life in the European area than anywhere else in the world and to maintain a global sense of the significance of the military balance. In fact in other parts of the world, military alliances crumbled away reasonably quickly in response to the practical consequences of the new conditions. But it was not to be until the mid-1980s that new developments in the very nature of power began to force a change in the relative significance allotted to military power, and with it a willingness on the part of Russia to abandon her persistent attempts to bridge the gap between herself and the US by military methods. Until then, the long forward shadow cast by this particular characteristic of the post-1945 era preoccupied governments and military staffs to the point where it frequently seemed to be both the most permanent and most compelling item on the agenda of international politics.

Other consequences flowed from the intrusion of balance of power attitudes and mechanisms into what was for practical purposes an even distribution between the superpowers, and they continued to be significant well beyond the Berlin airlift, the Korean War or the Indochina settlement of 1954, all of which might have seemed signs enough of an emerging stability. One of the most overwhelming was the strength of the notion that the foreign policy of a state was determined by the political colour of its domestic regime. Until a substantial number of new states had rejected the notion, either by deliberate acts of policy like that achieved at the Bandung conference in 1955, or as a result of their internal instability and tendency to change sides too rapidly and too often to leave much significance left in the act itself, the embrace demanded by both superpowers was python-like. It could be pursued by the application of straightforward force, more commonly by Russia, but used by both, and it could be advanced by economic bribery on a grand scale, more commonly by the US, but done by both. The frisson that could be caused by the merest hint of a rift within one or other bloc during the 1950s, as occasionally between Britain and the US, or between the USSR and China, is eloquent testimony to the force of this factor. Eventually the need to conscript every conceivable ally, and, as the US was to discover, some inconceivable ones, gave way to the routine attacks by de Gaulle on the Americans, and by Ceausescu on the Russians, and then to the extraordinary upheaval caused by Chancellor Brandt's *ostpolitik*. But not until the 1960s was this so, and even then there remained a residual importance attached to the ideology of individual régimes which earlier centuries would not have understood. It is the longlasting significance of this factor which has given point to accusations made by American revisionist historians of the origins of the cold war that the particular weight of Russian oppression in Eastern Europe was caused by the determination of the US not to accept Russian security needs on her western frontiers, while at the same time being prevented by the realities of power from actually ejecting her. Russian anxiety used the space between the two positions to make certainty doubly sure.

Another consequence which deserves discussion concerns the effect of 'cold war' ideological differences in preventing active co-operation between the superpowers after they had been forced to recognise the realities of the situation *de facto*. It is a difficult estimation to make. In one area it can be readily done: the UN; in others, not at all. After 1815, the consequence of a perception of stability in the distribution of power was to yield a general wish to defend, rather than seek to test or alter, the *status quo*. After 1955, a similar response can be discerned. The reaction of the superpowers to Suez was basically similar, and the US did not seek to intervene in Hungary when the Russians suppressed the revolution of 1956. At a lower level of significance, however, disturbances which the old great powers would have regarded as obliging them at least to attempt to stop, the US and USSR tended to leave alone, with the consequence that there was greater anarchy, if of a broadly unthreatening kind, in the system than need have been. The conflict surrounding the existence of Israel is the most persistent example, but there are many others, and it is quite impossible to know what a superpower concert would or could have done about it.

In the case of the United Nations, however, the consequences of the cold war can be seen running their full course. The intended mode of operation of the UN in 1945 owed much to the sense that the League had not been powerful enough, and the duties and powers given to the security council indicate the intention to remove that problem clearly enough. The *quid pro quo* for this was an acknowledgement, not made by the League covenant, of the superior sovereignty of the then great powers. Plainly the expectation was that the UN would effectively be run by an oligarchy of the greater states, and that their shared need to defend the *status quo* would supply the necessary common basis for action. Without anything like the same institutional support, this had been the basis of the old Concert of Europe. In a very short time, it was quite clear that the Cabinet of Oligarchs was irretrievably divided and possessed no common basis. The system broke down amid cries of abuse, and so far from being above the stress of the international environment became a part of it. The US adopted the UN, in which *pro tem* it had a comfortable majority, and turned it into a vehicle of propaganda; the Russians responded at first by absenting themselves, and subsequently by making constant use of their veto power. Little purpose was served by the UN until both powers had an interest in using its mediating function over Suez and, shortly after that episode, the arrival of the new states in significant numbers gave the organization a new rôle which came in the end to be uncomfortable to both superpowers, and caused them both to continue to seek propaganda points at general assemblies, but otherwise to ignore it. The legacies of the cold war continued to make a public and common defence of the existing order impossible – whatever was done privately. Very recently the situation has changed in a way that points to what might have been. Faced with an increasingly damaging Gulf War, in the context of declining Russo-American tension and with West Germany and Japan both members of the Security Council as well as the permanent members, it was possible for a skilful secretary-general to bring about a UN involvement along the lines originally intended, and to bring the war to an end.

A further medium term consequence of the manner in which the status quo was confirmed militarily after the Second World War flowed from the need felt by the Americans to respond to Russia's insistence on maintaining a highly military security stance in the cheapest way. American opinion would only accept the need to take measures such as the Marshall plan after blatant shock tactics, and it was clear that in terms of military strength, Congress would seek to rely on the superiority already enjoyed by the US in nuclear weapons rather than emulate the Russians in the scale of their conventional armament. The result was an ongoing disbalance of type in the style of military force deployed by the superpowers that was to make any self denying ordinance unachievable long after the underlying reason for such competition had died away. Like was not offered for like, and when breakthrough came, it was in a completely different context, in which the very basis of power had altered to the point where both parties had a greater interest in trying to protect their economies from the advances of others than in maintaining a military stalemate *vis-à-vis* each other.

We may perhaps conclude, therefore, that it is plainly important to try to understand the emergence of the cold war as the final stage of a process of transition, begun in the 1890s, from one kind of even distribution of power across five major states to another, global in scale, devolved upon two. In the process, claimants to similar status with those two – Germany and Japan – made a bid for expansion. In the suddenness of their failure between 1941 and 1945 lie some of the reasons for the need for an extension of the period of adjustment, by contrast with what had happened in 1815. This in turn led to the confusion of the cold war which took on characteristics of its own, characteristics which endured to colour the detailed moves of a long phase of fundamentally stable international conditions and even to conceal the fact from some of its major participants. These characteristics are themselves easier to identify and assess in the context of long-term movements in the distribution of power, a privilege available to the international historian, but much less, if at all, available to those engaged in the excitement of ideological struggles, with all their definable points of right and wrong, still less perhaps to those locked into a strategic and tactical battle, with all its risks of triumph or destruction – or both. Grotius would have well conceived the condition; Kant might have correctly predicted its result.

St. John's College, Cambridge

Ending the Cold War

GERALD SEGAL[1]

They say the cold war is over. The superpowers and their allies seem sure that the latest round of *détente* is so different from any other that in effect the match is ended. Although the Soviet Union will not admit it, and the west is careful not to claim victory too loudly, Moscow's former East European allies are clear that they are free because the west has won.

And yet it is important to keep these changes in perspective. It has been far too often forgotten that the cold war was always a process with relative degree of warmth. Much as there was never a 'second cold war', but merely a different phase of the first one, so caution is required in declaring the death of the cold war in early 1990. It may simply be a matter of tying up loose ends, but it is important to remember that the superpowers are still armed to their nuclear teeth and there are far more tanks and troops in Europe than one might expect in peacetime. COCOM is still in force but by far the greatest degree of caution must come from the fact that all these changes have come so fast, and not all of them are irrversible. As *perestroika* gives way to *catastroika*, there can be little confidence that all will now be peaceful in international relations.[2]

Of course, the puncturing of the tyre of Soviet power has just occurred and it takes some time for the shrinkage to be evident. Given the explosive potential of such change, not to mention the chances of erratic movement, it is best to be careful when re-structuring international security. The cautious will recall how the rhetoric of earlier *détentes* leapt ahead of reality, only to be yanked back when the aspirations went unfulfilled.

Of course, despite the speed of recent change in Europe it is unlikely that the liberation of Eastern Europe could be undone, even by a reactionary Soviet leader. Unlike in other phases of *détente*, East Europeans have been allowed to choose their own governments and even political systems. It is true that the Soviet Union itself might backtrack on reforms, but it can no longer regain its lost allies. Thus, if the cold war referred to a state of significant tension between a large number of states apart from merely the superpowers, then it certainly seems to have ended in 1989. A new form of cold war that focuses on the United States and the Soviet Union, or Europe and the Soviet Union, is certainly possible, but it would be a different conflict – a genuine second cold war – much as Sino-Soviet tension was always very different from that between the Soviet Union and the United States.

In order not to confuse these cold wars, it is best to agree that we are talking mainly about the ending of the east-west tension in Europe, and far more still needs to be done in the strictly bilateral relationship between what was once referred to as the two superpowers before an overall end to the cold war can be declared. Conflict in the developing world remains far less a manifestation of superpower conflict than a result of mainly local disputes.[3] But it is useful to note that the variant of the cold war in Asia mostly ended long ago, and virtually nothing of it remains today. Thus if we are to understand why the cold war is ending, it is essential to note that regional and local factors are often every bit as important as the changes in Moscow and Washington.

If the central objective of this analysis is to suggest why the cold war ended, it is best to acknowledge that we are looking at a process, or rather several processes that are taking place on several levels. Yet, for the purposes of clear analysis, it is necessary to distinguish between major components of these processes. Let us start with the decisions in Moscow, for at least as far as most pundits are concerned, it was the tacit acceptance of defeat in the Kremlin that made the new world possible. But even when considering the choices in Moscow, it is essential to recall that without important developments in the international system, let alone the essential local conditions in Eastern Europe, the revolution would not have taken place.

Decisions in Moscow

The nature of the reforms in the Soviet Union is changing even as this is written. Yet it is already clear that Soviet foreign policy was revolutionized to a sufficient extent to have led to the recognition that even basic elements had to be changed. One can identify at least four major reasons for the new policies in Moscow, all of which are interconnected.

The first reason is of course the failure of the Soviet system to produce sufficient prosperity to satisfy the people's desires or to ensure the continuing legitimacy of the ruling communist party. This failure was both economic and political and any solution would require changes in both economic and political practices. The failure was also a long time in coming. Although many observers argued that such crises were bound to come, few knew just how deep the problem was and how quickly the recognition and reaction in Moscow would be.

Mikhail Gorbachev was not the first leader to recognise the looming problems. Nikita Khrushchev and even Leonid Brezhnev had their phases of reform, although neither felt as much pressure to change. When Yuri Andropov came to power in 1982 reform was back on the agenda, but this former KGB chief was too ill and too stuck in the old system to really set about kicking it to pieces. Following Andropov's death, the year-long retreat to inaction under the guidance of Konstantin Chernenko was a last effort by the system to strike back. Chernenko's death, and the ridicule that his leadership had earned the Soviet system both at home and abroad, meant that Gorbachev was given his chance in the spring of 1985.

It is true that Gorbachev was not unopposed, but he was remarkably swift in consolidating power. And yet the equally rapid shift to more radical reforms which necessitated the purges of conservatives could hardly be described as under Gorbachev's control. Just as the systemic crisis 'required' reforms, so the recognition of the depth of the problems required faster and more thorough changes. There were various points at which the reforms were visibly speeded, but it became increasingly clear by the autumn of 1988 that Gorbachev was riding a tiger. He was still a bold enough leader to hang on, but the precariousness of his position led few to think about taking his place. For the time being the speed of the tiger was Gorbachev's best insurance.

The fact remains that Gorbachev did not appreciate what he had let himself in for. His original motive was to reform the system in order to create a better socialism. But the iron law of revolution dragged him forward as it became clear that the systemic problems were very deep.

Gorbachev had no idea what was at the end of this ride, even if he often needed to suggest he was in control.

As reform slipped into great reform and even revolution, the analyses of Sakharov, Djilas and even the PCI, Havel and Koestler seemed more true than ever-the system was more or less finished and mere reform was not enough. But for all his wisdom in recognizing the need for far-reaching change, Gorbachev was not in the business of simply creating capitalism and pluralism in the Soviet Union. The aspiration for kinder, gentler (not to mention more efficient) socialism remained his objective. For the time being at least, neither Djilas or the old nationalism of Solzhenitsyn was accepted by the Gorbachev reformers.

Gorbachev was certainly not accepting the argument of foreigners such as President Reagan that outside pressure was vital in setting an objective for the changes. But it was certainly a factor in the calculations in the Kremlin that there was an alternative to the present-day Soviet reality. Although President Reagan's hard line in the early 1980s no doubt made the crisis in the Soviet system more apparent by forcing yet another debilitating arms race, this was not so much a cause of change as much as a matter of speeding up the pace. A far more important dimension was the positive models offered by other parts of the outside world.

As Soviet reformers looked around for ideas about reform, they had a wide range from which to choose. Consideration was given to the Hungarian experience, but then Hungary was seen as a special case if only by virtue of its size. In any case, by the time reformers in the Soviet Union took a serious look at Hungary, the reforms were stuck. China was more similar to the Soviet Union in size and Peking's reforms were still seen to be successful. But China was also a poor, peasant state that many in the Soviet Union saw as merely catching up with earlier phases of Soviet reform. Yet, others did accept that at least some of the reforms in China might have application to the Soviet Union, if only in the realm of how to deal with the outside world through joint ventures and special export zones.[4]

More adventurous reformers in the Soviet Union looked beyond the distorted mirrors of socialism to the more successful economies of Europe, Japan and even some of the east Asian NICs. The so-called Swedish model was sometimes held up as a good mix of welfare and wealth. Japan and the NICs were applauded for their mix of central planning and market forces. More generally, all of the west, but especially the Japanese and the Europeans were a shock to the Soviet system if only because they existed as evidence of what the Soviet system had failed to achieve. Japan surpassed the Soviet Union as the world's second largest economy and the NICs demonstrated that their *per-capita* GNP could quickly out-pace that in the socialist motherland. It is not so much that the outside world forced the Soviet Union to recognize their own incompetence, but rather that merely by being there, they would provide powerful evidence to those within the Soviet Union who eventually recognized that there was an alternative. The impact of the international system was important, but unintentional.

Indeed, the more some people in the west, most notably President Reagan, tried to rub the Soviet Union's nose in this reality, the less likely it was that reform could be contemplated in the Kremlin. It was only in the second Reagan administration, when the carrot replaced the stick and *détente* was offered, that Soviet reformers felt freer to think more radical thoughts. The leadership in Moscow was far too proud to bend to overt pressure and it might even be argued that the ending of the cold war might have come earlier in the Gorbachev age if the United States had been less confrontational.

The Gorbachev era began in the spring of 1985 just as President Reagan began his second term. This coincidence, as well as the clear signs from Moscow that some of the old thinking in foreign policy would be abandoned, helped turn the vicious circle into its virtuous relative. The early initiatives clearly came from the Soviet side, with bold ideas from Gorbachev about INF negotiations and even strategic weapons cuts. It was not so much that the Soviet Union was forced to the bargaining table by the firmness of President Reagan, but more that there was finally a Soviet leader wise enough to take the United States up on an INF deal (zero-zero) that was partly proposed in the expectation that it would never be taken up. Simultaneously both superpowers retained some curious notions about strategic weapons (SDI and non-nuclear world, to name but two), which ensured that talks about strategic weapons never made much progress in the decade since the SALT II treaty. Throughout this period, the Europeans remained far more careful about nuclear issues and the balance of power, all the while trying to calm the wilder emotions and euphorias in Moscow and Washington.

It is not surprising that a major feature of the Soviet Union's new foreign policy was the much abused concept of a common European home.[5] In some ways this was merely a code-phrase for Soviet admiration for the success of Western Europe in creating prosperity though closer interdependence. Soviet reformers came to recognise that there was a new way to organize international relations that offered some prospects for the Soviet Union to be integrated into the international community. Such integration would not only help produce wealth, but it also might help press those parts inside the Soviet Union who were opposed to change. By bringing Europe inside the Soviet Union, the chances of success at home might be enhanced.

The international system was also important in a less positive way. The existence of imperial overstretch, like the phase of more hostile superpower relations, clearly added to the burden on those seeking to reform the Soviet system. By far the most obvious example of this process was the Soviet entanglement in Afghanistan, although many other examples of distant imperial burdens in the developing world could be cited. Afghanistan was particularly onerous because of the size of the Soviet commitment in troops and aid. Just as the Vietnam war helped sober American foreign policy in the previous decade, so the Soviet Union was pushed towards reform at a faster pace because of the drain of imperial commitments.

Of course, Afghanistan was more evidence of the crisis than a cause of reform. Gorbachev, if only because of his brief tenure in the *Politburo*, was able to jettison the policies of distant imperialism that had so blossomed in the age of Brezhnev. But much like the other European leaders who supervised the contraction of empire, Gorbachev soon discovered that along with returning soldiers came additional problems. The defeat by Muslim bandits in the hills in Afghanistan was evidence that the Red Army could be beaten. It was not only East Europeans, but also the various opponents of Russian rule within the borders that recognized this implication. Gorbachev bought time by withdrawing from Afghanistan and more distant engagements, but he also stored up far more important trouble. At each stage as these reforms gathered pace, the choice to continue forward seemed fairly obvious. But as was evident in internal Soviet reforms, this was a reform tiger gathering speed. Gorbachev had no time to catch his breath – there was no breathing space or even a real peace dividend after the withdrawal from Afghanistan or even the 1988 INF treaty. One feeding of the reform tiger merely meant another morsel would soon have to be offered.

Finally, some consideration should be given to the role of leadership in setting the pace and nature of Soviet reforms. As has already been suggested, Gorbachev was to some extent merely the right man 'chosen by historical forces' to fulfil the task of dismantling the decrepit old system. Because of the radical change that has taken place, there is the tendency to suggest that this is where Gorbachev intended to be all along. However, it is vital to recall that Gorbachev began as a party man looking for better ways to keep the party and the system in business. After five years of power, it seemed that neither objective was still attainable and so in early 1990 he moved to diminish the authority of the party while clinging to power.

Yet this is not to suggest that just because the Gorbachev-in-command model is wrong, it is correct to ignore the role that his specific personality has had on events. Lesser leaders might have chosen to dismount from the dashing tiger of reform and some might have been far less skilled in knowing how to hang on, or even steer the process to even a small extent. Great moments in history, and that is surely what we have just seen in the last months of 1989, are usually more the product of larger historical forces. Yet, personality remains important if only because of the extent to which so many people are concerned that he might not survive to see the process through. Like Lenin, and in contrast to Peter the Great, the nature of the revolution can be altered when its guiding figure is no longer there to give 'history a shove'.

Eastern Europe: Local Conditions

They will probably remember Mikhail the Enabler rather than Mikhail the Creator, for the greatest part played by Gorbachev in ending the cold war was 'merely' to recognise the reality of the crisis of communism and to allow the East Europeans to go their own way. Gorbachev has not created a new world as part of a coherent vision, but rather he has let matters take their natural course. This is not to belittle the role of the Soviet reforms, but merely to suggest that a reformed Soviet Union by no means had to lead to the end of the cold war. After all, the Soviet Union might have merely been seeking a breathing space in order to engage in deeper rivalry with the west.

What made all the difference was the conditions in Eastern Europe. If the East Europeans had not been dying to break away from Russian imperial power, then little would have happened to the balance of power when the Gorbachev reforms were implemented in Eastern Europe. Thus the real death of the cold war must be sought in both the deeper and more immediate causes of the collapse of communism in between the Soviet frontier and Western Europe.

It is not merely with hindsight that we can say the East Europeans never took to communism. Only Yugoslavia and Albania had an indigenous communist revolution. All others were installed by Stalin and sustained by the Soviet Union and the cold war tension. As we now know, none had sustained economic success when compared to the growth in Western Europe.

Of course, Stalin's harsh approach was soon replaced by the you-cannot-herd-people-into-paradise policy of Khrushchev. But de-Stalinization soon led to the uprisings in Poland and Hungary in 1956. Reforms in the 1960s Soviet Union soon encouraged Czechoslovakia to try its luck in testing the limits of Soviet control. Each time the answer was the same – a Soviet invasion. In the last of the 12-year cycles in 1980, Poland again pushed against imperial rule, only to find that Moscow was able to get its way without having to use Soviet troops. Although this was a somewhat more liberal application of the doctrine (erroneously called the Brezhnev Doctrine) that 'once a socialist state, always a socialist state', the reality remained the same. In no case was the leading role of the communist party to be given up.[6]

In the depths of East European despair in the winter of 1981 when martial law was imposed in Poland, it seemed that no matter how unsuitable communist rule was to East European conditions, no change seemed likely. And yet, these were also the dying days of the Brezhnev period, even if the East Europeans were not to know that Andropov and Gorbachev were not far away. The despair was deepened by the realisation that reform communism in individual East European states regularly failed to break through what looked like an immutable problem of mixing market and Marx. The Hungarians more than the Poles had experimented with economic reforms, but at no time did they achieve more than fleeting and false gains.

As despair spread, reservoirs of already limited legitimacy shrunk to all-time lows. Worst of all, confidence ebbed as well. While it was clear that only radical change would do, it seemed equally clear that radical change was not on offer. That is until Gorbachev-the-Enabler re-kindled hopes, much as Khrushchev did in the de-Stalinization period. It is difficult to know at what time the Soviet Union decided that it really could live with the so-called Sinatra Doctrine (they can do it their way). It certainly seems that by the summer of 1989 the Soviet Union was letting it be known that it would not stop radical reformers in Eastern Europe taking the banner of reform further than the Soviet Union had done. No doubt part of the Kremlin's calculus was that successful reform in Eastern Europe would help reformers in Moscow. There was also a probable hope that more liberalization in Eastern Europe would lessen the economic burden on the Soviet Union and certainly earn a better press and more support from the west.

Did Gorbachev really know in June 1989 that by the end of the year he would lose control of his East European allies? It seems unlikely. What seems far more probable is that Gorbachev might have guessed as much, but he hoped that in this case, as with his own domestic reforms, that somehow events would provide him with a chance to catch his breath and catch up with history. But in Eastern Europe as in the Soviet Union, the system was so bankrupt that all that happened was swift collapse.

The specific trigger for the collapse in 1989 is hard to identify. The Poles and Hungarians could be said to have led the way with moves to relatively democratic elections in the first half of 1989. In both cases, but especially for the Poles, the economic problems had become so severe that genuine government was no longer possible. The opposition had to be brought into government in order to legitimize the necessary radical changes. At first the pace was careful, with an almost tangible testing of Gorbachev's promise of restraint. East Europeans remembered how previous Soviet reformers balked when they were faced with the reality of surrendering control. But as the delicate dance of reform grew more confident, all eyes soon swung east to China to see the implications of the challenge that faced all reform communists.

China, whose economic reforms were far more daring than nearly anything seen in Eastern Europe, steadfastly refused demands in the spring of 1989 for political reform as was emerging in Eastern Europe.

While all concerned knew that China and east Asia came from a very different political tradition, they all had also grow more accustomed to China as a major participant in modern debates about reform communism. It was not too much earlier that East European leaders had vied for the opportunity to be the first to restore party-to-party relations with Peking after Moscow gave the go-ahead.[7]

The Peking massacre was the most obvious response for a communist leadership which perceived a challenge to its leading role. China had used troops in such a cause before, as had various East Europeans. But what was so striking about the lessons learned in Eastern Europe was that not only was it horrific to have to do what the Chinese comrades had just done, but that the Soviet Union was not pleased with such bloodshed. Although the Soviet Union was officially cautious in its response to the Peking massacre, East Europeans were in no doubt that Gorbachev was appalled. When it came to choosing between the bullets in Peking on 4 June or the ballots in Warsaw on the same day, the Soviet Union was happier to see democratic pluralism than communism from the barrel of a gun.

As a result, the Soviet Union realised that it had little choice but to give a bright green light for real reform in Eastern Europe. Indeed, in general there was a palpable loss of faith in the communist system in Eastern Europe. Hungary, which saw closer integration with West Germany and Austria as crucial to solving economic problems, was determined to develop its own political reforms. As Poland chose its first non-communist government and communists were humiliated in the first genuinely free vote in Eastern Europe since 1945, Hungary saw the opportunity to follow suit. Leadership changes were engineered at first without the benefit of free elections, and in some sense the Hungarians were frustrated at being seen to follow a Polish lead.

In East Germany, long influenced by the images of a more prosperous world in West Germany, the reluctance of their aged leadership to contemplate similar reforms grew more intolerable. As the Honecker regime praised the actions of China's leaders in June, more East Germans sought to leave for the west. Of course, such pressures were not new, but this time the Hungarians, anxious to please West Germany and demonstrate liberal credentials, refused to help the East German regime by stopping the exodus of Germans via Hungary. The trickle of people soon turned into a flood in September. In a matter of weeks even the removal of Honecker was insufficient to calm the unrest. That all important hand-maiden of political legitimacy – confidence – had ebbed and the regimes soon tumbled. Honecker had reportedly asked Moscow's opinion about the tactics of Tiananmen, but the Soviet Union refused to sanction such slaughter. If force would not be used to defend communism, then its days were numbered.

Just how small the number of days remaining was a surprise to all concerned. In a desperate effort to stem the tide of people, Honecker's successor tried to open the Berlin wall in the hope that if people saw they could leave, they would choose to stay. The first breach of the wall was made on 9 November, and if the pedantic want a date to mark the end of the cold war, that is the best one to choose. The Wall, so long the symbol of a divided Europe, was also the manifestation of the notion of the 'iron curtain'. Germany was divided by the great power politics of the 1940s and was the front line of the cold war that followed. The prospect that the German question would be solved by reunification removed the major feature of the old great power-imposed order and set a new agenda.

What followed was not quite anti-climactic, if only because it was so dramatic. Bulgaria lurched down the road of reform as a result of what was more of a palace coup. But with demonstrators on the streets, the much cowed Czechs felt embarrassed into forcing the end of their own communist leaders. Peaceful protests in Prague, whose struggle was still an emotive symbol for all Europeans who remembered 1968, ran a brief risk of going the way of Tiananmen, only to suddenly break open into communist defeat. With the dissident playwright Havel at its head, the old order was overturned.

Among the Warsaw Pact allies, only Romania refused to join the revolution. But by December 1989, and after the bloodiest scenes since Tiananmen, the Ceaucescu regime toppled. At years' end it all seemed like a European dream come true – communism had collapsed in six countries in six months, and with the exception of Romania, hardly a shot was fired. This was no longer mere reform, this was revolution.

At the time of writing in the spring of 1990, the revolution looked like spreading inside the borders of the Soviet Union. The Baltic states looked set to gain their freedom as part of a general reassessment of the frontiers of the Soviet empire. But regardless of whether more states joined the ranks of the freed East Europeans, the evidence suggested that Moscow could not regain control of its old empire. The agenda for European and superpower politics would never be the same again – an understandable state of affairs considering the fact that the old certainty of the cold war was gone.

As the rubble of the old order was still being cleared away, the new order was not yet fully visible. Nevertheless, some important structures were already beginning to take shape. Not only were the two Germanies hurrying to reunification, but elections were scheduled and then moved forward in order to race to complete the formal stages of democratic transition. This was more akin to the politics of southern Europe in the 1970s than anything ever seen in the communist world. East Europeans also vied with each other in telling Moscow to pull its troops out and how to quickly abandon the old CMEA relationships. West Europeans began unilateral military reductions and defence budgets were slashed. Arms control negotiators sat forlornly on the sidelines as political reality raced farther ahead than even the most visionary of the diplomats. CFE talks could at most ratify the process of *de facto* arms control, but even that role seemed unlikely for some time as the Germans sorted out their relationship with themselves and their neighbours. Superpower arms control remained on the notional negotiating agenda, but in reality far too little thought had been given to the implications of all the political revolutions on nuclear weapons strategies: Now was the time for strategic visionaries rather than strategic nit-pickers.

Making Sense of History

Strategic shift used to take place as a result of war, but in the nuclear age this was never a likely prospect. At the start of 1989 it already looked like it would be a momentous year for global strategy as the Sino-Soviet summit was set for May. This *détente*, the most important shift in the balance of power since the Sino-American *détente* of the early 1970s, was also the single most important improvement in the Soviet strategic position since the consolidation of power in Eastern Europe some 40 years earlier.

As if these shifts were not enough, the Soviet Union swung its attention back to Europe where even more important trends were underway. The loss of its allies in Eastern Europe is the single greatest strategic setback suffered by the Soviet empire since Hitler's invasion of Russia. It was also the single greatest improvement in the security of West Europeans and the United States since the defeat of the Axis powers in 1945. This year of superlatives was capped by the recognition that the risk of major war involving developed states had not been this low since the 1920s.

Given the magnificence of these strategic shifts, no simple explanation is possible. It seems most fair to say that without Gorbachev it might not have happened in 1989, but it would not have been long in coming. The fact that the end of the cold war happened so peacefully was a miracle that must go beyond the specific actions of individual leaders. It was certainly a masterpiece of crisis management. But real causes of the collapse of the struggle must be mainly found in the systemic collapse of communism. Whether it was the Soviet Union's version, or that far less entrenched manifestation in Eastern Europe, in either case the crisis was internal and not generated or manipulated by the west. The west won more by positive example.

That communism collapsed so quickly is not necessarily evidence that we never understood the nature of the conflict. None of the protagonists, including Gorbachev, knew the end would come so swiftly. The west did know well before Gorbachev that communism was doomed, although they never quite knew how right they were.

But before the west gets carried away with its victory, it might do well to ponder the most obvious of the implications of the new world they are facing. We simply do not know what lies underneath the cold war overlay in Europe. Some of the old nationalisms, such as that within the German people, looks like being absorbed into the West German success that is so closely tied to a post-1992 European integration. Other nationalisms, such as in the Balkans, have far more potential for war and entangling alliances as in the run-up to the First World War.

Of course, the ending of the cold war is not likely to take us back to the days of Balkan intrigue that consumed European civilization. The international economy is far more interdependent and the United States seems less likely to slip back into isolation. New social orders and internal communications makes war in Europe far less likely. But we also seem far less likely to spend our diplomatic time on arms control, except in the most general terms of confidence-building measures and general discussions about regional security in a CSCE mould.

Superpower arms control talks will be more concerned with nuclear issues, but with less of the de-stabilizing problems of commitment of allies.

The logic of minimum deterrence seems so much stronger. But nuclear weapons look set to remain on the agenda of international relations and as such, a sort of cold war between the superpowers looks set to continue. In some very real senses, nuclear weapons made a cold war possible and their continued existence seems to make cold war between old rivals who still hold these arsenals, more difficult to dissolve. The ideological base of the old superpower struggle has undeniably been undermined, but the existence of two, probably rival great power, seems likely to linger much longer. Of course, the oldest and most important cold war, that in Europe, is now over. This is no small mercy for which to be thankful.

Royal Institute of International Affairs, London

NOTES

1. This draft has benefitted from the comments of Neil Malcolm, Eric Herring, and Adrian Hyde Price.
2. The argument about the existence of a second cold war is best taken up by Fred Halliday in *The Making of the Second Cold War* (London: Verso, 1983). See a more conservative assessment of some of these issues in J.L. Gaddis, *Strategies of Containment* (Oxford: Oxford University Press, 1987) and Raymond Garthoff, *Detente and Confrontation* (Washington: Brookings, 1985).
3. For a different discussion of this point see Fred Halliday, *Cold War, Third World* (London: Century Hutchinson, 1989)
4. These issues are discussed generally in Alex Pravda and Toshio Hasegawa, *Soviet Perestroika* (London: Sage, for the RIIA, 1990)
5. Neil Malcolm, *Soviet Policy Perspectives on Western Europe* (London: Chatham House Papers, 1989) and 'The Common European Home and Soviet European Policy' in *International Affairs* No. 4, 1989.
6. These now dated discussions are discussed in various chapters of Edwina Moreton and Gerald Segal eds., *Soviet Strategy Towards Western Europe* (London: Allen and Unwin, 1984).
7. These issues of linkage between China and east Europe are discussed in Gerald Segal, 'Taking Sino-Soviet Detente Seriously', *The Washington Quarterly*, Summer 1989 and 'Sino-Soviet-Japanese Relations' in *The World Today*, March 1990.
8. For a discussion of the basics of the German question see Edwina Moreton ed., *Germany Between East and West* (Cambridge: Cambridge University Press, 1988).
9. Lawrence Freedman 'The Politics of Conventional Arms Control', *Survival* Sept./Oct. 1989.

Is the Cold War Over?

URI RA'ANAN

In the 1940s the BBC used to run an amusing show called 'The Brains' Trust', in which the philosopher Cyril Joad played a prominent role. To each question sent in by a listener, he responded, 'Well, it all depends on what you mean by . . .'. That approach is entirely appropriate for the question posed in the title of this chapter.

Few phrases have been bandied about more indiscriminately than the term 'the cold war'. In the case of almost each Soviet leadership change since Stalin's death, western commentators have adjusted the definition of 'cold war' to describe simply whatever the preceding Soviet administration had done, and have contrasted that with the period of supposed *détente* for which the Soviet successor regime has been given credit. Thus, the Geneva summit of the Spring of 1955 was greeted as the 'springtime of nations', or as the beginning of the 'thaw', and as the end of the bleak Stalin years, otherwise known as the cold war.

That rosy atmosphere was enhanced as a result of Khrushchev's 'secret speech' at the 20th CPSU congress and the beginning of the process of de-Stalinization. The period was marked by the 'unprecedented' withdrawal of Soviet troops from foreign soil, to wit, the Soviet occupation zone of Austria and the Soviet base in Finland, as well as a sizeable demobilization of Soviet forces. Moreover, communists outside the Soviet empire, starting with the Italian party, displayed the first signs of what was to become known as 'Eurocommunism.'

With the Soviet invasion of Hungary and the sharply doctrinaire overtones of the extraordinary 21st CPSU congress, these optimistic appraisals had to be shelved temporarily, only to be resuscitated during Khrushchev's 1959 visit to the US and the resulting 'Spirit of Camp David', the locale of his summit with President Eisenhower.

That idyll was shattered by a series of Soviet actions, including the unilateral Soviet breach of the moratorium on nuclear tests and the raising of the Berlin wall, culminating in the Cuban missile crisis.

Within a short period following Khrushchev's overthrow in 1964, and in part as a result of the increasingly shrill tones of the Sino-Soviet conflict, the new Brezhnev–Kosygin leadership came to be hailed as standard-bearers of *détente*, with the PRC rapidly replacing the USSR as the perceived prime adversary of the United States – at least as far as the western media and many analysts were concerned. (Khrushchev, it was suddenly realized, had been an adventurer dangerous to international stability and in 1962 had resuscitated the cold war.)

As the wave of Brezhnev's popularity in the west crested, Warsaw Pact troops invaded Czechoslovakia. For a brief period, the prevalent euphoria was replaced by cold sobriety. However, as early as 1969, the Soviet leadership, acting as if nothing had happened, sent Marshal Grechko to suggest a joint US–Soviet nuclear strike against the PRC; since heaven protects children, animals and the feeble of mind, this 'invitation' fortunately was declined.

By the the early 1970s, such 'glitches' had been forgotten and the spring of 1972 came to be remembered as yet another beginning of *détente*, with the Moscow summit and the conclusion of SALT I. The Brezhnev period – denounced by President Reagan in retrospect as the time to which the term 'the Evil Empire' really applied, as opposed to the subsequent idyll of the *Gorbachevshchina* – in fact was marked by an ongoing series of summit meetings and negotiations on arms control, each one hailed at the time as a historic turning point in relations with the USSR.

Indeed, one loses count of the number of times when the media and analysts, particularly during summits, have used the phrase 'historic turning point'; it seems axiomatic that, if this has happened on dozens of occasions, only one at most can have deserved this appellation. That is, unless they were 'turning points' in opposite directions, some pointing forward and others being retrograde. However, that clearly is not what the phrase was supposed to mean.

In fact, periods of *détente*, far from constituting a unilinear trend onward and upward, have turned out to be part of a pendular pattern. For instance, just when Brezhnev's renewed springtime of relations with the west had been accepted as the norm, *détente* tripped over two untoward events: the invasion of Afghanistan and the imposition of martial law in Poland. One presumes that President Reagan was moved by the memory of those developments when he tied the phrase 'Evil Empire' to Brezhnev's personality – forgetting all the encomia of western praise heaped on that Soviet leader during 1972–78.

It was poor Jimmy Carter's voice which gave expression to western bewilderment at the Manichaean attributes of Soviet behavior, when he said that the Soviet invasion of Afghanistan had destroyed all of his previous optimistic views of the USSR. Incidentally, it was also he who seems to have found the most appropriate means of responding to periodic cold war manifestations. His decision to orchestrate a boycott of the Moscow Olympics turned out to be quite painful for the Soviet leadership, since the population was quick to note that 'they' (also known as the *nomenklatura*) had been denied the international legitimation which comes from universal participation in their Games.

Upon considering the zigs and zags of Soviet policy, the reader is entitled to ask 'What occurred during the cold war that ceased to occur as a result of *détente* and vice versa?' That question is remarkably difficult to answer. For instance, at the supposed height of the cold war, during Stalin's last years, the Soviet leader encountered one case of particular recalcitrance by an East European client, namely Tito's defiance. Stalin responded with his traditional covert efforts to undermine an adversary, if possible to have him removed, but . . . the Red Army did not invade Yugoslavia.

As noted, the Hungarian revolution and the Prague Spring occurred during periods of *détente* (or thaw), but the result was armed Soviet intervention, of the bloodiest kind in the first case, and relatively bloodless in the second instance only because the Czechs did not resist.

Again, the final period of Stalin's life, despite current impressions to the contrary, was not really a time marked by deliberate escalation of tensions to the level of full-scale superpower armed confrontations, either just before or just after the US nuclear monopoly was broken:

Stalin tried to blockade Berlin, but acted with great circumspection: The operation was conducted at all times under total control of the Soviet *Kommandantura* in Berlin, which could turn it on and off at will and within minutes. Now you saw it, now you didn't. Termination of the blockade required no humiliating surrender, and no visible retreat. One day the USSR simply stopped applying the forms of pressure which had been used previously. US nuclear power was not tested.

In Korea, Stalin acted via surrogates, and surrogates of surrogates. When the North Koreans, to their and Stalin's surprise, encountered an armed US response, Stalin pressured the PRC (as we now know) to come in and rescue Kim Il Sung's troops. Stalin discreetly avoided any hint of direct Soviet involvement, irrespective of the conflict's outcome – so discreetly that the presence of some Soviet military personnel in Korea during the war was discovered only 37 years later, as a result of a *Pravda* article.

This contrasts vividly with international confrontations during *détente* – or at least 'post-Cold War' – periods that had unmistakable nuclear implications, just to mention the Cuban missile crisis, in which Khrushchev left himself only two options: undisguisable retreat, with Soviet vessels on the high seas turning 180° upon encountering the US 'quarantine', or escalation to nuclear conflict. In the same context one might recall also Brezhnev's adventurous step in moving to insert his airborne divisions into the Middle East conflict, on October 24–25, 1973, leading to a US nuclear alert (DefCon 3).[1] On both occasions, a nuclear confrontation was precipitated shortly after a summit, 16 months after the Vienna summit, in the first case, and four months and sixteen months respectively after the Washington and Moscow summits, in the second instance.

Now, obviously no one would claim that Stalin's last years constituted a period of milk and honey for the world, not to speak of the Soviet population, or that the Khrushchev and Brezhnev periods amounted to unrelieved gloom and doom. The purpose of comparing the events cited, however, is to demonstrate to what an astounding degree the terms 'cold war' and '*détente*' are misleading, certainly as far as international relations are concerned.

Presumably then, to be meaningful, the question 'is the cold war over?' really asks us to determine whether the Gorbachev period constitutes a qualitative break with *all* previous periods of post-World War II Soviet policy, both those subsumed previously under the 'cold war' and the *détente* categories. (Implicit in the question is the strange assumption that the cold war prevailed uninterruptedly until Gorbachev's ascent to power.) Moreover, even if the answer should be positive, one would have to determine whether the shift is unilinear and irreversible.

In this context, one would have to say that while many of Gorbachev's departures obviously are of major proportions, others are not unprecedented, and this applies also to the encomia of praise the west has heaped upon him, often uncritically, as it did earlier with Khrushchev and Brezhnev.

To address this issue seriously, however, it is not enough to deal with Gorbachev's international policy. One must realize that much of the Gorbachev image in the west has been the result of measures that were essentially domestic, so that one cannot answer the question in the title of this chapter without addressing his impact on the Soviet population.

Here, it is essential to note that *glasnost* with its attraction for the west (which viewed it as equivalent to democratization) reached its peak in 1988 and has suffered occasional setbacks since then. One need only compare the manner in which Moscow television (especially *Vremya*) has covered Lithuania, reverting to a 'party line' approach in reporting (actually not reporting) developments in that republic, with the babel of critical and dissenting voices that prevailed only a couple of years earlier even in the central Soviet press, radio and television.

On May Day of 1990, the coverage by Soviet television evoked haunting memories of an ominous precedent. Gorbachev, accompanied by his advisers, appeared on the dais to take the salute as bused in and organized contingents of marchers moved past. Immediately thereafter, however, a spontaneous demonstration took place as thousands followed in the wake of the organized group, carrying the flags of Lithuania and other union republics wishing to be independent, as well as the tricolor of Russia's democratic February Revolution. Many placards carried anti-Gorbachev slogans. As Gorbachev, apparently taken aback, turned to leave the dais, he was loudly booed by the demonstrators, whereupon Soviet television abruptly ceased broadcasting the event. Traditionally, May Day and October Revolution ceremonies have been covered in excruciating detail from beginning to end. With all of the obvious qualitative differences, there was a sense of *déja vu* . . . the finale of Ceausescu's Bucharest.

Even so, clearly the Soviet population in the pre-Gorbachev era would not have dared to express disapproval in this manner. Moreover, had there been such an incident then, the consequences might have been nightmarish. The question, however, is whether Gorbachev is carrying his early policy departures to their logical conclusion or whether he is beginning to retreat.

Unfortunately, Gorbachev's behaviour pattern has displayed increasingly autocratic, umbrageous, and erratic tendencies. His monopolization of power, in a period of a few years, constitutes a record in Soviet history. In addition to becoming General Secretary of the CPSU, supreme commander of the armed forces (originally by virtue of his chairmanship of the State Defence Council), and Chairman of the Presidium of the Supreme Soviet, he has appointed himself USSR president, with powers that can be compared only in jest with a US- or French-style presidency.

Thus, if the Supreme Soviet should prove disagreeable to him, he can simply dissolve it, not in order to hold new popular elections, but rather for the Congress of People's Deputies to select a new Supreme Soviet for him. (One has to remember that the CPD with 2,250 members – of which one-third are not popularly elected, but represent 'social organizations', such as the CPSU and the Komsomol – is a more easily controllable body.) He can establish laws by simple edict, if the Supreme Soviet fails to oblige. He can veto acts of the Supreme Soviet and he demanded the right to overrule that body, should it attempt to override his veto. He can impose martial law on any portion of the Soviet Union without proper regard to the rights of the union republics that are theoretically sovereign in their own territory.

He adamantly opposed members of the Supreme Soviet who called for popular election of such an all-powerful leader, insisting that, in his case, submission to such an ordeal should be required only five years hence.

He defended his request for these extraordinary powers as necessary to enable him to enact drastic economic reforms. However, no sooner were these powers granted, than he started to explain why such reforms were not feasible at the present time.

Admittedly, under Gorbachev the apparatus of the CPSU's Central Committee appears to have been downgraded considerably, but it may be questioned whether that is an unmixed blessing. For instance, the CC's Department for Administrative Organs, the party's watchdog over the KGB, has been dissolved; as a consequence, the security organs now appear to be free of any oversight. This may explain the KGB's increasing muscle flexing, not only internationally (as has been noted by US security experts), but also domestically.

For many years the actions of the KGB and its predecessors had been veiled in complete secrecy. Brezhnev initiated an era of popularization of its achievements abroad; movies, novels, even comic books for children extolled 'the exploits of our brave Chekists', including Kim Philby, Sorge, and others. However, one year ago, the KGB also started flaunting its power to affect decisions of the CPSU. Recently, the sons of Khrushchev and Mikoyan, respectively, published accounts of Khrushchev's overthrow. Immediately thereafter, the head of the KGB at that time, Semichastny, gave an interview in which he stated that, of course, it was the KGB that was responsible for Khrushchev's ouster and that persons like Kosygin only joined once they were assured of KGB support.

Gorbachev, it will be recalled, was the protégé of Andropov, one-time head of the KGB – one of the few aspects of Gorbachev's career on which there seems to be general consensus. However, this is not the only part of the security apparatus that has received a boost.

The Ministry of Internal Affairs (MVD) now has at its disposal special action forces (some 300,000 troops) for population control, with the power to open fire on 'demonstrations and congresses' (by definition meaning peaceful assemblies) and to break into homes for search and seizure operations. These forces participated in the bloody events of April 1989 in Tbilisi, and subsequently in Baku.

Furthermore, the Procurator's Office has been equipped with a particularly ominous clause that was added to the penal code, and which allows imprisonment for words or actions that 'could discredit . . . state and party officials and institutions'.

In his new capacity as President, Gorbachev has included representatives of all the security organs in his cabinet, adding moreover two particularly notorious members of the chauvinistic Russian extreme right, including (*nomen est omen*) one Rasputin.

While still presiding over the Supreme Soviet, Gorbachev had started already to display some arbitrary and autocratic facets of his temperament. Andrei Sakharov, shortly before his death, had warned of the dangers which Gorbachev's accumulation of power posed. When Sakharov attempted to address the assembly, Gorbachev told him rudely to shut up and turned off his microphone. In the sessions that preceded the creation of the new all-powerful presidency, Gorbachev gavelled down speakers who insisted on popular elections for president, and repeatedly refused to bring unwelcome motions to a vote.

His lack of self-control had been noted on previous occasions, and was demonstrated by the outbursts that punctuated his brief visits to Armenia and Lithuania. Taking offence that Armenians and Lithuanians had dared to speak back to him, he started to display particular arbitrariness where these two nationalities were concerned. In the face of repeated appeals, he remained strangely passive for more than a year while Armenians were victims of Azeri pogroms. On the other hand, he rushed to order repressive measures, including a blockade (an act of war under international law), against Lithuania for attempting to break away at a time when the Soviet constitution specifically allowed each union republic to secede (and before the Supreme Soviet, at his behest, passed legislation rendering such secession well-nigh unfeasible).

For years westerners have argued that Gorbachev's domestic policies provided a solid base for the assumption that the cold war is ending, because radical economic reform and democratization cannot go hand in hand with a militarily offensive and ideologically expansionistic international posture. The same analysts cannot now turn around and posit that the deterioration in his performance at home is irrelevant as an indicator of what may be expected of the USSR in the global arena.

Given all their positive features until recently, Gorbachev's current international operations are not entirely devoid of ominous portents, having to do largely with projection of power, particularly into areas of regional conflict. In 1989, Soviet arms transfers to such trouble spots as the Middle East, south and south-east Asia, and Latin America exceeded $17 billion. In most of these cases, moreover, the recipients were regimes that have not repaid past debts incurred for weapons, are not capable of repaying, and have not even promised to do so. In other words, Soviet economic problems have preciously little to do with this flow. On the contrary, they are being exacerbated. (Western governments do supply weapons to third world countries, but usually in return for hard cash, particularly petrodollars.)

In the year *after* the withdrawal of Soviet combat forces from Afghanistan, over $3 billion of Soviet hardware streamed into that country, more than in any one year when 100,000 Soviet soldiers were still there. Syria and Cuba have been other major recipients. The amount of economic drain this represents does not constitute the only problem, but one should also note that state-of-the-art technology is being transferred. Weapons which were not given to most Soviet allies in the Warsaw Pact, when that organization was still fully intact, have been sent to third world recipients, including the MiG-29, the Sukhoi-24, the T-72 and even some T-80 tanks, as well as the SS-23 missile. This applies particularly to Syria, whose armored forces today exceed the number of Soviet and German tanks, combined, in the largest armoured battle of World War II, at Kursk.

(In this respect, discussions on the reduction of conventional forces in Europe, if successful, could have a further deleterious impact on the third world. Weapons no longer useful for such forces in Europe almost inevitably would be transferred overseas.)

In several cases, the amounts and qualities of arms supplied have exceeded by far the absorptive capacity of the recipients' armed forces; that is true of countries like Libya, the population of which numbers only a couple of million. The question has to be raised why such quantities should be transferred to states of that type. There are indications that these weapons are intended for pre-positioning, in places like the Syrian port of Tartus, to be used potentially by Soviet forces. In October of 1973, the USSR was considering the possibility of armed intervention in the Middle East, relying heavily upon its airborne divisions. Its lift capacity, however, was equal at most to transferring one or two of the seven divisions over a brief period, if hardware had to be brought in as well as the troops. Pre-positioning, of course, would take care of such problems.

In this context, special attention has to be devoted also to another white elephant, economically speaking, that is the continued heavy Soviet investment in at least three additional aircraft carriers, which would be vulnerable in a global nuclear confrontation. However, they could play a major role in Soviet power projection into third world areas, where shore-based facilities might not suffice to provide an adequate air umbrella for regional combat. The carriers would constitute the core of task forces that could operate with relative self-sufficiency in the eastern Mediterranean, the Red Sea, or the Indian Ocean, and could reinforce clients and intimidate their adversaries, as Admiral Gorshkov stressed in his classic work on the use of seapower in times of war and peace.

These endeavours must be viewed side by side with the measurably enhanced Soviet intelligence activities, both in such areas and in and around the US itself, as noted by Judge Webster. These have not only proliferated in number, but have become almost overt, in some cases flaunting their seeming invulnerability to western countermeasures. Of course, this goes hand in hand with the upgraded role of the KGB within the USSR, as noted earlier.

Moscow's diplomatic posture in the third world which, for a brief period, appeared to be advocating restraint on the part of Soviet clients, occasionally has reverted to its previous stance. Thus, an ominous statement following the Gorbachev–Assad meeting at the end of April indicated Soviet support for undefined Syrian measures to cope with Israel's alleged nuclear capability. Only some months earlier, so western diplomats were informed, the Soviet Union had cautioned Syria that, if it went to war, it could not expect to be rescued by the USSR.

Shortly after the Soviet–Syrian summit, the Soviet ambassador to Damascus announced that the USSR was about to 'modernize' the Syrian arsenal. Considering the quality and quantity of Soviet weapons already in Syria's possession, as described earlier, it is difficult to imagine what may be implied.

After a very encouraging initial approach to changes in Eastern Europe, Gorbachev is showing signs now of foot dragging over the removal of the Soviet military presence from several East European countries. With regard to Soviet troop withdrawal from Hungary and Czechoslovakia, earlier positive Soviet signals have been replaced by increasing orchestration in the Soviet media of the theme that this would be beset by difficulties and obstacles. Thus, publications are proliferating concerning troop relocation problems, in terms of shortage of transportation, lack of adequate facilities in the Soviet Union for returning soldiers, lack of work for those to be demobilized, and so on.

The alleged shortage of facilities has to be viewed sceptically considering that the Soviet draft has been curtailed. This reduction was due primarily to demographic realities, although it was publicized as one of Gorbachev's gestures toward the west. The fact is that 37 per cent of all potential recruits in 1990 emanated from the so-called Moslem nationalities, which are considered not only politically unreliable, but also suffer from linguistic, educational and technological handicaps.

Incidentally, western eagerness for an agreement on the reduction of conventional forces in Europe has a potentially adverse affect on Czechoslovakia's and Hungary's chances to be rid of the Red Army. They are requesting that *all* Soviet soldiers leave, whereas a western agreement with the USSR would provide merely for a *reduced* Soviet military presence, which would be legitimated in effect.

In the Polish case, Soviet pressure of a more subtle kind has persuaded the premier to call for the continued deployment of Soviet military communication units on Polish soil, supposedly as a guarantee against a united Germany. In fact, their presence would be needed primarily if Soviet troops continued to be deployed in the eastern zone of a united Germany. Increasingly, it appears that Gorbachev, despite earlier signals to the contrary, will insist on retaining a substantial military presence in the eastern zone.

Particularly disquieting are continued Soviet deception activities, even concerning relatively petty issues on which one would not expect that the risk of exposure was worth the game. Evidence of this tendency is the case of the SS-23 missiles which, under the 1987 agreement between the US and the USSR, were supposed to be eliminated. At the time, Washington was given to understand that only the Soviet Union possessed these weapons. Recently, however, East Berlin revealed that Moscow transferred the missiles to the former East German régime and, since then, it has been discovered that Czechoslovakia and Bulgaria also were given the SS-23.

When the truth emerged, Soviet sources told Washington that the transfers had been made without the knowledge of Soviet leaders; however, soon thereafter the same sources stated on behalf of these leaders that the 1987 agreement had not been violated anyway, since the missiles were passed on to the east Europeans before it was signed! In either case, of course, this constituted deception since the US was left deliberately under the impression that the agreement meant the destruction of *all* of these weapons. There is cause for concern, especially because hiding away some SS-23s would affect the balance in that part of Europe marginally if at all. Why, therefore, bother to go through such subterfuge and to endanger far more important agreements in the works?

The actions discussed did not predate the Gorbachev era; in fact, some of them are of very recent vintage. The old saw that the leader does not know and that only some evil-minded underlings are to blame simply will not hold. Operations that involved not merely the Soviet armed forces but at least three East European regimes as well, not to mention possible repercussions concerning the US, could not have been implemented without a green light from the highest source.

The discussion of these frequently ignored symptoms of an under-lying malaise is not meant to denigrate in any way the importance of the dramatic events that have occurred in the Soviet Union and in much of Eastern Europe during the Gorbachev period. What is at issue, however, is whether they constitute a qualitative, unilinear break with the past, and, even if the answer were to be positive without a caveat, whether such a change is irreversible.

The substance of this chapter indicates: (a) the terms 'Cold War' and '*détente*' have been bandied about indiscriminately and without clear definition; (b) Soviet actions and policies in the post-world war II period have not been unilinear, but pendular, moving relatively often between these two poles; (c) some of the developments associated with Gorbachev are not necessarily unprecedented, even if they have been dramatic; (d) both domestically and on the international arena, his own actions have been pendular in character, and there has been occasional backsliding from the peak of *glasnost* some 18 months ago; (e) in Eastern Europe, after a very encouraging opening, Gorbachev is beginning to equivocate over troop withdrawl probably in response to increasingly centrifugal developments; and (f) Soviet operations concerning the third world, as well as related intelligence activities, constitute continuation of policies usually associated with the Brezhnev period, Gorbachev's posture over Iraq–Kuwait notwith-standing.

Yogi Berra, the baseball hero whose sayings have become classics of Americana, used to assert 'it ain't over 'til it's over'. If the reader has difficulty with Berra's response, the fault lies not with the answer but with the question, which is not really meaningful as this chapter has tried to demonstrate.

Institute for the Study of Conflict,
Ideology and Policy, Boston University

NOTE

1. Earlier steps along these lines, respectively by Khrushchev and Bulganin, in threatening to annihilate London, Paris, and Jerusalem in November of 1956, and by Brezhnev, in moving his Mediterranean naval unit to the Syrian coast on 10 June 1967, were recognized at the time as constituting mere bluff, since they were taken after those two middle eastern wars essentially had terminated.

The Problem for United States Foreign Policy

JOHN A. THOMPSON

It is not necessary to endorse the claim that *perestroika* is the fruit of the Reagan administration's arms build-up in order to see the end of the cold war as a success for American foreign policy. In 1947, George F. Kennan called for 'a long-term, patient but firm and vigilant containment of Russian expansive tendencies' on the grounds that this would 'promote tendencies which must eventually find their outlet in either the break-up or the gradual mellowing of Soviet power'.[1] Since then, the strategy of containment has taken various forms, but it has remained the constant, overriding goal of US foreign policy.[2] Its object would now appear to have been attained.

In this sense at least, America has won the 'cold war'. The term is, of course, a metaphor, although for the United States it has involved two very real wars, in Korea and Vietnam. But the metaphor has the merit of sharply raising the question whether, following victory, Americans will demobilize and concentrate upon domestic issues and private concerns. Such used to be their habit, manifested after World War I and, briefly and to a lesser extent, after World War II also. These examples, however, come from the period before the United States became involved in international politics in a continuous and extensive way.[3] During the last 43 years, a whole complex of interests both at home and around the world have become entwined with US foreign policy, and these will not simply fade away. In order to estimate the likely effects of the end of the cold war, it is necessary to probe the nature of the connections between that conflict and the global projection of American power in the post-World War II era.

I

One such connection is that fear of Soviet or communist expansion has led other governments to seek American assistance and protection. This was particularly apparent in the early days of the cold war. Some of the first Soviet–American confrontations occurred in the near east where, as Bruce Kuniholm has pointed out, 'US involvement in the affairs of Iran and Turkey was encouraged by those countries, because their governments wanted the United States to serve as a counterweight to the USSR, whose influence was resented and feared'.[4] Likewise, the extent to which the impetus for the North Atlantic treaty (NATO) came from the European allies has been emphasized by much recent historiography.[5] If the consequence is seen as constituting some form of American empire, it was largely a case, in Geir Lundestad's happy phrase, of 'empire by invitation'.[6]

Like more coercively-imposed imperialisms, however, this one has exacted a price. The establishment of American military bases in other countries has been intrinsic to it, and has, indeed, sometimes been welcomed as a guarantee of the US commitment. But the presence of foreign forces essentially beyond the jurisdiction and outside the control of the host government inevitably involves a diminution of sovereignty. Moreover, all America's allies have had, to a greater or lesser extent, to accommodate their policies to those of their more powerful partner or patron. Their position has been made no easier by the fact that the United States has largely carried over from its isolationist past the habit of making its own policy unilaterally. From Wilson's handling of the pre-armistice negotiations in 1918 through Kennedy's imposition of a blockade on Cuba in 1962 to Reagan's air raid on Libya in 1986, America's allies have found their interests implicated in actions that they had no opportunity to influence beforehand. Nurtured by an introverted political culture and reinforced by the role of Congress, this unilateralist tendency has reflected the disparity of dependence between the United States and even the most important of her allies.

Readiness to accept American 'leadership' on these terms has been based on two factors – the desire for security, and faith in American power. NATO arose from the conviction that, in Lawrence Kaplan's words, 'only the United States had the resources and the power to save the west'.[7] This feeling derived most of its urgency from fear of Soviet-communist expansion, but it was not entirely dependent on it. An American commitment to European security had been sought by British and French statesmen since at least the days of World War I, and both the North Atlantic treaty and the re-committal of US troops to Europe in 1950 were seen as protection against a resurgent Germany as well as the USSR.[8] Outside the European theatre, the desire of nations as diverse as Israel, Pakistan, Australia and New Zealand for alliance with the United States owed much less to an imminent communist threat. Indeed, as the geographical scope of US action has expanded over the decades, regimes and contenders for power in many regions have become adept at clothing more local anxieties and enmities in cold war rhetoric in order to gain American aid. Meanwhile, the developed nations of the far east as well as those of Europe and North America have come to look to the United States to take the lead in maintaining world order against threats of all kinds.

Over the years, then, authentic fear of Soviet expansionism has come to play a smaller part in generating the external 'pull' on American foreign policy. This is not only because other demands have grown but also because the fear itself has declined even in those places where it has been of primary importance, particularly western Europe. Although the need to balance the power of the Warsaw pact has remained NATO doctrine, it had already in recent years become increasingly difficult to secure political support for the deployment of new missiles or their 'modernization'. The greater sense of security has also been manifested in the increased readiness of the European allies to distance themselves from US policy – and even on occasion, as over the gas pipeline issue in the early 1980s, to defy it. From this point of view, the collapse of the Warsaw pact and the sharp diminution in the credibility of the threat from the east represents the acceleration of a trend rather than its reversal. The dramatically changed situation will no doubt affect NATO's force levels, and quite possibly also its structure, but it is unlikely that the cry of 'Yankee, go home' will be the dominant one. Leaving aside the additionally de-stabilizing effects of an American withdrawal, the nuclear balance seems bound to remain dependent on the United States. Moreover, as they confront the problems of a post-cold war Europe, leaders in most countries (not least, perhaps, the Soviet Union) are likely to value any contribution to a new system of security that can be made by a great power that is largely detached from the continent's historic antagonisms and tensions. As in the 1940s, they would, doubtless, also welcome an input of American resources to help solve the economic problems – this time of Eastern Europe.

If in this latter respect expectations are lower than they were in the immediate post-war years, this reflects the general feeling that American resources are less abundant than they were. It is certainly the case that the United States no longer possesses the remarkable economic pre-eminence that it enjoyed in the late 1940s. At that time, the American output of goods and services was approximately half the world's total and no other country had a gross national product (GNP) even a third as large. By the late 1980s, the USA's share of world output was no more than 23 per cent, while its share of world exports had declined from almost 17 per cent in 1950 to just over ten per cent.[9] Such statistics as these have led many to conclude that the economic basis of American hegemony is inexorably shrinking and that, in Paul Kennedy's words, 'the task facing American statesmen over the next decades, therefore, is to recognize that broad trends are under way, and that there is a need to "manage" affairs so that the *relative* erosion of the United States' position takes place slowly and smoothly'.[10]

This statement is more qualified than the reception of Kennedy's book would have indicated, and the moderation is wise. As Kennedy himself recognizes, American power was 'artificially high' in 1945 since the economies of all the other industrial nations, defeated and 'victorious' alike, had been so severely damaged by the war.[11] By its nature, this situation was exceptional and unsustainable but the American economy remains by far the biggest in the world, almost twice as large as that of its nearest rival, Japan. Militarily, America's pre-eminence is even more marked, in terms of the variety and range as well as the size of its forces. Altogether the United States is now, and perhaps always was, the world's one 'superpower'.[12] But this status is related to such facts as that it has over half a million of its servicemen abroad (including 65,000 afloat)[13], and that it has for the last 40 years spent a higher proportion of its GNP on defence than any major country except the USSR. Acting the role of a great power is a matter not only of strength but also of will – as nothing demonstrates better than the history of US foreign policy itself earlier this century.

II

This leads to the second, more direct, connection between the cold war and the role the US has played in world affairs in recent years, which is its effect on American motivation. The question takes one to the heart of the controversy over the origins of the cold war. The traditional or 'orthodox' view was that from the American point of view the cold war was simply a defensive response to Soviet expansionism and that it did not take shape until the Truman Doctrine of 1947. In its pristine version, the revisionist interpretation reversed this account by suggesting that Soviet actions were themselves a defensive response to the expansionist surge of American power as it sought to establish an 'open door world' extending into Eastern Europe and to thwart all forces, left-wing and nationalist alike, that resisted incorporation into this international capitalist system. The first view would lead one to expect that as the Soviet threat declines so will the American response, the second that US policy, driven by an internal dynamic, will remain essentially unchanged.

In these 'post-revisionist' days, few historians would endorse either of these extreme positions. Despite the claims for a long-term continuity in American 'expansionism' made by some prominent revisionists, few would deny that the 1940s witnessed something approaching a 'revolution' in America's foreign policy.[14] But the changes came in stages and in response to a variety of stimuli. Following the fall of France in 1940, the United States abandoned anything that could properly be called 'isolationism' or 'continentalism', although it took Pearl Harbor to move her to full-scale belligerency. Moreover, long before any serious confrontation with the Soviet Union developed, it was clear that participation in the Second World War, unlike that in the First, would have a profound and lasting effect on American policy. This was because of the widespread acceptance of the view that the war could have been prevented if the US had played an active part in the League of Nations and that the depression which had contributed so much to Hitler's rise to power was produced and aggravated by economic nationalism. By the end of the war the United States had decisively abandoned isolationism, diplomatically by joining the United Nations, economically by taking the lead in setting up the International Monetary Fund (IMF), the World Bank and the 'Bretton Woods system', and strategically to the extent that even the army had come to accept the need for a defence posture extending well beyond the western hemisphere.[15] On the other hand, it was later events that led to the launching of the Marshall Plan, the subsequent establishment of a worldwide network of commitments, pacts and military assistance agreements, and the assumption of a level of defence spending that no one had envisaged in 1945. These unforeseen events included the economic plight of western Europe in 1947 and the rapid decline of British power as well as the apparently limitless expansionism of the Soviet Union. George Kennan, for one, was keen to dispel the impression 'that the United States approach to world problems is a defensive reaction to communist pressure and that the effort to restore sound economic conditions is only a by-product of this reaction and not something we would be interested in doing if there were no communist menace'.[16]

The impression Kennan deplored was that created by the Truman Doctrine speech of 12 March 1947. The form of that speech had reflected a deliberate attempt, in Robert Pollard's words, 'to use anti-communism to galvanize Congressional and public support for aid to Greece and Turkey'.[17] The efficacy of this approach had been indicated the previous year during the difficult progress of the British loan through Congress when, as Lord Halifax reported from Washington, 'the main propulsive force . . . behind the loan is felt to be none other than Stalin, whose tactics have created a greater volume of sentiment in favour of support for Britain than our own unaided efforts could probably ever have achieved'.[18] The same phenomenon was to be apparent during the passage through Congress of Marshall aid itself in 1947–48.[19] Ever since, the requirements of the cold war have provided the principal justification for almost all the demands that American foreign policy has made upon American resources.

The importance of this function needs to be underlined. A common image is that foreign policy is 'made' by the President and his advisers and then 'sold' to Congress and the public – Truman himself referred to his task in persuading the US to participate in European politics as 'the greatest selling job ever facing a President'.[20] But the image is misleading and slights the role of public opinion in the formation of policy. For one thing, in certain crucial areas the 'product' does not exist until it has been 'sold'. Without congressional appropriations, there would have been no European recovery programme – or any other foreign aid, apart from those limited amounts that can be disposed of at the discretion of the executive. Likewise, the authority of the President to commit US forces to action or to enter into binding obligations to other countries, although nowadays stretched beyond what a strict reading of the constitution would indicate, remains circumscribed. In practice, the significance of these constitutional constraints in any particular case depends upon the political context and the state of public opinion. An administration can do much to shape the latter, given its power to set the agenda and manipulate the media as well as the natural inclination of most Americans to rally behind their president during foreign crises. Emphasizing these factors, one scholar has concluded that public opinion gave Truman 'a free hand' to 'define and carry out his foreign policy preferences'.[21] Yet presidents certainly can find their foreign policy initiatives rejected – Wilson and the League of Nations remains the most famous case but in more recent years we have seen the cutting off of military aid to Indochina in 1973 and to the Nicaraguan contras in 1984 despite the fervent pleas of Nixon and Reagan respectively. As these examples remind us, the President is an elected official operating in a competitive political environment. In these circumstances, his own 'foreign policy preferences' are likely to be affected by his assessment of the prospect of mobilizing support for them.[22]

The difficulty of obtaining such support rises in proportion to the costs of the policy in question. This is true in any country, but historically Americans have been particularly reluctant to make sacrifices for foreign policy objectives. In part, this may be seen as an aspect of a broader prejudice against governmentally organized public enterprises, the reflection of a libertarian and voluntarist tradition that has been reinforced by the fragmented political structure. In respect of foreign policy itself, the legacy of isolationism is commonly held to have exercised a continuing influence. However, the nineteenth century is now long past and it may be more relevant to recognize the extent to which the conditions that gave rise to that posture have persisted. If nineteenth-century Americans hardly felt that their own welfare and safety depended upon the success of US foreign policy, it is not clear how far their twentieth-century successors have felt differently – or have had reason to.

In economic terms, indeed, the United States has been rather more self-contained in the twentieth century than it was earlier. Whereas in the second half of the nineteenth century exports constituted 6–8 per cent of GNP, in the period 1920–70 the figure was no more than 3–5 per cent. (These percentages, low as they are in comparative terms, would be reduced even further if the North American economy were considered as a unit, since between a fifth and a quarter of US exports have been to Canada and Mexico.)[23] Imports have until recently tended to run at a slightly lower level than exports, and although they have included a few raw materials unavailable in the United States, a policy of stockpiling and the extent of potential substitution has meant that there has been no 'vital' dependence on these.[24] Petroleum, where net imports now amount to more than a third of the enormous American consumption, is clearly a special case. But, even here, the United States remains far less dependent on oil from strategically vulnerable regions like the Middle East than are Japan and most Western European countries.[25] Moreover, the example of oil also illustrates the even more important point that the overseas activities of America business have not required the support of diplomatic or military commitments. The multinational oil companies have had their own ways of protecting their interests and, indeed, sometimes (as in Angola and Libya) these have not been precisely in harmony with US foreign policy.[26] More generally, the very size of the American economy has meant that its economic relations have always been more important for the other country involved than for the United States, and this imbalance has created a bargaining leverage that has rarely needed to be supplemented.[27] It is true that at times advocates of foreign policy initiatives, such as the acquisition of the Philippines or the Marshall Plan, have maintained that they were necessary for the nation's future prosperity, but such arguments have always been plausibly contested.[28] Indeed, in debates over American policy, it has been more often the opponents of intervention who have attributed it to economic interests. This fact, particularly evident in the cases of the First World War and Vietnam, has reflected not only the assumption that such economic interests must be essentially sectional rather than national in character but also the related belief that, although they could conceivably justify a foreign aid programme or diplomatic pressure, they were not worth the lives of American boys.

In order to mobilize the military might that in the last resort gives the United States its weight in world politics, American leaders have had to invoke the requirements of 'national security'. Self-defence, the sole justification for war allowed by the United Nations (UN) Charter, has remained for ordinary Americans the only really compelling reason for fighting – certainly with conscripted servicemen. But in this respect, too, the case for extensive foreign commitments has not been easy to make. Those who have sought to argue it have stressed the extent to which the conditions of American security in the nineteenth century – physical distance from major military powers, British command of the seas, and the European balance of power – have been eroded by subsequent technological and political developments. There can be little doubt that such developments have brought to an end 'the era of free security' for the United States, and since the birth of the 'new navy' in the 1890s, Americans have gradually become accustomed to devoting to national defence a far higher proportion of the GNP than the less than one per cent which had been its historic norm.[29] But the implications for foreign, as distinct from defence, policy have been less clear. For the very growth of American power has reduced the nation's reliance on others to protect it from attack. Even in the atomic age, when 'defence' has become a matter of deterrence, the United States remains self-sufficient in this regard. Since the core of the nation's retaliatory capacity resides in missiles based on American soil or under the oceans, the US does not really need any allies at all from a strictly military point of view. Indeed, it has been persuasively argued by hard-headed analysts that alliances have come to have a negative effect on America's physical security, since 'although the loss of allies, even the most important allies, would not significantly alter the prospects of an adversary surviving an attack upon the United States, the risks that might have to be run on behalf of allies could lead to a nuclear confrontation that would escape the control of the great protagonists'.[30]

In these circumstances, it is not surprising that while national security has been the central and indispensable element in any effective justification of costly overseas involvement, it has acquired meanings that go beyond purely military considerations. In the two world wars, the precipitant of US intervention was an outraged sense of national honour – the German submarine campaign and the Zimmermann telegram arousing the same sort of response, if less intensely, as the attack on Pearl Harbor. This was augmented by a moral and ideological hostility towards what Wilson called 'selfish and autocratic power', and Franklin Roosevelt described as 'the dictator nations'. Such terms appealed to the traditional idea of an American mission to uphold the cause of liberty in the world, but it is significant that they were less evangelical in character than defensive. Wilson stated that 'the world must be made safe for democracy', while Roosevelt emphasized that 'military and naval victory for the gods of force and hate would endanger the institutions of democracy in the western world'.[31] Historically, the American mission had been seen as essentially exemplary,[32] and it has only been capable of inspiring a strenuous effort abroad when linked to the perceived needs of national security.

Just such a link was established, of course, by the cold war. Indeed, it would be hard to conceive of a cause better suited to muster the breadth and depth of support necessary to sustain the sort of extensive, forceful and continuous role in international politics that the United States had never before played, despite having been potentially the most powerful actor on the world stage throughout the twentieth century. It was a conflict with a complex rationale that touched several nerves and appealed to diverse constituencies. Militarily, the Soviet Union was the only state which could be seen as having the capability of achieving that domination of the Eurasian continent that American strategists and policymakers had come to believe would pose an unacceptable threat to American security.[33] The ruthless manner in which it expanded its sphere of control in the aftermath of World War II aroused the antagonism of Americans of Eastern European origin who had not normally formed part of 'the foreign policy public', and soon also alarmed that east coast elite who had long felt intimately connected, in a variety of profound ways, with the countries of *Western* Europe. The international behaviour of the Soviet Union, in conjunction with the internal character of the Stalinist regime, seemed to conform to that model of 'totalitarianism' that had been vividly imprinted on people's minds by the events of the very recent past.[34] Although not specifically alluded to in the Truman Doctrine speech, the particular ideology espoused by Moscow was also of the utmost importance. It was not only that resisting the spread of communism provided a Democratic administration with the best possible grounds for gaining the bipartisan support needed to secure congressional approval for its revolutionary foreign policy, it also tapped a most powerful current in American opinion. Public opinion polls had shown that as late as 1939, most Americans, if forced to choose between communism and fascism, would have preferred the latter.[35] This reflected a depth of antagonism fostered by countless denunciations of communism as the enemy of all that most Americans believed in – not only the free enterprise system but also religion. Such denunciations, particularly by Catholic spokesmen, were not stemmed by World War II, and in 1941 Roosevelt had made a point of emphasizing that 'the Nazis are as ruthless as the Communists in the denial of God'.[36]

The diversity of elements compounded in the rationale for the cold war has not been entirely a source of strength. It also introduced an ambiguity over whether the adversary was the Soviet Union or communism as an ideology. This became particularly relevant with the extension of containment from Europe to the rest of the world, which never commanded quite the same level of support. The commitment of US troops to Vietnam created a division in 'the foreign policy elite'[37] long before the costs and difficulty of that war produced a wider public reaction to it. It could well be argued that since Vietnam the 'cold war consensus' has never been quite the same, since not only have all subsequent presidents been careful to avoid any similar involvement but even the defence build-up of the early 1980s (which never reached the level of that of the early 1950s) was not financed by painful taxes. Nevertheless, in the words of an authoritative American textbook, 'every time that containment has appeared to be fading or to be undergoing a metamorphosis, the illusion has been shattered as the premises of containment logic have reasserted their hold on American foreign policy thinking'.[38]

The behaviour of the Soviet Union has played a crucial part in sustaining these premises (as is apparent now it has so manifestly changed), but their durability has also owed much to the dynamics of policy-making in the United States. Some special interests have obviously been involved, not only the military and their suppliers but also all those whose careers have become bound up with planning and executing cold war strategy. More generally, the rivalry with the Soviet Union has provided a focus for the competitive spirit which is so strong in American culture but had not previously found expression in foreign policy (apart, perhaps, from naval relations with Great Britain between the wars). Furthermore, it has served to give US policy not only force but also a much needed sense of direction. The American decision-making process is notoriously fissiparous and porous, with several different and generally competitive bureaucracies involved in making foreign policy in addition to Congress, always susceptible to pressure from well organized lobbies. In this context, it has never been easy to impose coherence on policy and establish an orderly sense of priorities, and the absence of an overriding goal or objective would make it even more difficult. If the Bush administration initially seemed a little reluctant to recognize the end of the cold war, it is hardly surprising.

The question clearly arises whether an alternative focus could be found for American policy that would perform the same functions. In an article castigating 'even our more enlightened bureaucrats' for their slowness 'to free themselves from their entrenched attitude that the cold war is the only framework in which policy should be formulated', George Ball suggested that the US should seek to work with the Soviet Union towards solving regional problems 'under the reassuring flag of the United Nations'.[39] The idea that American power should be devoted to the establishment of world order through the mechanism of an international organization is, of course, not a new one, and its history is hardly encouraging. The Senate's rejection of membership in the League of Nations in 1919 was emphatically endorsed in the election of 1920.[40] In the late 1940s, the Truman administration deliberately decided that US aid programmes should be independent of the new United Nations.[41] In 1977, Carter came into office intending to make world order (and human rights) rather than the cold war the basis of American policy, but he was unable to hold to this line. One difficulty in the way of such an approach has been that the cooperation involved would run counter to the unilateralist tradition of US foreign policy. A greater problem, however, is that a serious commitment to the goal of world order would certainly demand considerable resources and quite possibly the lives of American servicemen. It is hard to imagine a public readiness to bear such burdens for a task that seems less than necessary and worse than thankless.

Even if the cold war loses all credibility, US foreign policy will not be unaffected by it for some time to come. Its legacy will include the impression made on Americans by the experiences of the past 40 years. Not the least of these was the trauma of defeat in Vietnam which contributed to the emergence in the late 1970s of a belligerent national mood that has been sustained perhaps by a sense of declining importance on the world scene.[42] In this climate, the raid on Libya in 1986 and the intervention in Panama in 1989 met with an enthusiastic public response. But it is of the essence of such exercise that they are not only swiftly successful but inexpensive. In this era of deficits, it will take some much more serious purpose to enable foreign policy to maintain its claim to the proportion of the nation's resources that it has absorbed in recent decades.

III

Although the decline of the perceived Soviet threat will reduce the urgency of the desire for American protection, particularly in Europe, many nations will continue to look to the United States for assistance, and even leadership, in containing and alleviating the other serious problems that will continue to confront them. However, such an external 'pull' is unlikely of itself to produce a substantial deployment of America's still ample power – as Chinese as well as European statesmen of an earlier generation could testify. In each case, there will no doubt be some Americans, including quite possibly a number in high places, who will want to see their country make an effective response. But in order to generate resources on any scale, they will have to persuade a firm majority of their countrymen that significant interests of their own are at stake. The difficulty of establishing clear and direct connections between the security and prosperity of the American people and the achievement of any particular foreign policy objective has been a perennial problem for those who have wished to see the United States play an active and forceful part in world affairs. For over 40 years, the cold war has provided an answer to this problem. It is not easy to see what could take its place.

NOTES

1. 'The Sources of Soviet Conduct', *Foreign Affairs*, 25 (July 1947), pp. 566–82 at pp. 575, 582.
2. The various forms are lucidly analysed in John Lewis Gaddis, *Strategies of Containment: A Critical Appraisal of Postwar American National Security Policy* (New York, 1982).
3. Before 1945, in the words of one authority, 'the United States was not involved in international politics continuously enough or with enough consistency of purpose to permit the development of a coherent national strategy for the consistent pursuit of political goals by diplomacy in combination with armed force'. Russell F. Weigley, *The American Way of War: A History of United States Military Strategy and Policy* (New York, 1973), p. xix.
4. 'Comment' on Melvyn P. Leffler, 'The American Conception of National Security and the Beginnings of the Cold War, 1945–1948', *American Historical Review*, 89 (April 1984), p. 389. See also Bruce Robellet Kuniholm, *The Origins of the Cold War in the Near East: Great Power Conflict and Diplomacy in Iran, Turkey, and Greece* (Princeton, NJ, 1980).
5. See, for example, Timothy P. Ireland, *Creating the Entangling Alliance: The Origins of the North Atlantic Treaty Organization* (London, 1981), especially pp. 48–79; Lawrence S. Kaplan, *The United States and NATO: The Formative Years* (Lexington, Kentucky, 1984), pp. 50–1, 61–4, 79, 89, 113, 183–4.
6. Geir Lundestad, 'Empire by Invitation?: The United States and Western Europe, 1945–1952', *Journal of Peace Research*, 23 (Sept. 1986), pp. 263–77. On the utility of the concept of an 'American empire', see John Lewis Gaddis, 'The Emerging Postrevisionist Synthesis on the Origins of the Cold War', *Diplomatic History*, 7 (Summer 1983), pp. 181–8, and for a refinement, urging the applicability of an 'Athenian' rather than 'Roman' model of empire, see Charles S. Maier, 'Alliance and autonomy: European identity and US foreign policy objectives in the Truman years' in Michael J. Lacey (ed.), *The Truman Presidency* (Cambridge, 1989), pp. 274–5.
7. Lawrence S. Kaplan, *NATO and the United States: The Enduring Alliance* (Boston, 1988), p. 7.
8. Ireland, *Creating the Entangling Alliance*, especially pp. 222–3.
9. Paul Kennedy, *The Rise and Fall of the Great Powers: Economic Change and Military Conflict from 1500 to 2000* (London, 1988), p. 369; Carl-Ludwig Holtfrerich (editor), *Economic and Strategic Issues in US Foreign Policy* (Berlin and New York, 1989), p. xiii; *The Economist*, 24 Feb. 1990, p. 11.
10. Kennedy, *Rise and Fall of the Great Powers*, p. 534.
11. Kennedy, *Rise and Fall of the Great Powers*, p. 357.
12. The term was apparently minted in 1944 by William T.R. Fox, who included Britain as well as the USSR with the US in the category. William T.R. Fox, *The super-powers: The US, Britain and the Soviet Union – their responsibility for peace* (New York, 1944).
13. Kennedy, *Rise and Fall of the Great Powers*, p. 521.
14. See, for example, William G. Carleton, *The Revolution in American Foreign Policy: Its Global Range* (New York, 1963). On the supposedly continuous character of American 'expansionism', see William Appleman Williams, *The Roots of the Modern American Empire: A Study of the Growth and Shaping of Social Consciousness in a Marketplace Society* (New York, 1969), and, for a critique of this interpretation, J.A. Thompson, 'William Appleman Williams and the "American Empire"', *Journal of American Studies*, 7 (April 1973), pp. 91–104.

15. On the strategic issue, see Leffler, 'The American Conception of National Security', pp. 349–55; John Lewis Gaddis, *The Long Peace: Inquiries Into the History of the Cold War* (New York, 1987), pp. 24–5; Mark A. Stoler, 'From Continentalism to Globalism: General Stanley D. Embick, the Joint Strategic Survey Committee, and the Military View of American National Policy during the Second World War', *Diplomatic History*, 6 (Summer 1982), pp. 303–21.

16. The Director of the Policy Planning Staff (Kennan) to the Under Secretary of State (Acheson), 23 May 1947. *Foreign Relations of the United States 1947*, III (Washington DC, 1972), pp. 223–30 at 229.

17. Robert A. Pollard, *Economic Security and the Origins of the Cold War, 1945–1950* (New York, 1985), pp. 119–25, quotation on 122.

18. Quoted in Peter G. Boyle, 'The British Foreign Office View of Soviet–American Relations, 1945–46', *Diplomatic History*, 3 (Summer 1979), p.318. I am grateful to Dr Boyle for providing me with a corrected version of this quotation.

19. See Pollard, *Economic Security*, pp. 145–53.

20. Pollard, *Economic Security*, p. 123.

21. Thomas G. Paterson, 'Presidential Foreign Policy, Public Opinion, and Congress: The Truman Years', *Diplomatic History*, 3 (Winter 1979), pp. 1–18 at 10, 18.

22. For an attempt to show how far this was true even in the case of Woodrow Wilson, see J.A. Thompson, 'Woodrow Wilson and World War I: A Reappraisal', *Journal of American Studies*, 19 (Dec 1985), pp. 325–48.

23. US Bureau of the Census, *Historical Statistics of the United States: Colonial Times to 1970* (Washington DC, 1975), pp. 887, 903. During the 1970s, the proportion of the American economy involved in international trade almost doubled, but it has since fallen back again. See the figures (calculated on a somewhat different basis) in US Bureau of the Census, *Statistical Abstract of the United States: 1989* (Washington DC, 1989), pp. 774, 421.

24. On this point, see Kenneth N. Waltz, 'The Myth of National Interdependence' in Charles P. Kindleberger (editor), *The International Corporation* (Cambridge, MA, 1970), pp. 210–12.

25. *Statistical Abstract of the United States: 1989*, p. 563.

26. For the Angolan case, see Robert S. Litwak, *Detente and the Nixon Doctrine: American Foreign Policy and the Pursuit of Stability, 1969–1976* (Cambridge, 1984), p. 217.

27. For examples of such asymmetries, see Waltz, 'The Myth of National Interdependence', p. 213.

28. For the debate over the acquisition of the Philippines, see Robert L. Beisner, *Twelve Against Empire: The Anti-Imperialists, 1898–1900* (New York, 1968), especially pp. 101–6, and for that over the Marshall Plan, Pollard, *Economic Security*, pp. 145–53; and, in this connection, John Gimbel, *The Origins of the Marshall Plan* (Stanford, California, 1976), pp. 270–2.

29. C. Vann Woodward, 'The Age of Reinterpretation', *American Historical Review* 66 (Oct. 1960), pp. 1–9 at 3–4.

30. Robert W. Tucker, *A New Isolationism: Threat or Promise?* (New York, 1972), pp. 46–7.

31. Wilson quotations from his war message to Congress, 2 April 1917. Arthur S. Link, *The Papers of Woodrow Wilson*, 41 (Princeton, NJ, 1983), pp. 519–27 at 523, 525; FDR quotations from annual message to Congress, 6 Jan. 1941 and Address at the University of Virginia, 10 June 1940. *The Public Papers and Addresses of Franklin D. Roosevelt. 1940*, (London, 1941), pp. 663–72 at 665 and 259–64 at 261–2.

32. As eloquently expressed by John Quincy Adams on 21 July 1821 in a passage put into currency in recent times by George F. Kennan, who quoted it in testimony before the Senate Foreign Relations Committee in 1966: 'Wherever the standard of freedom

and independence has been or shall be unfurled, there will be America's heart, her benedictions and her prayers. But she goes not abroad in search of monsters to destroy. She is the well-wisher to the freedom and independence of all. She is the champion and vindicator only of her own.' See *The Vietnam Hearings*, with an introduction by J. William Fulbright (New York, 1966), p. 115.

33. On the acceptance of this view, see Leffler, 'The American Conception of National Security', p. 356; Gaddis, *The Long Peace*, pp. 21–5.

34. On none was the impression more vivid than President Truman himself. See Gaddis, *The Long Peace*, pp. 35–6, and for more wide-ranging evidence of the phenomenon Les K. Adler and Thomas G. Paterson, 'Red Fascism: The Merger of Nazi Germany and Soviet Russia in the American Image of Totalitarianism, 1930s–1950s', *American Historical Review*, 75 (April 1970), pp. 1046–64.

35. John Lewis Gaddis, *The United States and the Origins of the Cold War, 1941–1947* (New York, 1972), p. 32.

36. Radio Address, 27 May 1941. *The Public Papers and Addresses of Franklin D. Roosevelt 1941* (New York, 1950), pp. 181–94 at 184.

37. Which could be illustrated by the position in 1966 not only of Kennan but also of Senator J. William Fulbright, chairman of the Foreign Relations Committee before whom Kennan testified. See note 32 above.

38. Charles W. Kegley and Eugene R. Wittkopf, *American Foreign Policy: Pattern and Process* 3rd edition (London, 1987), p. 5

39. 'New World', *London Review of Books*, 22 June 1989.

40. The extent to which the election of 1920 *did* represent a judgement of the League of Nations is made clear in the most recent account. See Lloyd E. Ambrosius, *Woodrow Wilson and the American Diplomatic Tradition: The Treaty Fight in Perspective* (Cambridge, 1987), Ch. 9.

41. Pollard, *Economic Security*, p. 135.

42. On this public mood, see Daniel Yankelovich and Larry Kaagan, 'Assertive America' in 'America and the World 1980' issue, *Foreign Affairs*, 59 (1981), pp. 696–713.

Economic Influences on the Decline of the Soviet Union as a Great Power: Continuity Despite Change

CHRISTOPHER MARK DAVIS

> And on the pedestal these words appear:
> 'My name is Ozymandias, king of kings:
> Look on my works, ye Mighty, and despair!'
> Nothing beside remains. Round the decay
> Of that colossal wreck, boundless and bare
> The lone and level sands stretch far away.
>
> 'Ozymandias' by P.B. Shelley (1792–1822)

1. Introduction

Nations usually achieve the status of great power through the inter-related development of both economic strength and military capabilities. A strong economy is needed to sustain the political legitimacy of governing groups through improvement of citizens' living standards, to exert influence during peace time in the international arena, to generate modern weapons technologies, and to provide support of military efforts in periods of protracted warfare. Military power traditionally has been used to expand and defend nations and empires, to obtain wealth, and to promote a country's interests in the world political system. Excessively ambitious military build-ups by a nation over an extended period, however, can weaken its economy and result in a decline in its power relative to competitors. In his book on *The Rise and Fall of the Great Powers* Paul Kennedy shows that in the course of history there are many examples of major nations that have assumed onerous military burdens and have paid the price of gradual eclipse (e.g. the Dutch in the seventeenth century and the British in the twentieth) or catastrophic military defeat (e.g. Napoleon's France and Hitler's Germany).[1] Given this inter-relationship, one of the most important skills of statecraft is to maintain a correct balance in the distribution of national income between consumption, investment and defence.[2]

Early Marxist theorists argued that there was a decisive inter-connection between the economy and the capabilities of the armed forces in slave, feudal and early capitalist societies.[3] In the period since the October 1917 revolution, Lenin and subsequent Soviet leaders have recognized the importance to their ideologically-determined programmes and goals of the economy–military link and have adopted policies intended to provide a strong economic foundation for the military power of the socialist state.[4] During the Civil War the Bolsheviks introduced the measures of war communism, which successfully mobilized the limited available resources to support the military efforts of the Red Army.[5] One of the primary justifications for the Stalinist programme of rapid industrialization in the 1930s was that the growing threat of war by 'imperialist' states in Europe and Japan required the accelerated development of defence-related heavy industries.[6] In World War II, the Soviet Union's effective transition to a war economy, in which all activity was subordinated to production for the armed forces, made a vital contribution to its eventual victory.[7] The post-war Stalinist leadership of the USSR gave a high priority to ambitious and expensive scientific-industrial programmes to develop atomic and hydrogen bombs as well as missile delivery systems.[8]

Although the Stalinist economic system was effective in generating military power during 1928–53, it neglected living standards and was characterized by inefficiency, low factor productivity and poor quality of industrial output.[9] In the period 1953–85 Soviet leaders paid greater attention to consumer welfare (but consumption retained a relatively low priority status) and repeatedly attempted to reform the economy to improve technological innovation and efficiency. However, delusions about the efficacy of state ownership and central planning undermined remedial efforts.[10] Furthermore, a combination of cold war competitive pressures, worst-case threat assessments, over-ambitious foreign policy goals, failure to appreciate fully the limited utility of conventional military power in the modern world, and possibly the lack of accurate information about the scale of military expenditures resulted in Soviet defence burdens that were exceptionally heavy by world standards and that grew from the early 1960s to the middle of the 1980s. In the Brezhnev-Andropov-Chernenko years of 'stagnation' (henceforth called the Brezhnev period) the arrogance, self-deception, and incompetence of the Soviet leadership and the manifold failures of analysts in the USSR ensured that insufficient attention was paid to the issue raised by Kennedy concerning the sustainability of great power status by a nation that overdevelops its military capabilities and allows its economic performance to lag behind world standards.[11]

From the time M.S. Gorbachev was appointed General Secretary of the CPSU (March 1985) to the present (June 1990) influential figures in the USSR appear to have recognized the widening gap between that nation's military commitments and its economic capabilities, as well as the dire long-term consequences of maintaining ambitious, confrontational cold war policies. Attempts have been made to introduce increasingly radical reforms in the political system, national security area, and the economy. To date the new policies have made positive contributions to cultural life and democratization in the USSR, have improved east–west relations, and have established an environment conducive to arms control negotiations. From the perspective of influential elements of the Soviet population, though, there have been important negative aspects of *perestroika*. For example, the Gorbachev regime's policies have resulted in the loss to the communist community of several east European countries, the weakening of the Council of Mutual Economic Assistance and the Warsaw Treaty Organization, domestic political instability, and a worsening of consumer welfare.

This essay extends, with reluctance, the list of criticisms of *perestroika* by arguing that the Soviet Union under the enlightened leadership of Gorbachev has not actually achieved by the middle of 1990 a more balanced relationship between economic power and military commitments than it had in 1985, at the end of the Chernenko regime. Due to unfortunate circumstances, adherence to traditional dogmas and ineffectual reform policies, and inept management, economic performance in the USSR has deteriorated and economic growth has been retarded during 1985–90. Although military expenditures have been cut, the defence burden on the Soviet economy is not significantly lower than when Gorbachev assumed office and the gap has widened between Soviet economic power and that of other major nations.

2. Features and Objectives of the Traditional Soviet System

The characteristics of the Soviet cold war political, international security and economic institutions and policies evolved out of the Stalinist system.[12] In the political sphere the USSR was ruled in a dictatorial manner by a party elite that had as its primary objective the maintenance of the Soviet-style communist system.[13] The leadership employed ideological, economic and coercive instruments to control the population and to protect itself against any domestic threats. Although large numbers of citizens participated in political rituals, such as single candidate 'elections', and experts provided inputs to the policy process, there was severely limited freedom and democratic activity in the society.

During the cold war period Soviet international security requirements were overambitious and related policies tended to be excessively military-oriented for a variety of reasons: the USSR occupied a difficult geostrategic position; its population has been traumatized by World War II; policy makers wanted to achieve absolute security against any future invasions or attacks by dominating Europe and other border regions; the Marxist-Leninist ideology that was accepted, or at least espoused, by the political elite obliged the USSR in principle to support class struggles and liberation movement in other countries; the leadership viewed western ('imperialistic') nations as inveterately hostile and it engaged in worst-case external threat assessments; and Soviet history and political culture fostered the fear that the fate of the nation might be determined by military conflict, despite the official policies of peaceful coexistence and economic competition between socialist and capitalist nations that were adopted in the Khrushchev era.

The economic system introduced in the Stalin period was designed to maximize the possibility that the relatively backward economy could support the ambitious domestic political, economic and international security goals of the elite. This was accomplished in the first instance by minimizing private ownership and expanding state controls through nationalization of industry, collectivization of agriculture, and establishment of a state monopoly of foreign trade. The economic mechanism adopted was not dependent on prices, markets and competition but rather on central planning and quantity controls, such as rationing. With respect to end uses of national income, the traditional Soviet economy typically favoured defence and investment in heavy industry and allocated insufficient resources to consumption and investment in light industry and services. At the time of its creation and for much of its existence the leadership in the USSR probably expected that the centrally planned economy would grow faster and perform more efficiently than capitalist economies and would facilitate the mobilization of scarce resources to support the highest priority military and defence industry programmes.[14]

Over the period 1928–85 the Soviet economy grew rapidly to become the second largest in the world, improved the technological levels of its industries, and raised living standards in absolute terms. However, the combination of economic institutions, procedures and policies spawned an unique economic system that can be described as a socialist shortage economy, which discouraged efficiency in production, the drive to raise product quality, and technological innovation.[15] It may be the case that the co-existence of the command-administrative economic system and heavy defence burdens in the USSR resulted in an intensification of the adverse economic effects of overambitious military programmes discussed by Kennedy with respect to capitalist economies.

3. Soviet Military Power: 1965–85

In 1965 the Soviet elite probably perceived a considerable gap between their assessment of the nation's security status and their objectives.[16] They therefore supported an ambitious programme to enhance national security that placed much greater emphasis on the development and use of military power than on threat reduction measures such as diplomacy, propaganda and arms control. In doing so, they were acting in a manner that was consistent with past Soviet practices and the prevailing cold war approach to security promotion.

Although attempts were made to reduce threats, the quality and effectiveness of services produced by institutions such as the Ministry of Foreign Affairs, the Central Committee International Information Department, and arms control negotiating teams were low. So the national security status of the USSR was primarily determined by developments in the external threat and in Soviet military power.

The Brezhnev regime awarded the defence sector generous, increasing allocations of resources (e.g. labour, capital, and intermediate goods) and special high priority protection from the adverse features of the shortage economy.[17] The CIA estimates that defence spending in constant (1982) roubles went up from 60 billion roubles in 1965 to about 110 billion roubles in 1985.[18] The sustained commitment of the Soviet leadership to the build-up of the military power of the USSR resulted in the expansion of all defence institutions and improvements in their capabilities.[19] The size of the armed forces grew from 3,150,000 men in 1965 to 5,300,000 thousand in 1985.[20] In this period there were substantial increases of deployed conventional weapons in a number of categories (e.g. tanks, surface-to-air missiles, and helicopters) and upgradings of the technical capabilities of all weapons systems. During 1965–85 there was growth in the number of ICBMs and SLBMs from 331 to 2,377 and of nuclear warheads from about 1,000 to 8,832.[21] The Soviet Union greatly improved the reliability and accuracy of its missiles, achieved strategic parity with the US around 1970 and by the early 1980s had sufficient strategic warheads to cover all important targets.[22]

Despite these obvious achievements, it became clear by the early 1980s that the gap was widening between the demands of the Soviet military for technological innovation and the supply capabilities of the defence industry and military R & D. Furthermore, the growing complexity of weapons production and reliance of the defence industry on numerous branches of the malfunctioning civilian shortage economy made it increasingly difficult to protect defence institutions.[23] In consequence, the armed forces and defence industry became afflicted by many of the same problems that existed in other spheres of the economy and society.[24]

In the late cold war period the USSR was confronted by growing challenges with respect to external threats and power projection. If the Soviet leaders had been more astute they could have anticipated that other great powers would react to the military build-up of the USSR by developing countervailing capabilities of their own armed forces and that citizens and politicians in foreign countries would become increasingly worried by the Soviet threat and support more confrontational policies. But the security elite of the USSR apparently remained oblivious to their share of the responsibility for the acceleration of the arms race. In consequence, the external threat confronting the USSR and its geostrategic isolation grew markedly from about 1978 onwards.

In the case of power projection, it became increasingly difficult for the USSR, and other great powers, to make decisive use of even vastly superior military power in low-intensity conventional warfare.[25] As a result of this situation and the existence of the nuclear balance the credibility of the threat of the use of military force and the effectiveness of political intimidation were undermined. This meant that increments to Soviet military capabilities were generating diminishing returns with respect to the USSR's ability to influence the behaviour of other nations.

Taking all these factors into account, it appears that throughout the Brezhnev period the Soviet Union failed to satisfy its ambitious national security requirements.[26] From 1965 to about 1977 the gap between actual security status and goals closed due to the reduction in external threats (with the exception of that posed by China) and the Soviet military build-up. After that, though, the combination of worsening threat environment and declining security contributions from military power increments progressively lowered in absolute terms the national security status of the USSR.

4. Soviet Economic Power: 1965–85

Soviet leaders in the Brezhnev period recognized the need to expand their nation's economic power for domestic and international reasons.[27] In order to accomplish this, they adopted ambitious plans to accelerate technological innovation, raise living standards, and shift economic development from an extensive to an intensive basis. As argued above, though, they also supported the conflicting policy of maintaining the high growth rates of defence spending associated with the military build-up. Furthermore, they did not correct the major defects of the command-administrative economic system through various tinkering reforms (e.g. 1965, 1973, 1979). This combination of systemic deficiencies and inconsistent policies helped to sustain the unfavourable trends in the performance of the Soviet economy.

The severity of the challenge confronting the Soviet Union in its attempt to keep up in the cold war arms race can be appreciated by considering the dynamics of Soviet national income relative to those of the other great powers. According to official Soviet statistics the average growth of produced national income in five year periods declined as follows: 7.8 per cent in 1966–70; 5.7 per cent in 1971–75; 4.3 per cent in 1976–80; and 3.2 per cent in 1981–85.[28] CIA estimates of GNP growth in constant (1982) prices for the same periods also exhibit a downward trend but are consistently lower: 5.0 per cent, 3.1 per cent, 2.2 per cent, and 1.8 per cent.[29] Virtually all analysts now accept that the growth of the Soviet economy decelerated.[30]

Despite this unanimity concerning growth trends, arguments have arisen about the estimates of the actual rates.[31] Soviet economists such as Khanin and Selyunin and western ones such as Aslund argue that if Soviet growth is adjusted for hidden inflation then it averaged 2.2 per cent per annum during 1966–85 instead of the CIA estimate of 3.0 per cent and the official claim of 5.4 per cent.[32] The critics also assert that real national income growth was near zero (0.6 per cent) during 1981–85 in contrast to the officially reported growth of 3.6 per cent and the CIA estimate of 1.8 per cent.[33]

Kennedy believes that in assessing trends in power balances it is necessary to focus on relative performance.[34] If CIA estimates are considered, then the Soviet GNP growth rates were those given above and the equivalent US ones were: 3.0 per cent in 1966–70; 2.2 per cent in 1971–75; 3.4 per cent in 1976–80; and 2.4 per cent in 1981–85.[35] The comparison indicates that the Soviet economy grew more rapidly during 1966–75 but relatively slowly during 1976–85. Taking into account these rates and estimates of national income, the ratio of Soviet to US GNP (both expressed in US dollars) rose from 50 per cent in 1965 to a peak of 58 per cent in the mid-1970s but then dropped back to 53 per cent in 1985. Over the same period, according to the CIA, the ratio of Japanese to Soviet GNP increased from 37 to 65 per cent and the USSR share of world GNP declined from 15.3 per cent to 13.8 per cent. These statistics indicate that during the late Brezhnev period the size of the Soviet economy fell relative to other great powers.[36]

The critics of the official and CIA national income statistics mentioned above believe that the size of the Soviet economy is smaller than conventional estimates because of the poor quality of Soviet products, hidden inflation, and falsified reports of output. According to their adjusted calculations the actual ratio of Soviet-to-US GNP (expressed in US dollars) should be in the 28–38 per cent range for the mid-1980s, not 53 per cent as estimated by the CIA or 66 per cent according to official Soviet calculations in roubles.[37] If this ratio was in fact 34 per cent or lower, then by 1985 Japan would have had the second largest economy in the world, not the USSR.[38]

Kennedy identifies technological innovation as a major determinant of trends in the economic and military power of nations.[39] In the USSR many features of the traditional economic system inhibited technological change and ensured that the technical level of Soviet industrial products, whether military or civilian, remained low relative to world standards.[40] For example, the CIA estimates that in the late 1980s the USSR lagged behind the US in key technologies as follows: 8–10 years for advanced microcircuits; 9–15 years for mainframe computers; 5–9 years for computer-operated machine tools; and 7–10 years in flexible manufacturing systems.[41] The continuing inability of the Soviet economy to innovate except in special circumstances, the evidence that a new scientific-technological revolution was occurring in the capitalist countries, and the acceleration of high technology conventional and nuclear arms races must have worried Soviet leaders and contributed to their re-examination of policy options.[42]

As a consequence of consciously established priorities of the elite and related resource allocation patterns, the living standards of the Soviet population were low in comparison with those of developed countries and fell in relative terms during 1975–85.[43] Given the nature of the Soviet system, consumers had little market power and official retail markets were characterized by excess demand, chronic shortages, supply of poor quality goods, queuing, rationing, and forced saving. Although the 'second economy' sold many deficit goods for higher prices, its size was constrained by legal and administrative measures.[44] In the public consumption sphere (e.g. housing, health, education, social security) there was under-investment relative to population needs, shortages and poor quality of services provided, and low wages paid to staff.[45] The deficiencies in consumption generated popular dissatisfaction, undermined incentives, and contributed to low labour productivity.

The international influence of a nation also can be measured by its degree of involvement in the world economy. According to the criterion of participation, the Soviet Union was not a great power in the Brezhnev period. Due to the existence of sellers' markets within the USSR, inhibition of technological innovation, and poor product quality most commodities produced by Soviet industry were not competitive in international hard-currency markets and their sales diminished in relative terms over time. This point was made in a 1983 study of the Economic Commission for Europe, which showed that the Soviet share of western imports of a broad range of manufactured goods fell from 0.8 per cent in 1965 to 0.5 per cent in 1981.[46] OECD imports from the USSR of products in the narrower category of 'Machinery and Transport Equipment' declined from 0.3 per cent in 1975 to 0.1 per cent in 1985.[47] The USSR did have some success in the arms trade. The value of its military export agreements rose from $ 3,185 million in 1975 to a peak of $ 14,635 million in 1980.[48] In general, though, the USSR maintained an export structure typical of a developing country with a predominance of primary products. By the early 1980s it was earning about 60 per cent of hard currency from sales of oil and gas.

Another economic problem was that of the rising 'costs of empire'. In the period 1965–85 the world communist system expanded, but most of the countries in it were relatively underdeveloped and required assistance from the USSR. According to a RAND study, in 1980 the approximate costs (expressed in current dollars) to the USSR of its empire included: trade subsidies (about $ 21 billion); trade credits ($ 6 billion); economic aid ($ 1 billion); military aid ($ 5 billion); incremental costs of Soviet forces in Afghanistan ($ 1 billion); and covert activities related to empire maintenance ($ 4 billion).[49] The estimated burden of empire expressed as a share of GNP rose from about one per cent in 1971 to three per cent in 1980.[50]

The growing defence burden (conventionally measured as a share of GNP) associated with the military build-up was an additional impediment to the balanced development of the Soviet economy in the Brezhnev period. In western and eastern Europe defence burdens fell in the 2–5 per cent ranges whereas that of the US was 6–7 per cent.[51] According to pre-*glasnost* Soviet statistics, the defence share of national income (net material product utilized) was small and declined over time from 6.1 per cent in 1970 to 3.6 per cent in 1980 to 3.3 per cent in 1985.[52] In 1989 Soviet authorities announced that this assessment had been altered and that the USSR devoted about nine per cent of GNP to defence.[53] In contrast, the authoritative CIA evaluation is that the Soviet defence burden rose from 12–14 per cent of GNP in 1965 to 15–17 per cent in 1985.[54]

David Epstein, a Department of Defense analyst, argues that although the CIA estimate may be accurate it does not reflect the full cost to the Soviet economy of the security sector, the high priority protection of defence institutions, and the empire. He proposes supplements to conventionally-defined defence spending that take into account these factors. According to his calculations, the extended security burden for 1982 was in the range of 23–26 per cent of GNP.[55]

It should be recalled, though, that there is a dispute concerning the size of Soviet GNP. If Birman and Aslund are correct that the national income of the USSR expressed in dollar terms was around 33 per cent of US GNP, rather than about 50 per cent in 1965 and 53 per cent in 1985, and one accepts the CIA defence spending estimates, then the narrowly-defined burden actually grew from about 20 per cent in 1965 to 26 per cent in 1985.[56] If Epstein's extended measurement of security is compared to the lower GNP then the security burden in 1985 would have been about 40 per cent.[57]

As is evident from the statistics presented above, during the Brezhnev period there was a growing imbalance between the military and economic power of the USSR. The Soviet economy fell ever further behind those of its major competitors both in terms of size and technological sophistication. Its defence burden grew exceptionally heavy and exerted negative feedback on the performance of civilian branches. These developments undoubtedly focussed the attention of the Soviet elite on the crucial trade-off problem identified by Kennedy:

Precisely because a top-heavy military establishment may slow down the rate of economic growth and lead to a decline in the nation's share of world manufacturing output, and therefore wealth, and therefore power, the whole issue becomes one of balancing the short-term security afforded by large defence forces against the longer-term security of rising production and income.[58]

5. Reform Under Gorbachev: Policies and Outcomes

The statements and actions of Soviet leaders during 1985–90 make it clear that they have recognised the many problems of the traditional system in the USSR and are determined to remedy them. Since Gorbachev became General Secretary of the CPSU there have been significant changes in the political sphere, national security promotion strategy, and economy. The crucial issues of relevance to this essay, however, are whether these reform policies have significantly lessened the defence burden on the Soviet economy or closed the economic power gap that exists between the USSR and developed western nations.

(a) Political Reform

There have been numerous important changes in the Soviet political environment and system.[59] First, the Gorbachev faction has consolidated its power in the party apparatus and state, which has facilitated the introduction of reform policies. Second, *glasnost* and *demokratizatsiya* have contributed to an improvement in human rights and a diminution of the role of the CPSU in the political system. Third, the reform of the electoral system and parliamentary bodies (i.e. the Congress of People's Deputies and the Supreme Soviet) have resulted in more open debates of outstanding issues. Fourth, the democratization of the political system has enabled at least the reformist element of the elite to express more forcefully its preferences concerning end uses of national income and sectoral priorities. Not surprisingly, these are for more resources to be devoted to consumption and less to defence. Fifth, the central authorities increasingly have lost control of political processes in the USSR. An example of this was the election of Boris

Yeltsin as President of the RSFSR Supreme Soviet in May 1990 despite the concerted, if inept, efforts of the top party leadership to prevent this outcome. Sixth, political reform has allowed nationalist forces openly to organize, to resist Moscow's rule, and to press for the autonomy or independence of regions and republics.

(b) Reform of the National Security Promotion Strategy

Since Gorbachev came to power the Soviet leadership appears to have been influenced by the *novoe myshlenie* (new thinking) in security affairs.[60] This has resulted in major developments affecting the Soviet national security promotion strategy and related policies.[61] The Gorbachev regime has vigorously applied the *perestroika* program to both threat reduction and defence institutions in order to make them more effective and efficient.[62] As a consequence of the new strategy there has been a shift of emphasis within the national security production process in favour of the threat reduction programmes of the re-vitalized diplomatic, propaganda, espionage, and arms control institutions. The importance of defence sector activities has been diminished in relative terms.[63]

This re-alignment had only a minor impact on the defence sector and defence–civilian economic relations during 1985–88. In this period the reform policies of the Gorbachev regime concerning the defence sector included: purge of the leadership of the military–industrial complex; alteration of military doctrine to give it a defensive orientation; introduction of new personnel policies (e.g. anti-alcohol campaign, strengthening of material incentives; stress on human factors) to improve lower level performance; and changes in the economic mechanisms governing the operations of defence institutions.[64]

In the case of defence spending, official Soviet statements have been contradictory concerning trends during 1985–88.[65] Most western analyses indicate that the defence sector maintained a high priority status in this period and that real defence spending rose by two to three per cent per annum.[66]

There was much discussion in the USSR of the necessity of altering the pattern of transfers of resources between defence and civilian sectors during 1985–88 at the micro level, but only modest actual change. The Soviet defence industry continued its traditional programme of providing the civilian economy with numerous commodities and achieved some success.[67] In the case of labour, there were flows out of the defence sector as the result of lay-offs and retirements from industry and research institutes. Some workers in missile factories affected by the INF treaty were shifted to production lines for civilian goods. On the other hand, the transfer to defence industry ministries of the enterprises of the old light and food industry machine-building ministry augmented the defence sector labour force.

Although there was little actual disarmament in the USSR before 1989, the situation changed after Gorbachev's speech at the UN in December 1988 in which he outlined the new national security strategy:

> After all, it is now quite clear that building up military power makes no country omnipotent. What is more, one-sided reliance on military power ultimately weakens other components of national security ... We are witnessing the emergence of a new historic reality – a turning away from the principle of superarmament to the principle of reasonable defence sufficiency. We are present at the birth of a new model of ensuring security – not through the build-up of arms, as was almost always the case in the past, but on the contrary, through their reduction on the basis of compromise.[68]

At that time he announced major unilateral arms reductions in the period 1989–90 of 500,000 men (450,000 within the USSR and 50,000 stationed outside), 10,000 tanks, 8,500 artillery pieces, and 800 combat aircraft.

After that speech the disarmament process accelerated and by the end of 1989 the manpower of the armed forces was reduced by 265,000 men.[69] In addition, about 7,000 tanks, 1,100 artillery pieces and 600 combat planes were taken out of service. The announced size of the Soviet armed forces fell from 4,258,000 on 1 January 1989 to 3,993,000 on 1 January 1990.[70]

During 1989–90 there was an intensification of the production of civilian commodities by the defence industry and the initiation of an apparently large-scale defence industry conversion (*konversiya*) effort.[71] The Chairman of the Military–Industrial Commission, I.S. Belousov, has stated that the targets of the new conversion program include: a reduction in the output of 'military technology' by the defence complex during 1989 of 4.5 per cent from the 1988 level (before conversion the planned growth rate for the year was 5.5 per cent); a cumulative 19.5 per cent reduction in the defence industry's output of arms and military equipment by 1991 from the 1988 level; and the increase in the civilian goods' share of defence industry output from 40 per cent in 1988 to 60 per cent in 1995.[72]

Developments in Soviet defence spending during 1989 are unclear despite the statements made by leading party and state officials concerning this topic and the new data provided.[73] Given the absence of claims of a reduction, it would appear likely that the announced figure of 77,294.2 million roubles was the same as that of 1988 or somewhat higher. However, the preliminary CIA/DIA estimate is that real defence expenditure declined by 4–5 per cent in 1989.[74] The Soviet leadership has called for an 8.2 per cent cut in the 1990 defence budget that would reduce spending to 70,975.8 million roubles. If expenditure plans are not modified due to unanticipated developments (e.g. imposition of martial law in a republic) or problems (e.g. difficulties in absorbing demobilized troops in the civilian economy or in implementing the conversion programme), then there should be reductions in 1990 on outlays on military procurement, operations, wages, and R & D.[75] The various freezes and cuts are supposed to generate savings of 30 billion roubles during 1986–90 relative to the total approved in the 12th Five Year Plan.

From the perspective of the traditional Soviet communist elite the national security results of the 'new thinking' strategy have been mixed. On the benefit side, political relations with the US, western Europe, and China have improved. The INF treaty has been signed and implemented and progress is being made in arms control negotiations concerning CFE and START treaties. On the debit side, the policies of the Gorbachev regime allowed, if not encouraged, the revolutions in Eastern Europe that led to the movement of most countries in the region out of the socialist bloc, the further discrediting of communism and Soviet-style economic policies, the rapid progress toward the reunification of Germany, and the transformation of the Warsaw Pact into an ineffectual body no longer dominated by the USSR. Furthermore, the reform policies have produced growing unrest within the USSR that threatens not only the existing communist political system but also the territorial integrity of the nation. In sum, the enlightened policies of the Gorbachev regime appear to have worsened the national security status of the USSR in the period 1985–90 if domestic developments are considered as well as those in the international sphere.

(c) Economic Reform

The initial economic strategy and policies of the Gorbachev regime reflected the moderately reformist Andropov programme of purging unsuitable high-level personnel, tightening labour discipline, combating corruption, carrying out large-scale economic experiments in decentralized industrial enterprise management, and improving consumption on a low cost basis.[76] The 12th Five Year Plan for 1986–90 was supposed to express the concept of 'acceleration of the socio-economic development of the country' which was adopted at the April 1985 Central Committee plenum. Its main, publicly announced goals were to accelerate economic growth, to shift to intensive development, to stimulate technological progress and to improve the quality of industrial goods.

It was known at the time of its formulation that the 12th Plan was to be implemented in a period of economic reform. However, the assumption of the Soviet leadership probably was that new policies would continue to be of the conservative, 'tinkering' type similar in essence to those introduced in 1985–86. As Aslund has shown, however, the reform process became more radical over time, with key events being the January 1987 and June 1987 Central Committee plenums and the June 1988 party conference.[77] In the period from October 1988 through June 1990 efforts have been made to extend self-financing in industry and leasing of land in agriculture, reduce state orders, expand wholesale trade, encourage co-operatives and joint ventures, increase private ownership of property, and further decentralize foreign trade decision making.[78]

The Soviet economy did not respond well to the plans and reform policies of the Gorbachev regime.[79] Throughout 1986–90 plan targets in crucial industries, such as machine-building and metal production, have been chronically underfulfilled. This has generated supply deficits and production bottlenecks in industry that are characteristic of a Soviet-type shortage economy. Furthermore, wage growth has exceeded that of labour productivity, output targets for consumer goods and agricultural production have been underfulfilled, and only modest increases in imports have been made. All this has contributed to growing government budget deficits (about 400 billion roubles, or ten per cent of GNP, in 1990) and excess demand in retail markets, and thus to phenomena in the consumption sphere such as pervasive shortages, queueing, forced substitution, and forced saving.[80]

These various problems have been reflected in growth rates of GNP which were, according to CIA estimates, 0.7 per cent in 1985, 4.1 per cent in 1986, 1.3 per cent in 1987, 2.2 per cent in 1988 and 1.4 per cent in 1989.[81] According to official Soviet statistics the economy performed poorly in 1989 and real produced national income rose by only 2.4 per cent.[82] However, Khanin argues that real growth actually declined by 4–5 per cent in that year.[83] In 1990 the economy appears to be out of control to an increasing degree and performance at micro and macro levels is deteriorating. During the initial four months the value of national income has fallen by 1.7 per cent, the population's income has increased by 13.4 per cent, state orders have been significantly underfulfilled and absenteeism of workers has been greater than in all of 1989.[84]

The poor performance of the Soviet economy during 1985–90 can be explained by a variety of factors. In part it was due to unpropitious circumstances in the economy, weather, and foreign trade.[85] Numerous obstacles also existed in the political and economic systems. First, many reform measures adversely affected the interests of party officials, planners, ministry bureaucrats, managers, and workers and therefore were resisted. Second, the socialist shortage economy possesses numerous macroeconomic and microeconomic feedback control mechanisms which tend to counteract reform efforts and return the system to its 'normal' disequilibrium state.[86] Third, the uncontrolled upsurge of nationalist unrest and localism disrupted the economy.

The policies of the Soviet government also contributed to the continuation of economic imbalances and performance deficiencies. The 12th Five Year Plan had unrealistically ambitious goals and such taut planning is a well known source of disequilibrium. The reform program was timid until at least mid-1987 and the announced measures were not radical enough to deal with existing problems.

The failure to rectify the deficiencies in the economic information system meant that it was difficult at all levels to make rational decisions.[87] With respect to implementation, there was insufficient preparation of decision-makers to enable them to function effectively in the new economic system and the timing of the introduction of the various reform policies was problematic. For example, enterprises were supposed to operate on a market-oriented, self-financing basis well before prices were reformed to reflect scarcity values. One other problem was that the reform process undermined the command-administrative system of the Soviet economy but did not develop market mechanisms to replace it. In consequence, confusion increased among decision makers at macro and micro levels.[88]

(d) The Military-Economic Power Balance Under Gorbachev

In assessing developments affecting the great power status of the USSR during the Gorbachev period attention can be focused on indicators of the defence burden and the economic power gap. In the case of the former, it was argued above that there was only limited progress in disarmament during 1985–88. The Soviet leadership intended to increase defence spending at a rate greater than that planned for national income during the 12th Plan period. The western consensus is that real defence spending actually went up by about two to three per cent a year through 1988. So if military expenditure was 102.7 billion 1982 roubles in 1985 (15.0 per cent of a GNP of 684.7 billion roubles) then the more plausible three per cent growth rate would produce a level of 112.2 billion roubles in 1988.[89] According to the CIA, the Soviet GNP in that year was 731.9 billion roubles, so the burden would have been 15.3 per cent.

The most recent CIA/DIA estimate is that 1989 defence spending declined by five per cent from the 1988 level (to 106.6 billion 1982 roubles) and real GNP increased by 1.4 per cent (to 745.8 billion roubles). This implies that the burden fell to 14.3 per cent in 1989. However, given the margins of error associated with the estimation of both military expenditure and economic growth it is prudent to consider alternative possibilities. For example, if real growth in defence spending was zero in 1989 and GNP rose by 1.4 per cent, then the burden would have diminished only slightly to 15.1 per cent. In the case that the real growth of Soviet GNP was lower than that estimated by the CIA (extending the arguments of Khanin/Selyunin and Aslund) the impact on the 1989 defence burden with military spending of 106.6 billion constant (1982) roubles can be seen from the following: zero growth implies 14.5 per cent; -1 per cent implies 14.6 per cent; and -2 per cent implies 14.8 per cent.

With respect to 1990, it is unclear at this stage whether defence spending will be reduced proportionately more than aggregate economic output will fall. But it is safe to assume that in the first half of this year that there has not been a dramatic lessening of the defence burden.

The economic power gap clearly has widened in the Gorbachev period because even the CIA-estimated growth rates of Soviet GNP have been lower than those of other major nations. According to the CIA, the average growth rate for the economy of the USSR during 1985–89 was 1.9 per cent.[90] In contrast, the average annual growth rates of the other major nations during 1985–89 were as follows: the US 3.4 per cent; Germany 2.4 per cent; Japan 4.5 per cent; and the average for all OECD countries 3.5 per cent.[91]

To conclude, the Gorbachev regime has initiated profound and varied reforms of the political system, national security strategy, and economy of the Soviet Union. Its policies have been beneficial domestically and internationally in many respects, but have not been successful to date (June 1990) in either significantly lowering the defence burden or in closing the economic power gap. Furthermore, the living standards of the Soviet population have fallen since 1985 and technological innovation has not accelerated because of the failure of the economic reform. Given these adverse developments it is obvious that the current Soviet leadership has been presiding over the continuing fall of the USSR as a great power.

In the future it is possible that more radical remedial policies, than those outlined in Ryzhkov's recent speech about the 'transition to the regulated market economy' could arrest this relative decline in power status.[92] Alternatively, developments could prove correct the pessimistic assessments of 'Z' and Brzezinski that reform of communist systems is not feasible and that disintegration of the Soviet Union is likely.[93] In sum, crucial questions remain unanswered about the fate of the USSR as a great power in the post-cold war world of the 1990s.

NOTES

Acknowledgements: Research for this paper was supported by grants from the Ford Foundation through the project 'The Economics of the Soviet Defense Sector' and the British Economic and Social Research Council through the project 'Central Control, Disequilibrium and Private Activity in Socialist Economies'. I would like to thank Roy Allison, Vladislav Balashov, Erik Goldstein and Philip Hanson for their comments on the first draft of this essay as well as members of IISS, especially Hans Binnendijk, for their discussion of this paper following its presentation at a seminar there on 24 April 1990. This article is dedicated to my late father-in-law, the historian Professor Marcus Cunliffe (1922–90).

1. This paper attempts to apply to the analysis of trends in the power status of the Soviet Union the arguments of Paul Kennedy presented in *The Rise and Fall of Great Powers: Economic Change and Military Conflict from 1500 to 2000*, London, Unwin Hyman, 1988. His basic message of relevance is summarised on page 439. '. . . there exists a dynamic for change, driven chiefly by economic and technological developments, which then impact on social structures, political systems, military power, and the position of individual states and empires. The speed of the global economic change has not been a uniform one, simply because the pace of technological innovation and economic growth is itself irregular . . . this uneven pace of economic growth has had crucial long-term impacts upon the relative military power and strategical position of the member of the states system . . . all the major shifts in the world's military power balances have followed alterations in the productive balances . . . the rising and falling of the various empires and states in the international system has been confirmed by the outcomes of the major Great Power wars, where victory has always gone to the side with the greatest material resources.' In his book Kennedy provides plausible accounts of the adverse consequences for economies of heavy defence burdens based upon historical evidence. But he does not either elaborate in theoretical terms the inter-relationship between trends in military power and economic performance or rigorously test related hypotheses. This article accepts his general interpretation of the dynamics of global power balances while recognizing the need for further investigation of the specific factors (e.g. excessive military expenditure) that generate changes in economic performance.

2. Ibid., pg.446

3. For Soviet discussions of the writings of Marx and Engels on defence economics see: K. *Marks, F. Engels, V.I. Lenin O Voine i Armii*, Moscow, Voennoe Izdatelstvo, 1982; A.I. Pozharov *Ekonomicheskie Osnovy Oboronnogo Mogushchestva Sotsialisticheskogo Gosudarstva*, Moscow, Voennoe Izdatelstvo, 1981; and A.A. Epishev *KPSS i Voennoe Stroitelstvo*, Moscow, Voennoe Izdatelstvo, 1982. On pg.49 Epishev cites the well known observation by Engels: 'Nothing so depends upon economic conditions as the army and navy. The arms, staff, organization, tactics and strategy at a given time depend first of all on the attained stage of production and on the means of communications.'

4. The basic book on Soviet defence economics is Pozharov, op. cit. The military-economy interconnection is also discussed in the more recent Y.E. Vlas'evich, A. S. Sukhoguzov, and V.A. Zubkov *Osnovy Voenno-Ekonomicheskikh Znanii*, Moscow, Voennoe Izdatelstvo, 1989. For example, on p. 47 they summarize the relationship as follows: 'The foundation of the military potential, and consequently the military power, of the state is its economic potential. This characterizes the economy from the point of view of all available objective possibilities for the production of material wealth and the provision of services.' Despite the long tradition of work on defence

economics in the USSR, Soviet writings suffer from a number of deficiencies. One is that considerably more stress has been placed on the importance of the economy for the defence sector than on the adverse consequences for the socialist economy of a heavy defence burden.

5. For information on the economics of defence during the civil war period see: A.N. Lagovskii *V.I Lenin ob Ekonomicheskom Obespechenii Oborony Strany*, Moscow, Voennoe Izdatelstvo, 1976, pp. 69–116; Pozharov, op. cit., pp. 40–43; and S. Malle *The Economic Organisation of War Communism 1918–21*, Cambridge, Cambridge University Press, 1985. It should be recognized that economic policies and performance did not determine victory in the civil war, but rather assisted in its achievement. Ideological, political, social and military-technical factors exerted decisive influences on the outcome of the conflict.

6. Ya. E. Chadaev *Ekonomika SSSR v Gody Velikoi Otechestvennoi Voiny*, Moscow, Mysl', 1985, pp. 21–76; Lagovskii, op. cit., pp. 134–165; and E. Zaleski *Stalinist Planning for Economic Growth, 1933–1952*, Chapel Hill, University of North Carolina Press, 1980.

7. Sources on the Soviet economy during World War II include Chadaev, op. cit., and M. Harrison *Soviet Planning in Peace and War 1938–1945*, Cambridge Cambridge University Press, 1985. As in the case of the civil war, non-economic forces (e.g. patriotism, military strategy, NKVD repression) helped the USSR to triumph in its struggle with the Nazi regime. See for example the chapter on the war in M. Heller and A.M. Nekrich *Utopia in Power*, New York, Summit Books, 1986.

8. M.M. Kir'yan *Voenno-Tekhnicheskii Progress i Vooruzhennye Sily SSSR*, Moscow, Voennoe Izdatelstvo, 1982, pp. 218–55; D. Holloway *The Soviet Union and the Arms Race*, London, Yale University Press, 1983, pp. 20–35.

9. Zaleski, op. cit.

10. M. Ellman *Socialist Planning* (Second Edition), Cambridge, Cambridge University Press, 1989 and P.R. Gregory and R.C. Stuart *Soviet Economic Structure and Performance* (Fourth Edition), New York, Harper & Row, 1990. The delusions of the Soviet leadership concerning the economic system were fostered by their ideological biases and sustained by the inaccurate statistical information with which it was provided about the true state of the economy.

11. It is probable that in the Brezhnev period Soviet leaders had an understanding of the determinants of great power status that was considerably different from that of Kennedy (op. cit.). They appear to have attached considerable importance to factors such as strategic nuclear parity, development of the space programme, maintenance of a large military and defence industry capacity, and symbols of national power such as success in international sports competitions. Although they were aware of the need to accelerate technological progress and improve the competitiveness of Soviet industrial products, they were insufficiently committed to the attainment of these goals to reform economic policies and mechanisms in the necessary manner.

12. Given the constraints on this essay it is only possible to summarize these features. More detailed descriptions and analyses are available elsewhere. The political system in: D. Lane *Politics and Society in the USSR*, London, Martin Robertson, 1978; J.F. Hough and M. Fainsod *How the Soviet Union is Governed*, Cambridge, Harvard University Press, 1979. International security in: Holloway, op. cit.; J. Valenta and W. Potter (eds.) *Soviet Decisionmaking for National Security*, London, George Allen & Unwin, 1984; and W.T. Lee and R.F. Staar *Soviet Military Policy Since World War II*, Stanford, Hoover Institution Press, 1986. The economy in: M. Ellman *Planning Problems in the USSR*, Cambridge, Cambridge University Press, 1973; Ellman, 1989, op. cit.; A. Nove *The Soviet Economic System*, London, George Allen & Unwin, 1977; and Gregory and Stuart *Soviet Economic Structure*, op. cit.

13. An interesting critical analysis of the Soviet political system is presented in the article: 'Z' (pseudonym) 'To the Stalin Mausoleum', *Daedalus*, vol. 119, no. 1 (Winter 1990).
14. Soviet efforts to mobilize the economy in support of defence programmes are analysed in J. Sapir *L'Economie Mobilisée*, Paris, Editions La Découverte, 1990.
15. Empirical and theoretical analyses of the socialist shortage economy are presented in the books by J. Kornai: *Overcentralization of Economic Administration*, London, Oxford University Press, 1959 and *Economics of Shortage*, Amsterdam, North-Holland, 1980. For a discussion of the historical evolution of the shortage economy in the USSR see C. Davis and W. Charemza 'Introduction to models of disequilibrium and shortage in centrally planned economies' in C. Davis and W. Charemza (eds.) *Models of Disequilibrium and Shortage in Centrally Planned Economies*, London, Chapman and Hall, 1989.
16. It is argued elsewhere by this author that Soviet defence and international security activities can be interpreted using a model of the national security production process. In brief, this process is controlled by the political leadership in the USSR and has as its objective the optimization of national security status. This involves establishing objective or subjective goals and indicators for national security, assessing external threats (military, economic, political), developing a national security promotion strategy that involves both threat reduction programmes (diplomatic, propaganda, arms control, and espionage) and military activities, and allocating necessary domestic resources. For further information see the papers by C. Davis: 'Interdependence of the Defence and Civilian Sectors in the Contemporary Soviet Economy: Concepts, Problems and Reform' in C. Davis, H.-H. Hohmann, and H.-H. Schroder (eds.) *Rustung Modernisierung Reform: Die sowjetische Verteidigungswirtschaft in der Perestrojka (Defense, Modernization and Reform: The Military Sector of the Soviet Economy in the Perestroika Period)*, Koln, Bund-Verlag, 1990 (an updated, English language version of this chapter was presented at the AAASS convention in Chicago in Nov. 1989) and 'Economic Plans, National Security Strategy, and the Priority of the Soviet Defence Sector: 1985–95', Santa Monica, Paper presented at the Hoover-RAND symposium on 'The Defense Sector in the Soviet Economy', 29–30 March 1990.
17. The mechanisms and policies used to protect the institutions of the defence sector in the USSR are discussed in C. Davis 'The high priority military sector in a shortage economy' in H.S. Rowen and C. Wolf Jr. (eds.) *The Impoverished Superpower: Perestroika and the Burden of Soviet Military Spending*, San Francisco, Institute for Contemporary Studies, 1990.
18. Estimated from Figure 4, p. 10 in CIA *Revisiting Soviet Economic Performance Under Glasnost: Implications for CIA Estimates*, Directorate of Intelligence, SOV 88–10068, Sept. 1988. Further information about trends in Soviet defence spending is provided in A. Becker *Sitting on Bayonets: The Soviet Defense Burden and the Slowdown of Soviet Defense Spending*, Santa Monica, RAND JRS-01, 1985 and N.D. Michaud 'Current developments in Soviet military spending' in Rowen and Wolf Jr. *The Impoverished Superpower*, op. cit.
19. Authoritative assessments of developments in the Soviet defence sector during 1965–85 are provided in the annual issues of the International Institute for Strategic Studies *The Military Balance* and the US Department of Defense *Soviet Military Power*. See also Lee and Staar, op. cit., and C. Davis 'The production of military power by the Soviet defense sector 1975–85', Birmingham, Discussion Paper, August 1986.
20. D.R. Jones (ed.) *Soviet Armed Forces Review Annual: No. 10, 1985–1986*, Gulf Breeze, Florida, Academic International Press, 1987, p. 33.
21. Jones, ibid., p. 79; International Institute for Strategic Studies *The Military Balance 1985–1986*, London, IISS, 1985, pp. 21–30; Lee and Staar, op. cit., p. 74.
22. R.P. Berman and J.C. Baker *Soviet Strategic Forces: Requirements and Responses*,

Washington DC, The Brookings Institution, 1982; Lee and Staar, op. cit.

23. Davis, 'The high priority', op. cit.

24. In the case of the armed forces the main defects included: stagnant senior military leadership; laziness, drunkenness, and lack of initiative among officers; poor living conditions of enlisted personnel which contributed to low morale and substandard execution of duties; low states of readiness of military units; and reliance on an extensive development strategy (see A. Cockburn *The Threat: Inside the Soviet Military Machine*, New York, Vintage Books, 1984 and C. Davis '*Perestroika* in the Soviet defense sector, 1985–87: National security elite participation and turnover', Birmingham, Paper presented at the conference on elites and political power in the USSR, 1–2 July 1987). A more recent and scathing Soviet critique of the armed forces is made in A. Pankin 'Otechestvo v opasnosti!?', *Novoe Vremya*, 1990, no. 16 (April 1990). Among defence industry problems were: uneven quality of enterprise management; failures in defence industry planning; the backwardness of technology relative to western standards; flaws in product designs; negligent supervision and shoddy workmanship; and slack discipline, alcohol abuse, and corruption among workers and staff (Cockburn, op. cit.; Davis, 'The high priority', op. cit.; and P. Almquist *Red Forge: Soviet Military Industry Since 1965*, New York, Columbia University Press, 1990).

25. These constraints were evident in the European theatre even in Khrushchev's time.

26. Kennedy, op. cit., p. 512 characterizes the pre-Gorbachev security situation as follows: 'To the decision-makers in the Kremlin, heirs to a militaristic and often paranoid tradition of statecraft, Russia appears surrounded by crumbling frontiers -in Eastern Europe, along the 'northern tier' of the Middle East, and in its lengthy shared border with China; yet having pushed out so many Russian divisions and air squadrons to stabilize those frontiers has not produced the hoped-for invulnerability.' Evidence in support of the argument that the Brezhnev regime failed to achieve its security objectives is presented in the following papers by C. Davis: 'Economic and political aspects of the Military-Industrial Complex in the USSR' in H. -H. Höhmann, A. Nove and H. Vogel (Eds.) *Economics and Politics in the USSR: Problems of Interdependence*, London, Westview Press, 1986; 'Perestroika', op. cit.; and 'Economic plans', op. cit.

27. This statement is supported by the analysis of Paul Dibb in *The Soviet Union: The Incomplete Superpower* (Second Edition), London, IISS, 1988. On p. 70 he observes with respect to the Brezhnev leadership that: 'The importance of the economy for the USSR goes beyond the generation of military strength as the most easily recognizable measure of its state power. It is not only military strength which is largely determined by the Soviet Union's economic strength, but also its international political reputation. As the world's first communist power, the USSR continues to measure its economic achievements by constant comparisons with the US economy, the leading capitalist power. The command economy and central planning, those most distinctive attributes of Marxism-Leninism, are seen as being responsible for the elevation of the USSR to Superpower status.'

28. *Narodnoe Khozyaistvo SSSR v 1988 g.*, Moscow, Finansy i Statistika, 1989, p. 10

29. CIA *Revisiting . . .*, op. cit., p. 9

30. There are a number of factors that influenced the deceleration in growth in the period 1975–85. First, the failure to reform the economic system meant that growth continued to be extensive rather than intensive in character. Second, there were declines in the annual increments to the labour force and capital stock and growing difficulties in extracting supplies of energy and other raw materials. Third, due to systemic problems Soviet factor productivity (e.g. output per unit of inputs) dropped over time.

31. Scholars in the USSR and western countries have criticized official Soviet growth rates as inflated and debated their actual magnitude for well over a decade. Among the Soviet

analysts who have made contributions to the debate are Ya. Kvasha, V. Faltsman, and G. Khanin. Western participants include A. Bergson, A. Nove, P. Wiles, P. Hanson, G. Ofer, M. Ellman, and S. Cohn. In recent years public interest in growth rates has been stimulated by the article of the Soviet economists G. Khanin and V. Selyunin 'Lukavaya tsifra', *Novyy Mir*, vol. 63, no. 2 (Feb.1987). Their alternative estimates are critically reviewed, together with the official Soviet and CIA rates, in R. Ericson 'The Soviet statistical debate: Khanin vs. TsSU' in Rowen and Wolf Jr. *The Impoverished Superpower*, op. cit. Support for the Soviet critics is provided in A. Aslund 'How small is Soviet national income?' in the same Rowen and Wolf Jr. volume. The Central Intelligence Agency's growth rate estimation methodology and results are defended in CIA *Revisiting . . .*, op. cit.

32. Calculated as the average of the growth rates for the five-year intervals during 1966–85 given in Aslund, op. cit., p. 44 and CIA *Revisiting . . .*, op. cit., p. 11.

33. Ibid.

34. For general statements of this idea see the quote from Kennedy, op. cit. in note 1 as well as the introduction and epilogue in his book. On pp. 430–31 he discusses the Soviet economic growth record relative to those of other great powers.

35. L. Kurtzweg 'Trends in Soviet Gross National Product' in US Congress, Joint Economic Committee *Gorbachev's Economic Plans*, Washington DC, USGPO, 1987, p. 136.

36. The calculations are based upon the following GNP estimates of the CIA in billion 1984 $ US:
    1965: World 6,780; US 2,076; Japan 384; USSR 1,037;
    1985: World 14,412; US 3,748; Japan 1,290; USSR 1,991;
    The 1965 figures are from CIA *Handbook of Economic Statistics, 1985*, Washington DC, Directorate of Intelligence CPAS 85–10001, Sept. 1985, pp. 34–35. The 1985 GNP numbers were calculated by applying to the 1984 figures in CIA *Handbook . . . 1985*, ibid. the following growth rates for 1985 given in CIA *Handbook of Economic Statistics, 1986*, Washington DC, Directorate of Intelligence CPAS 86–10002, Sept. 1986, pp. 34–35: World 2.9 per cent; US 2.3 per cent; Japan 4.5 per cent; and USSR 1.7 per cent.

37. The Soviet estimate that USSR national income was 66 per cent of that of the US in 1985, both measured in roubles, is given in *Narodnoe Khozyaistvo SSSR v 1985 g.*, Moscow, Finansy i Statistika, 1986, p. 581. The CIA ratio of 53 per cent can be calculated from estimates provided in endnote 36 that US GNP was $ 3,748 billion (1984 $) in 1985 and Soviet GNP was $ 1,991 billion. Aslund, op. cit., p. 43, implies that in the mid-1980s a reasonable estimate of the per capita GNP ratio is 33 per cent, which implies a GNP ratio of 38 per cent (calculations based on the US and Soviet GNP estimates given above and respective populations of 238.6 and 278.9 million from CIA *Handbook . . . 1986*, op. cit., pp. 54–55). In a March 1990 re-assessment presented at a RAND conference, Aslund favoured a 33 per cent ratio. In April 1990 a leading Soviet economist, V. Belkin, stated that Soviet GNP was only 28 per cent of that produced by the US (see R. Pear 'Soviet experts call CIA data too rosy', *International Herald Tribune*, 24 April 1990). It is assumed that he was referring to US dollar comparisons given the context of the conference debate.

38. According to the endnote 36 estimates derived from CIA *Handbook . . . 1985* and *Handbook . . . 1986* in 1985 the Japanese GNP of $ 1,290 billion was 34.4 per cent of the US GNP of $ 3,748 billion. If Soviet GNP was 34 per cent of that of the US, or $ 1,274 billion, it would have been lower than that of Japan.

39. The general argument of Kennedy, op. cit., that technology is an important determinant of the rise and fall of great powers can be found in his introduction and epilogue. See also the quote in note 1. He discusses technology problems in the USSR on pp. 494–95 and 500–01.

40. Analyses of the reasons for sluggish technological innovation in the USSR are provided in J. Berliner *The Innovation Decision in Soviet Industry*, Cambrige, MIT Press, 1976 and R. Amann and J.M. Cooper (eds.) *Industrial Innovation in the Soviet Union*, London, Yale University Press, 1982.

41. Central Intelligence Agency/Defense Intelligence Agency (CIA/DIA) 'The Soviet economy in 1988: Gorbachev changes course', Washington DC, paper resented to the US Congress Joint Economic Committee, April 1989, p. 8 (figure 3). Relative US/USSR technology levels in deployed weapons systems are discussed in US Department of Defense *Soviet Military Power: An Assessment of the Threat 1988*, Washington DC, 1988, pp. 140–157. The history of the relationship between US and Soviet weapons technologies is examined in M. Evangelista *Innovation and the Arms Race*, London, Cornell University Press, 1988.

42. It can be argued that in the current period the pace of technological innovation is accelerating in the developed west, that new weapons technologies will require inputs of a broad range of sophisticated technologies (e.g. microelectronics, materials, electro-optics), and that an unreformed USSR would experience greater difficulty in keeping up in future technological arms races. Evangelista, op. cit., pp. 254–61 assesses the challenges for the USSR of developments in deep-strike conventional weapons and in the programmes associated with the Strategic Defence Initiative.

43. Authoritative CIA analyses indicate that in the early 1980s per capita consumption in the USSR was about one-third that in the US and one-half that in western Europe (G.E. Schroeder and I. Edwards *Consumption in the USSR: An International Comparison*, Washington DC, report for the US Congress Joint Economic Committee, 1981 and G.E. Schroeder 'Soviet living standards: Achievements and prospects' in US Congress, Joint Economic Committee *Soviet Economy in the 1980's: Problems and Prospects*, Washington DC, USGPO, 1983). Igor Birman in *Ekonomika Nedostach*, New York, Chalidze Publications, 1983 criticizes the CIA methodology and estimates the USSR-to-US per capita consumption ratio to be in the 20–25 per cent range. His assessment is supported by Aslund, op. cit., pp. 33–36. According to CIA/DIA, 1989, op. cit., p. 41 the average annual growth of real per capita consumption in the USSR declined as follows: 1966–70 5.0 per cent; 1971–75 3.0 per cent; 1976–80 2.0 per cent; and 1981–85 0.8 per cent. Given this downward trend, it is safe to conclude that Soviet living standards worsened relative to those of all other great powers at least in the period 1976–85.

44. G. Grossman 'The "second economy" of the USSR', *Problems of Communism*, vol. 26, no. 5 (1977) and C. Davis 'The second economy in disequilibrium and shortage models of centrally planned economies', Durham, *Berkeley-Duke Occasional Papers on the Second Economy in the USSR: No. 12*, July 1988.

45. The impact of a low priority ranking on the provision of public services in the USSR is analysed in C. Davis 'Priority and the shortage model: The medical system in the socialist economy' in Davis and Charemza (eds.) *Models of Disequilibrium*, op. cit.

46. The import shares are taken from Table 3.7, p. 459 of 'Exports of Manufactures from Eastern Europe and the Soviet Union to the Developed Market Economies, 1965–81', *Economic Bulletin for Europe*, vol. 35, no. 4 (Dec. 1983).

47. The OECD shares were calculated by dividing the value of imports from the USSR of commodities in SITC category 7 ('Machinery and Transport Equipment') (\$ 371.8 million in 1975 and \$ 420.1 million in 1985) by total imports in this category (\$ 129,567.6 million in 1975 and \$ 366,093.0 million in 1985). The shares were 0.287 per cent in 1975 and 0.115 per cent in 1985. The source of data is OECD *Statistics of Foreign Trade, Series C: Trade by Commodities*, (for 1975, p. 104; for 1985, Microtables K05 and L05).

48. M.N. Kramer 'Soviet arms transfers to the Third World', *Problems of Communism*, vol. 36, no. 5 (1987), p. 55.
49. C. Wolf Jr., K.C. Yeh, E. Brunner Jr., A. Gurwitz, and M. Lawrence *The Cost of Soviet Empire*, Santa Monica, RAND R-3073/1-NA, Sept.1983. See also D. F. Epstein 'The economic cost of Soviet security and empire' in Rowen and Wolf Jr. (eds.) *The Impoverished Superpower*, op. cit.
50. The GNP shares are the rounded-off mid-points of the ranges of the 'costs of empire' burdens shown in Table 2, p. 20 in Wolf Jr. et al., *The Costs*, op. cit., of 0.86–1.37 per cent for 1971 and 2.32–3.00 per cent for 1980.
51. Davis 'Interdependence' and 'Economic plans', op. cit.
52. These official Soviet defence burdens were calculated by dividing reported defence expenditures in billions of roubles (1970 17.9; 1980 17.1; 1985 19.1) by utilized national income in billions of roubles (1970 285.5; 1980 454.1; 1985 568.7). The sources of data are *Narodnoe Khozyaistvo SSSR 1922–1982*, Moscow, Finansy i Statistika, 1982, p. 562 and *Narodnoe . . . 1988*, op. cit., pp. 16, 625.
53. Some western analysts such as F.D. Holzman support this low figure. See his article 'Politics and guesswork: CIA and DIA estimates of Soviet military spending', *International Security*, vol. 14, No. 2 (Fall 1989) and his section of 'Correspondence: CIA estimates of Soviet military spending', *International Security*, vol. 14, no. 4 (Spring 1990). Holzman's methodology and conclusions are criticized by J.E. Steiner of the CIA in the same correspondence section.
54. CIA *Estimated Soviet Defense Spending: Trends and Prospects*, Washington DC, SR 78–10121, 1978; A. Becker *Sitting on Bayonets: The Soviet Defense Burden and the Slowdown of Soviet Defense Spending*, Santa Monica, RAND JRS-01, 1985; CIA *A Guide to Monetary Measures of Soviet Defense Activities*, Washington DC, SOV 87–10069, Nov. 1987; and Central Intelligence Agency/Defense Intelligence Agency (CIA/DIA) *Gorbachev's Economic Program: Problems Emerge*, Washington DC, DDB-1900–187–88, June 1988.
55. Epstein 'The economic cost', op. cit.
56. For the purposes of this calculation the following CIA estimates in billions of 1982 roubles were accepted: 1965 (defence spending 60, GNP 462) and 1985 (defence spending 110, GNP 685) (Sources: CIA *Revisiting*, op. cit., p. 10; CIA/DIA 'The Soviet economy', op. cit., p. 40; and the assumption of a 13 per cent defence burden in 1965). So the defence burdens were 13 per cent in 1965 and 16 per cent in 1985. If Soviet GNP was 33 per cent of US in 1965 (instead of 50 per cent as indicated in CIA *Handbook . . . 1985*, op. cit., pp. 34–35) and in 1985 (instead of 53 per cent), and there was a stable relationship between Soviet dollar and rouble GNP, then the respective rouble GNP figures for the USSR would be 66 per cent of that given above for 1965 (or 305 billion roubles) and 62 per cent for 1985 (or 423 billion roubles). With the same defence spending estimates the respective burdens would have been 20 per cent and 26 per cent.
57. The assumption is made that in 1985 the extended security spending as defined by Epstein, op. cit. was 171 billion (1982) roubles, GNP was 685 billion (1982) roubles, and the extended burden was 25 per cent. If Soviet GNP in dollars was 33 per cent of that of the US, and the assumptions of endnote 56 are valid, then the rouble GNP would have been only 423 billion (1982) roubles. So the actual extended burden would have been 40 per cent.
58. Kennedy, op. cit., p. 445
59. The most thorough recent assessment of change in the Soviet political system can be found in D. Lane *Soviet Society Under Perestroika*, London, Unwin Hyman, 1990. See also A. Brown (ed.) *Political Leadership in the Soviet Union*, Basingstoke, Macmillan, 1989 and R. Sakwa *Soviet Politics: An Introduction*, London, Routledge, 1989.

60. The influences of 'new thinking' are evident in numerous speeches of General Secretary Gorbachev and Foreign Minister Shevardnadze. For example, at the 27th CPSU Congress Gorbachev stated: 'The nature of today's weapons leaves no state the hope of defending itself by technical military means alone – let us say, by the creation of even the most powerful defence. The maintenance of security is taking the form more and more of a political task and it can be solved only by political means. First and foremost the will is needed to go along the path of disarmament.' (M.S. Gorbachev 'Politicheskii doklad Tsentral'nogo Komiteta KPSS XXVII S'ezdu Kommunisticheskoi Partii Sovetskogo Soyuza' in *XXVII S'ezd Kommunisticheskoi Partii Sovetskogo Soyuza: Stenograficheskii Otchet*, Moscow, Politizdat, 1986) Another important feature of 'new thinking' is the de-ideologization of international relations, which involves the minimization of the role of class struggle and emphasis on the need to cooperate to solve common global problems. An important recent article that reflects this new approach to security is S. Blagovolin 'Geopoliticheskie aspekty oboronitelnoi dostatochnosti', *Kommunist*, 1990, no. 4.

61. Authoritative western evaluations of 'new thinking' include: S.M. Meyer 'The sources and prospects of Gorbachev's new political thinking on security', *International Security*, Vol. 13 (1988), No. 2; S. Bialer '"New thinking" and Soviet foreign policy', *Survival*, July/Aug. 1988; E.L. Warner III 'New thinking and old realities in Soviet defence policy', *Survival*, Vol. XXXI (1989), No. 1; and R. Allison 'New thinking about defence in the Soviet Union' in K. Booth (ed.) *New Thinking About Strategy and International Security*, London, Unwin Hyman, Forthcoming.

62. Reform in the defence sector is discussed in: Davis 'Perestroika', 'Interdependence', and 'Disarmament', op. cit.; D.R. Herspring 'On *perestroika*: Gorbachev, Yazov, and the military', *Problems of Communism*, July-Aug. 1987; and numerous Soviet articles, such as D.T. Yazov 'Kachestvennye parametry oboronnogo stroitelstva', *Krasnaya Zvezda*, 9 Aug. 1988 and 'Na osnove novogo myshleniya', *Krasnaya Zvezda*, 13 April 1989. The perestroika in threat reduction institutions as of July 1987 is reviewed in: Davis 'Perestroika', op. cit.; Bialer, op. cit.; 'Round Table: Gorbachev and the Post-Chebrikov KGB', *Radio Liberty Research*, 22 Dec. 1989, pp. 16–30; Meyer op. cit.; and R. Allison 'Gorbachev's arms control offensive: Unilateral, bilateral and multilateral initiatives' in C.G. Jacobson (ed.) *Soviet Foreign Policy at the Cross-Roads*, London, Macmillian, 1989.

63. Critical assessments of the Soviet military that reflect this re-evaluation of security strategy by 'new thinkers' in the USSR can be found in: Pankin, op. cit.; the articles by A. Arbatov 'Gde predel razumnoi dostatochnosti?', *Novoe Vremya*, no. 17, 1989 and 'A esli bez lukavstva?', *Ogonek*, no. 17, 1990; and Yu. Ryzhkov 'Bezopasnost, kotoraya nam ne nuzhna', *Novoe Vremya*, 1990, no. 10 (March).

64. Davis 'Perestroika', 'Interdependence', and 'Disarmament', op. cit.

65. The Soviet leadership has made the following claims or announcements concerning defence expenditure during 1986–88: the 12th Five Year Plan called for growth in defence spending that exceeded that of the national economy; defence spending was frozen in 1987–88; and this freeze resulted in a saving of 10 billion roubles from the expenditure approved by the 12th Plan (M.S. Gorbachev 'Ob osnovnykh napravleniyakh vnutrennei i vneshnei politiki SSSR', *Krasnaya Zvezda*, 31 May 1989; M. Moiseev 'Oboronnyy byudzhet SSSR', *Pravda*, 11 June 1989; N.I. Ryzhkov 'Sluzhit interesam naroda', *Ekonomicheskaya Gazeta*, 1989, no. 24 (July); and D.T. Yazov 'Yazov reviews arms reduction and negotiations', *Summary of World Broadcasts*, SU/0564 A1/1, 18 Sept. 1989).

66. US government estimates of trends in Soviet defence spending during 1985–88 can be found in: US Congress, Joint Economic Committee *Allocation of Resources in the Soviet Union and China – 1986*, Washington DC, USGPO, 1988 and CIA/DIA 'Gorbachev's

Economic' (1988) and 'The Soviet economy' (1989) op. cit.. For academic assessments see D. Steinberg 'Defense economic trends under Gorbachev', Chicago, paper presented at the AAASS Convention, 2–4 Nov. 1989 and Davis 'Economic plans', op. cit. The US/NATO assessment that there was an upward trend during 1985–88 appears to be consistent with developments in specific expenditure categories: no significant reduction of armed forces employment, so the Ministry of Defence wage bill probably remained constant or rose slightly; military pension payments grew due to demographic factors; and spending on the procurement of weapons systems and on military R & D increased. However, there may have been some reduction in operations and maintenance costs due to reduced deployments of naval ships and the efficiency campaign throughout the armed forces.

67. Official Soviet statistical material indicates that eight branches of the defence industry increased their 1988 output of most types of civilian goods from 1987 levels but did not always fulfil their ambitious plans (See 'Proizvodstvo neprodovolst'stvennykh tovarov narodnogo potrebleniya v 1988 g.', *Vestnik Statistiki*, 1989, no. 5 and J. Tedstrom 'Is the contribution of the defence complex to civilian production growing?', *Radio Liberty Reports*, 16 June 1989).

68. M.S. Gorbachev 'Vystuplenie M.S. Gorbacheva v Organizatsii Ob'edinennykh Natsii', *Pravda*, 8 December 1988 (see also 'Mikhail Gorbachev's address to the UN general assembly', *Soviet News*, 14 Dec. 1988).

69. G. Krivosheyev 'Military plans for 1990' (interview with O. Moskovskiy), *Summary of World Broadcasts*, SU/0658 A1/1, 10 Jan. 1990. As the troop reductions proceeded it became clear that the two-year total would be in excess of the initial target of 500,000 men.

70. The 1989 figure is taken from 'Soobshchenie Ministerstva Oborony SSSR', *Krasnaya Zvezda*, 16 Dec. 1989. The size of the armed forces in Jan. 1990 was calculated by subtracting from the official 1989 total the 265,000 man cut mentioned by Krivosheyev, op. cit..

71. W.H. Kincade and T.K. Thomson 'Economic conversion in the USSR: Its role in perestroika', *Problems of Communism*, vol. XXXIX, no. 1 (Jan–Feb. 1990). See also the references to the conversion programme in Davis 'Disarmament', op. cit.

72. I.S. Belousov 'Konversiya. Chto eto znachit' (interview with A. Pokrovskii), *Pravda*, 28 Aug. 1989.

73. Among the important Soviet speeches, articles and announcements during 1989 on defence spending are: Gorbachev 'Ob osnovnykh', op. cit.; Ryzhkov 'Sluzhit interesam' op. cit.; Moiseev 'Oboronnyy', op. cit.; V. Deinega 'Oboronnyy byudzhet i ego realizatsiya', *Kommunist Vooruzhennykh Sil*, 1990, No. 3; A. Kireev 'Skol'ko tratit' na oborony', *Ogonek*, 1989, No. 19 (May); and 'Soobshchenie' op. cit.. An analysis of the published material in Davis 'Economic plans', op. cit., indicates that evidence concerning budget changes between 1988 and 1989 is so ambiguous that it is possible to argue that defence spending rose, remained constant, or fell.

74. CIA/DIA *The Soviet Economy Stumbles Badly in 1989*, Washington DC, Report presented to the US Congress, Joint Economic Committee, 20 April 1990.

75. Ryzhkov 'Bezopasnost', op. cit., mentions some of the difficulties and costs associated with conversion. See also the scenarios for disarmament in the 1990s and their associated implications for defence spending in Davis 'Disarmament', op. cit..

76. E.A. Hewett *Reforming the Soviet Economy: Equality versus Efficiency*, Washington DC, The Brookings Institutions, 1988.

77. A. Aslund *Gorbachev's Struggle for Economic Reform*, London, Pinter Publishers, 1989.

78. Recent developments in the economic reform are assessed in: CIA/DIA 'The Soviet economy' (1989), op. cit.; E.A. Hewett 'Perestroika "Plus": The Abalkin reforms',

PlanEcon Report, vol. V, nos. 48–49 (1 Dec. 1989); CIA/DIA *The Soviet Economy Stumbles* (1990), op. cit.; and N.I. Ryzhkov 'Ob ekonomicheskom polozhenii strany i kontseptsii perekhoda k reguliruemoi rynochnoi ekonomike', *Pravda*, 25 May 1990.

79. For good summary evaluations see the previously cited annual reports on the Soviet economy by the CIA/DIA: 'Gorbachev's Economic Program' (1988), 'The Soviet Economy in 1988' (1989), and 'The Soviet Economy Stumbles' (1990).

80. E. Gaidar 'Trudnyy vybor: Ekonomicheskoe obozrenie po itogam 1989 goda', *Kommunist*, 1990, no. 2; K. Kagalovskii 'Ekonomicheskii krizis. Gde iskat' vykhod?', *Kommunist*, 1990, no. 4 (March); Ryzhkov 'Ob ekonomicheskom', op. cit.

81. The 1985 growth rate is from CIA/DIA 'Gorbachev's Economic Program' (1988), op. cit. and those for 1986–89 from CIA/DIA 'The Soviet Economy Stumbles' (1990), op. cit., Table C-4.

82. 'Ekonomika strany: itogi goda. Sotsial'no-ekonomicheskoe razvitie SSSR v 1989 godu', *Izvestiya*, 28 Jan. 1990; 'Uskorit ozdorovlenie ekonomiki: Sotsial'no-ekonomicheskoe razvitie SSSR v 1989 godu', *Pravda*, 26 Jan. 1990; and Gaidar 'Trudnyy vybor', op. cit.

83. G.I. Khanin 'Krisis uglublyaetsya', *EKO*, 1990, no. 1.

84. Gaidar 'Trunyy vybor', op. cit.; Kagalovskii 'Ekonomicheskii krizis', op. cit.; 'Sotsial'no-ekonomicheskoe razvitie SSSR v pervom kvartale 1990 goda', *Izvestiya*, 27 April 1990; and Ryzhkov 'Ob ekonomicheskom', op. cit.

85. The unfavourable conditions were: the economy was already in disequilibrium at the start of the reform process; there was poor weather in 1985 and 1987 that adversely affected agriculture, raw material extraction, and transportation; the Chernobyl disaster; the Armenian earthquake; and worsening of the Soviet foreign trade position after 1985 due to the decline in the world price of oil and the strength of the US dollar (in which currency oil is priced).

86. In 1986 J. Kornai argued that the Hungarian shortage economy had survived despite energetic and radical reform efforts since 1968 (see 'The Hungarian reform process: Visions, hopes, and reality', *Journal of Economic Literature*, Vol. XXIV, no. 4 (Dec. 1986)). C. Krueger in '*Perestroika*: Reform in the Soviet Union?', Cambridge, Harvard Discussion Paper, 1987, put forward the argument that in the USSR shortage economy processes are more entrenched, the reforms have been less radical, and their effects have been less significant than in Hungary.

87. An excellent assessment of the coverage and quality of Soviet economic statistics in the Gorbachev period is contained in V. Treml 'Perestroika and Soviet statistics' in CIA *The Impact of Gorbachev's Policies on Soviet Economic Statistics*, Directorate of Intelligence, SOV 88–10049, July 1988.

88. Khanin, op. cit.; Gaidar, op. cit.; and CIA/DIA 'The Soviet Economy Stumbles' (1990), op. cit.

89. The 1985 GNP estimate is taken from CIA/DIA 'The Soviet Economy' (1989), op. cit., p. 40.

90. CIA/DIA 'The Soviet Economy in 1988' (1989) and 'The Soviet Economy Stumbles' (1990), op. cit.

91. The growth rates were calculated from OECD data about constant price GNP/GDP for the period 1984–89 obtained from the Datastream computer databank (series OCDGDP..D, USOCGNPDD, and JPOCGNPDD). Another source for the US and German growth rates was Economic Commission for Europe *Economic Survey of Europe in 1988–1989*, New York, United Nations, 1989, p. 16.

92. Ryzhkov 'Ob ekonomicheskom', op. cit.

93. 'Z' 'To the Stalin', op. cit. and Z. Brzezinski *The Grand Failure: The Birth and Death of Communism in the Twentieth Century*, London, Macdonald & Co., 1989.

Eastern Europe out of the Cold: Finlandization and Beyond

BENNETT KOVRIG

What does the political scientist know?
The political scientist knows the latest trends
The current states of affairs
The history of doctrines

What does the political scientist not know?
The political scientist doesn't know about desperation
He doesn't know the game that consists
Of renouncing the game

It doesn't occur to him
That no one knows when
Irrevocable changes may appear
Like an ice-floe's sudden cracks

And that the natural resources
Include knowledge of the venerated laws
Ability to wonder
And a sense of humour.

Themselves no strangers to generalization, political scientists may bristle at Artur Miedzyrecki's poetic tarbrush, but in truth the past year has been a sobering experience for self-professed experts in communist affairs.[1] To be sure, by the beginning of the decade few if any retained illusions about the popular legitimacy of East European regimes, or even about the reformability of socialism. The Solidarity crisis had exposed an unbridgeable gulf between governors and governed, leaving even altruistic communists bereft of workable formulas for creating material plenty and social peace. What Timothy Garton Ash called a 'revolution of consciousness' left no doubt that the socialist system was abhorred by a vast majority.[2] But the Kremlin's hegemonic will and the capacity of its client regimes to maintain order if not harmony seemed unimpaired.

By the time of Gorbachev's advent, an embryonic civil society, autonomous and profoundly estranged from the ruling party and its ideology, was flourishing in Poland and emerging in Hungary. Its contempt for the rituals of socialist democracy was tacitly tolerated by the rulers, and of course it lacked access to the levers of power. Elsewhere, sundry dissident intellectuals, environmentalists, champions of minority rights, religious activists, and conscientious objectors were drawing spiritual sustenance from the west's human rights campaign in the Helsinki process. They scarcely disturbed the neo-totalitarian rule of Bulgarian's Zhivkov, Czechoslovakia's Husak and his successor Jakes, East Germany's Honecker, or Romania's megalomaniacal Ceausescu.

The first tangible evidence of Gorbachev's permissiveness materialized in May 1988, when the Hungarian party unceremoniously dumped Kadar, once hailed as the father of goulash communism, and replaced him with a mixed bag of opportunists and radical reformers. Then General Jaruzelski swallowed his pride and, breaking earlier vows, opened a dialogue with Solidarity. Noting the near-bankruptcy of these two countries, western observers anticipated a protracted effort at conciliation by regimes seeking social support for the austerity measures and marketization urged on them by the International Monetary Fund.

The practitioners of Marxism-Leninism had made tactical concessions before. Much of Marxist economics was anachronistic and expendable, but political power in the Leninist conception was indivisible. Liberalization, it was confidently assumed, would stop short of the irreducible core of Leninism: the leading role of the party. The socialist pluralism evoked by Gorbachev and his East European disciples could not be translated into institutionalized political pluralism without putting into question the legitimacy and historical irreversibility of the socialist revolution. Economic hybrids were conceivable, albeit more as palliative than as remedy; that was the lasting lesson of the Hungarian experiment with a 'New Economic Mechanism'. Political hybrids were unworkable, a foredoomed squaring of the Leninist circle, in the most overused metaphor of the year.

Such caution was buttressed by doctrinal exegesis and ample experience with 'real existing socialism'. It failed to allow for the possibility that in the Kremlin's 'new political thinking', the East European empire was increasingly seen as economically burdensome, politically intractable, and strategically superfluous. The withdrawal of Soviet patronage was less predictable than the precipitous collapse of regimes in consequence of that withdrawal. The alienation of their subjects was evident, the fragility of their effective power and confidence less so. In the event, the cracks in the ice-cap were erased by a cataclysmic thaw that ultimately swept away the last dike of socialism, the Berlin Wall. After forty years of being victimized by utopian social engineering, the East Europeans chose revolutionary change. The capacity of socialist regimes to nurture and control evolutionary reform would be tested not there but in the Soviet Union, where Gorbachev was leading from behind to arrest structural disintegration, and in China, where the Tiananmen massacre signalled a will to counter-reform absent elsewhere in the socialist world.

In Europe, then, the comparatively stable and predictable post-Yalta order vanished with breathtaking suddenness. After a delay of 45 years, the East Europeans were allowed to claim the Yalta promise of national sovereignty. The delay had been immeasurably costly. At war's end, most East Europeans wanted respite from the excesses of state-sponsored nationalism and from the conservative authoritarianism that, except in Czechoslovakia, marked their prewar governments. The formidable task of rebuilding their ruined countries required strong leadership as well as foreign assistance; the prevailing mood favoured democratic institutions, social and economic reform, and national autonomy. Instead, with Stalin's help the communists delivered totalitarian rule and Procrustean imposition of the Soviet model of state socialism. In the early years, Soviet hegemony meant also economic exploitation (the wealth extracted from Eastern Europe roughly matched Marshall Plan aid to Western Europe) and cultural russification.

Counter-revolutions were brutally suppressed, and tinkering with the socialist economic system earned little legitimacy for regimes that had lost their revolutionary zeal but not their determination to preserve monopolistic power. To that end the requisites of modernization remained subordinated. The promise of social justice materialized in an equality of poverty. The promise of human liberation in a classless society turned into the denial of individual autonomy and civil rights. The communist type of totalitarian system, reflected Vaclav Havel in a moving address to the US Congress, left 'a legacy of countless dead, an infinite spectrum of human suffering, profound economic decline and, above all, enormous human humiliation.'[3]

Not to belabour the misdeeds perpetrated in the name of communist utopia, the experiment has left the East Europeans woefully unprepared for rejoining the world denied to them after Yalta. Their economies are monuments to inefficiency and mismanagement, incapable of satisfying either domestic consumer needs or the standards of the world market. Singapore exports more manufactured products to the OECD than all of Eastern Europe (including the Soviet Union), and the competitiveness of the latter has only declined over the past decade. Western credits were squandered, on consumption to buy social peace and in unproductive investments. Foreign debt, obsolete plants, unmotivated workers, an antiquated infrastructure (as anyone trying to place a telephone call in Warsaw or Budapest will testify), and some of the worst environmental pollution in Europe are a socialist legacy that strains the optimism of the most ardent advocates of market economics.

Nor was the damage only material. To be sure, as George Schopflin observes, the pre-socialist political traditions of the East Europeans could be characterized as backward.[4] Imperial rule had distorted and retarded their political as well as economic modernization compared to some Western European countries. Constitutionalism and democratic pluralism received due lip service in all the states of post-Versailles Eastern Europe, but in practice authoritarianism and etatism, draped in the cloth of nationalism, lingered on. In predominantly agrarian societies possessed of a comparatively small bourgeoisie and industrial working class, the cleavage between traditional peasant culture and modernizing, urban liberalism was papered over by the self-perpetuating rule of a political class that manned the typical governing party and state bureaucracy. This system of governance was neither explicitly monopolistic nor opposed to gradual modernization. It did cautiously promote social mobility and welfare as well as industrialization, and it accommodated limited political participation. The voices of peasant populism, liberalism, and democratic socialism could speak in the parliamentary arena.

Great diversity underlay this general pattern. The political culture of the Czech lands came close to western modernity, while that of the Balkans still suffered from the deadening legacy of centuries of Ottoman rule. Poles and Hungarians enjoyed a comparatively neutral rule of law and a lively if circumscribed political pluralism. Only with the onset of the Great Depression and with the ideologies of nationalism and fascism ascendant throughout Europe did their conservative political elites and those of the Balkans turn more authoritarian, and then mainly to forestall the challenge of domestic radicals of right and left.

Although the war shattered the legitimacy and social basis of this paternalistic order, the bureaucratic tradition of etatism served the communists well. In the Stalinist apotheosis of totalitarianism, the party marshalled a renewed and expanded bureaucratic army to direct every aspect of life in an atomized society. The slow emergence of civil societies was arrested. The very concept of individual and group autonomy was expunged from the political lexicon, its place taken by the myth of the will of unified masses. And since the masses had not reached a proper level of consciousness, the party substituted for them in articulating that will. In later years, when the parties came to acknowledge the existence of a plurality of socio-economic strata and of competing interests in the nominally classless state of 'real existing socialism', they would argue that the East Europeans were not sufficiently mature politically to be granted a more democratic choice of representatives and leaders.

One finds in the west today echoes of this patronizing concern, that the East Europeans may lack the blend of political assertiveness and tolerance necessary for a stable pluralistic democracy. The promise of Yalta implied that they were entitled, ready and able in 1945, and one may ask what has been lost, and what gained in this respect by two generations weaned on socialism. Havel observed gloomily in his presidential New Year's address:

> The worst thing is that we live in a contaminated moral environment. We fell morally ill because we became used to saying something different from what we think. . . . The previous regime, armed with its arrogant and intolerant ideology, degraded people into a productive force and nature into a tool

> of production ... it reduced gifted and autonomous people, skilfully working in their own country, to nuts and bolts of some monstrously huge, noisy and stinking machine, whose real meaning is not clear to anyone. ... We had all become used to the totalitarian system and accepted it as an unchangeable fact and thus helped to perpetuate it.[5]

In truth, communist rule had reinforced fearful respect for bureaucratic authority and sapped the will to autonomous action. In its messianism it had preyed on yearnings for final solutions and preached a concomitant contempt for competing values. And, in Ceausescu's and Zhivkov's aberrant version, it had exploited the darker side of nationalism in pandering to the intolerance of a *Staatsvolk*. This much for the debit side of the ledger.

Still, if the disease momentarily debilitated the East European body politic, the latter's reflexes did not wholly atrophy, and it developed some potentially useful antibodies. The triumph of the popular opposition in Poland, the burgeoning pluralism in Hungary, the revolutions in East Germany, Czechoslovakia, and Bulgaria displayed not only an abhorrence of communist dictatorship but also admirable individual and group initiative, civility, and tolerance. Only in Romania, where society is handicapped by being even less schooled in democracy than its neighbours, did an egregiously oppressive regime earn a violent end. On the whole, East Europeans responded with remarkable political maturity to the opportunity of escaping from Soviet hegemony and communist tyranny. As Sandor Petofi, poet of Hungary's 1848 revolution, observed, 'liberty is the greatest common good, and when one takes a piece, one takes it all'.

Both the negative example of 'socialist legality' and the elevation of human rights – in the Helsinki process, and by countless organizations in the west and dissident groups in the east – to a lodestar that transcends frontiers and cultural differences contributed to the conversion of most East Europeans to the liberal doctrine of immanent and indivisible individual liberties. That doctrine implies an unending pluralistic, constitutionally-governed contest for the allocation of scarce goods and services, but it does inhibit messianism, assimilative nationalism, and pseudo-scientific final solutions. It requires, in short, consensual agreement on the rules of the game, and as the East Europeans shed the totalitarian straitjacket they are, on the whole, rising to the liberal challenge.

Lest this be dismissed as a Panglossian view of their future, it must be anticipated that the euphoria of recaptured freedom will soon be dampened by the grim necessities of reconstruction. Sceptics bemoan the proliferation of new political parties, or alternatively the tenuous cohesion of a Solidarity movement charged with the thankless task of government. They fret that the East Europeans are trading one illusion for another, socialist utopia for the miraculous promise of market democracy. And they watch eagle-eyed for signs of regression to chauvinism, of anti-semitism, of official or popular intolerance of minorities, be they Bulgarian Turks, Romanian Magyars, or Polish Germans. Such concern and scrutiny are benign and potentially beneficial when they are not patronizing. Obviously the East Europeans have accumulated less experience with pluralistic democracy, and with market economics, than their more fortunate western neighbours. But even those mature democracies are not free of blemish when it comes to human rights and social justice, while in the east the recent experience of totalitarianism will long serve as a deterrent to deliberate compromise on human rights. As for the democratic pluralism, the principles are easily taught, but the political culture can only absorb it through the trial and error of experience.

That experience is beginning in this fourth springtime of nations (after the false start of 1848, the short-lived era of Wilsonian self-determination, and the aborted promise of Yalta), and at the time of writing the first round of truly free elections since the war is incomplete. The run-up to the elections was most remarkable for the similarity of political platforms. In converting themselves to a social democratic format, the former ruling parties renounced their doctrinal leading role, and state constitutions were amended accordingly. All contestants endorsed pluralistic democracy and the sovereignty of parliament, and all (apart from the odd forlorn band of unreconstructed communists) advocated market economics tempered by social justice. East Europeans welcomed Gorbachev's permissiveness but saw little promise in his incrementalist *perestroika*. Declared Lech Walesa back in April 1989:

I wish Gorbachev and his reforms all the best. But we still don't know what communism in its final form will look like. In contrast, we know very well which political and economic models in Europe and in the world have passed the test of time, and it is to these models that we must turn as opposed to attempting to 'reform' failed ideologies and concepts.[6]

Socialism, joke the East Europeans bitterly, is the hardest road from capitalism to capitalism. Its most positive consequence may well be the current broad consensus on the desirability of political and economic liberalism. But if consensus on the former should prove durable, the dilemmas of economic reconstruction will no doubt arouse sharp controversy. Democratic constitutionalism cannot quickly transform the economic and social order created by communists; it can only provide for the orderly representation of diverse interests and for the legislation of priorities enjoying majority support.

The first steps in this liberal revolution are relatively easy: to terminate the moribund communist parties' control over the key agencies of government and their monopoly of truth. The privileges of the party elite, the communists' hold over the police and armed forces, the party's presence in the workplace are readily legislated out of existence. The rights to free expression and association can also be promulgated and realized overnight. The hard choices and obstacles to implementation lie in the realm of social and economic policy. The obstacles are both structural and attitudinal. The administration of socialism involved massive political patronage, and if the *nomenklatura* system can be formally abolished, its army of beneficiaries remains in place. The problem bears no quick solution (one fanciful suggestion being a ruinous golden handshake to the least competent party hacks), and indeed it may underestimate the adaptability and professionalism of the many who of out existential necessity professed loyalty to the communist kings.

Popular mores and attitudes may be more resistant to quick conversion. The comfort of subsidized housing and staples, job security, and an admittedly penurious equality may weigh heavily in the balance against the discomforts and uncertainties of market economics. In the moment, the reality of queuing and shortages and the promise of market-generated economic growth conspire to induce a permissive consensus. The Poles have stomached with surprising stoicism the initial sharp drop in the standard of living precipitated by the 'big bang' programme of economic restructuring. But the substantial unemployment and greater income differentiation that loom will not fail to occasion some nostalgia for the egalitarian security of socialism.

Since no East European political party can credibly promise early improvement in the standard of living, the initial superficial harmony on fundamental issues will soon be superseded by political quarrels over distribution of a shrinking pie. In their attempts to forge a new social contract, economic liberals will be handicapped by the absence of a large entrepreneurial and propertied class, of a constituency that has an immediate vested interest in the market economy. The creative intellectuals who have been the catalysts of revolution in Eastern Europe may momentarily be swayed by the fashion for Friedmanite economics, but their heart lies closer to the paternalistic state than to the rough justice of the invisible hand. Peasants will not be pleased to discover that the free market favours agro-industry over the private plot. Nor will industrial workers welcome the demand for western-style productivity at eastern wages coupled with the threat of redundancy. Painful, too, will be the impact of budgetary austerity on services, such as health care, which are already in a lamentable state.

The outlook, then, is for political turbulence that will sorely test the fledgling democratic institutions. East Germany, thanks to the generosity of its big brother, may be spared much of the economic pain on its way to confederation or unification. That was the lure that drew East Germans to support what was in effect the West German Christian Democratic party in the March elections. Elsewhere in Eastern Europe, the reconstructed communist parties also stand little chance of securing popular recognition as the champions of social democracy, and their former allied parties (which enjoyed a nominal existence everywhere except in Hungary) are similarly tainted by their past. The new parliaments will more likely be dominated by newly-minted parties and reincarnations of pre-communist parties, such as the Hungarian Smallholders. These will share allegiance to democratic pluralism while dividing over issues of distribution and economic nationalism. The exigencies of impending bankruptcy have driven Hungarian and

Polish reformers to beg for foreign investment, but one can anticipate a nationalistic backlash against selling their countries to the highest bidder.

Even without the thoroughly discredited option of state socialism, many choices within the ambit of democratic socialism and welfare capitalism remain in contention. The Swedish model of a capitalist welfare state dedicated to full employment is a popular dream in Eastern Europe, but it is the product of unique historical factors and seems, in any case, to be running out of steam.[7] A strong and socially-conscious capitalist class, a consensual trust in the impartiality of government, a solid technological base are all lacking in the former Soviet sphere. The hard choices of economic reconstruction are only complicated by environmental issues and a mushrooming ecological movement. Socialist industrialization has bequeathed horrendous pollution, particularly in East Germany, Poland, and Czechoslovakia; by one estimate, three-quarters of East German industry fails to meet West German environmental standards. The replacement of obsolete industrial plants should eventually alleviate the problem, but the environmentalist agenda will not be easy to accommodate in the allocation of scarce resources. Hungarian Greens succeeded in halting the Gabcikovo-Nagymaros hydroelectric dam project on the Danube, much to the distress of the Czechoslovak partner. Greens in Bulgaria and elsewhere are campaigning against nuclear power-plants. Yet in such underdeveloped and energy-poor countries, environmentalism may be in the short run an unaffordable luxury.

And finally, the ethnic mosaic encompassed by the frontiers drawn at Versailles and Potsdam is bound to generate tensions in the pluralistic future. Poles, Romanians, and Bulgarians tend to regard ethnic minorities and their external cultural links as threats to national unity. Even some ostensibly democratic parties, such as the revived National Peasant party in Romania, are tempted to exploit nationalist intolerance. The two million-strong Hungarian community in Transylvania is once again the target of grass-roots Romanian chauvinism, and the new government in Bucharest will be hard pressed to implement the prescriptions for minority cultural rights enshrined in the concluding document of the Vienna CSCE meeting. By the same token, Germany and Hungary will champion ever more openly the rights of their co-nationals in other countries, and until these rights are effectively guaranteed, regional relations will not become truly peaceable.

In sum, the unfettered politics of Eastern Europe will not be free of divisive debate, and perhaps even of populist demagoguery. Leaving aside the special case of East Germany, the Czechoslovaks stand the best chance of shifting smoothly to an orderly market democracy, by virtue of their political traditions and comparative economic stability. More fractious politicking and coalition governments probably lie ahead in Hungary and Poland, whose economic distress may not be alleviated unless western lenders bite the bullet of debt forgiveness. The process of democratization in Romania promises to be even more acrimonious, with former communists draping themselves in the mantle of revolutionary legitimacy and the nationalism cultivated by Ceausescu continuing to poison inter-ethnic relations.

For the moment, East Europeans can at least relish the novelty of being masters in their own house, which many are eager to turn into an annexe of the European house anchored in Brussels. But the autonomy of small nations is always circumscribed by their powerful neighbours, and the clash of Russian and German interests in the lands between is merely entering a new phase as the division of Europe fades. If Gorbachev originally anticipated a replication of *perestroika*, a pluralism that could still be characterized as socialist, he gracefully accepted the more heretical choice of his former vassals. Making a virtue of necessity, he now envisages the Warsaw Pact as an essentially political alliance. Prague and Budapest have obtained the phased withdrawal of the Red Army. Their parliaments reclaimed the sovereign right to deploy their armed forces, a right which by earlier, secret agreements had been assigned to the Warsaw Pact (in fact, Soviet) command in times of war or apprehended hostilities.

As the East European governments cut defence expenditures, depoliticize their armed forces, and wave the Russians farewell, what is left of the Warsaw Pact? Certainly no battle-worthy military machine, and as democratically-elected leaders replace like-minded General Secretaries on its political council, no docile exponent of Soviet foreign policy either. The form will presumably remain as long as NATO survives, but the substance is rapidly disappearing. In the foreseeable future, it will be in the East Europeans' collective interest to retain a forum that can serve to assuage Russian insecurities (and lingering fears of German irredentism) and to air intra-regional disputes. But their vision of the common European home is focusd westward, their preference for some hypothetical pan-European security regime that facilitates their association with the European Community. They are lining up to join the Council of Europe, where most of them already have visiting privileges, and speculating about French and other models for disengaging from the Warsaw Pact. Hungary, in the succinct formula of a founding member of the Democratic Forum, would remain a pact member 'as long as necessary, but not one day longer'.[8]

With the prospect of formal integration with the Community still remote, the East Europeans are looking for transitional modes of autonomy. The hoary concept of Finlandization has been evoked more often as a threat to western solidarity than as an escape for the East Europeans from the Soviet embrace. Its applicability to much of Eastern Europe may be questionable, since in terms of Soviet security Finland's peripheral location is hardly comparable to the strategic importance of Poland, Czechoslovakia, or East Germany. And while Finland prospered, it had to pay political tribute to the Soviet Union in refusing to accept Marshall Plan aid, exercising considerable self-censorship (notably with regard to Soviet-communist attempts at subversion and blackmail), and refraining from official condemnation of the Soviet invasions of Hungary, Czechoslovakia, and Afghanistan. Still, if Gorbachev's version of *détente* is allowed to mature, the East Europeans will inevitably claim the Yalta promise of which, so far, Finland has been the sole beneficiary. Finland, in turn, may find its sovereignty less qualified and serve again as a test-case of Soviet permissiveness. Significantly, on a visit to Helsinki in October 1989, Gorbachev depicted Finland's neutrality as a positive feature rather than as a concession by the Soviet Union.

Hungarians and others are also drawn by the Austrian model of self-imposed neutrality, and its suitability as a road to the European Community is about to be tested. The State Treaty of 1955 prohibits economic and political union with Germany, but the concurrently-adopted neutrality law does not explicitly preclude broader international, non-military commitments. As Austria prepared to submit its application for membership, the Soviet attitude was that such a step was inconsistent with permanent neutrality.

Membership would bind Austria to follow 'all decisions taken in the framework of the Community', observed foreign ministry spokesman Gennadi Gerasimov, and 'the majority of the members of the Community are also members of NATO or of the Western European Union'.[9]

Neutrality presents problems for the Community as well at a time when the co-ordination of foreign and security policies mandated by the Single European Act is getting under way. If neutrality prevents Austria from accepting security obligations and joining the Community, there remain other mechanisms for closer association. But for its eastern neighbours (again, excepting East Germany, which rather undeservedly is promised preferential treatment), the road to European integration is bound to be even longer and more difficult to travel. Their greatest fear, that the single market will only accentuate the isolation of their faltering economies, can be partially addressed by bilateral trade concessions and aid programmes, including the new European reconstruction bank. But an emerging paradox of European reunification is that the more rapid the progress made by the Community toward political integration, the greater the hurdles will become for aspiring East European members. Conversely, attempts to accommodate the special geopolitical circumstances of the East Europeans may impede such progress. One happy circumstance is strong public support in the west for eventual adherence by the East Europeans to the Community; a survey in January 1990 showed large majorities in favour of that prospect in France and Britain as well as in Poland and the United States.[10] The notion of a pan-European confederation adumbrated by President Mitterrand strikes a responsive chord in the east, but such neo-Gaullist visions depict at best a distant future.

The lure of the west is only enhanced by the deepening agony of Comecon which, in its present form, offers neither the advantages of a regional free market nor the hypothetical benefits of rational planning by a strong supranational authority. It is, in the words of Czechoslovakia's former prime minister, Ladislav Adamec, an inefficient club of volunteers that 'became obsolete a long time ago and which does not serve us but, on the contrary, leads to immense dependence by the socialist countries on the capitalist countries'.[11] By the time the Comecon council met in Sofia in January 1990, every east

European member was in the midst of revolutionary transformation, and the question was whether the organization was reformable or ripe for euthanasia. Comecon, charged Hungarian foreign minister Gyula Horn, is 'not only unsuitable to meet its tasks, but also costs too much in its present form'.[12] A month earlier, Soviet prime minister Nikolai Ryzhkov had declared that by 1991 Comecon trade must be conducted in hard currency on the basis of world market prices, a reform that the Hungarians had been advocating for years. They, along with the Czechs and the Poles, emerged as the most impatient advocates of radical reform, of currency convertibility and of flexible transactions between enterprises instead of trade planned and directed by government agencies.

Consensus on a new Comecon will be elusive until the economic systems of its members are reformed to a modicum of symmetry. The conversion of regional trade to world market prices will have a severe impact on the terms of trade of energy-poor countries such as Hungary, whose manufactured exports to the Soviet Union have been tacitly over-valued. But the Hungarians, Czechs, and Poles appear willing to pay the price of short-term pain for the stimulus to energy-conservation, innovation, and productivity that such a reform would bring. In the final analysis, the interdependence of the Comecon's European members derives not from the institution itself but from their shared economic backwardness. Their common obsolescent technology will not be soon replaced by expensive western alternatives, and convertibility of their currencies will require a devaluation that in the short run at least will favour intra-regional trade at the expense of imports from the OECD. A marketized Comecon could thus serve as a free-trade holding pattern for the East Europeans even as they seek association with the more advanced economic groupings of Western Europe, EFTA and the European Community.

In the meantime, the leaders of the pack in economic reform, Hungary and Poland, assiduously court western investors. Already some large corporations such as General Motors, General Electric, and Suzuki have taken the bait, and the US ambassador to Budapest has traded diplomacy for the presidency of an American–Canadian investment consortium. A well educated labour force with wage rates lower than the lowest in the Community, proximity to the West European and Soviet markets, a pent-up domestic demand for producer and consumer goods, and fire-sale prices for state-owned enterprises should continue to draw foreign investors and traders to the region – and, inevitably, provoke grumbling about recolonization. Beggars such as Poland and Hungary have little choice but to put their assets on the block, court international lenders, and hope that the metamorphosis from stagnant socialism to productive capitalism can occur before the pains of adjustment become politically destabilizing.

To be sure, the Soviet shadow still hangs over the dawning new era in Eastern Europe, and the forceful reassertion of German national interest is conjuring up old spectres. By now it is doubtful that even ideological and military conservatives in Moscow believe the East European empire is retrievable, though they may yet draw the line at a united Germany in NATO while condoning *de facto* integration in a looser confederal structure. Among East Europeans, only the Poles openly oppose German unification. Fears of German irredentism will be superficially stilled by international guarantees of the Oder–Neisse frontier; the foreseeable expansion of German economic and political influence may, on the other hand, foster more ambivalent feelings about a renascent *Mitteleuropa*.

While waiting for admission to an expanded and federalized Europe, the East Europeans speculate about new and renewed linkages. Soviet hegemony induced a sense of common destiny, and its recession has stimulated, at least among some intellectuals and politicians, debate over a 'central European identity'. Nostalgia for an embellished Habsburg era and a sense of vulnerability in the new pluralistic, market environment lend momentary force to such quests. Budapest, Prague, and Warsaw talk of concerting strategy for their return to Europe. The Poles look northward to Baltic co-operation, the Hungarians to a Danubian federation (a variation on the existing, loose Alpen–Adria association) that includes Austria, Czechoslovakia, Italy, and Yugoslavia. The 'Eastern Europe' stretching from the Baltic to the Black Sea was a geopolitical fabrication, not a natural coalescence of strategic and economic interests. The integration imposed through the Warsaw Pact and Comecon scarcely reduced cultural diversity and divisions and the wide gaps in economic modernization among the East European nations. Voluntary linkages may now materialize and serve limited ends, but the vision of a united Europe should prove more enduring and fruitful if their western neighbours respond creatively to the challenge of welcoming home the victims of Yalta.

Trinity College, Toronto University

NOTES

1. The poem is quoted in Stanislaw Baranczak, 'Uncaptive Minds', *The New Republic*, 4 Dec. 1989, p. 30.
2. *Daedalus*, Vol. 119, No. 1 (Winter 1990), p. 110.
3. *Time*, 5 March 1990, p. 37.
4. George Schopflin, 'The Political Traditions of Eastern Europe', *Daedalus*, Vol. 119, No. 1 (Winter 1990), p. 55.
5. *The Globe and Mail* (Toronto), 24 Jan. 1990.
6. *Die Welt*, 24 April 1989.
7. See Angelo M. Codevilla, 'Is Olof Palme the Wave of the Future?' *Commentary*, Vol. 89, No. 3 (March 1990), pp. 26–32.
8. Geza Jeszenszky, quoted in RFE/RL Daily Report, 9 November 1989.
9. *Financial Times*, 18 May 1988.
10. *The Economist*, 27 Jan. 1990, p. 49.
11. RFE Situation Report, 14 April 1989.
12. Associated Press, 6 Jan. 1990.

The Re-emergence of 'the German Question': a United Germany and European Security and Stability

IEUAN G. JOHN

The sudden, dramatic and accelerating process of revolutionary change in Eastern Europe during winter 1989/90 and early 1990 has begun to erode the foundations of the Europe of Yalta. In particular the liberation of the East Germans from the repressive and stifling Honeker regime in the German Democratic Republic (GDR) has moved the issue of German reunification from the back-burner of history to the top of the contemporary European political agenda. The 'German question', in the last quarter of the nineteenth century and the first half of the twentieth the central issue of European diplomacy and strategy, has re-emerged albeit in a new European and global setting. I propose first to identify the main determinants of the German 'problem'; second, to describe and analyse briefly the role of a divided Germany in the bipolar balance of power in Europe through the alternating phases of acute tension which characterised the 'cold war' and relaxation of tension (the more precise meaning of the term *détente*); third, to trace and examine the relations between the Federal Republic of Germany (FRG) and the German Democratic Republic (GDR) before and after the popular movement of revolt sparked off by the exodus of East Germans to West Germany and assess the pace and scope of process of unification, and last to consider the implications for and consequences of the unification of the two Germanies for the future European order.

From a modern historical perspective, the 'German question' stems from three factors. Two of them could be described as perhaps objective factors: Germany's geographical location in the very centre of Europe with all its diplomatic and strategic consequences and the relative size, in comparison with its neighbours and other European states, of its territory, population, human and material resources and potential as well as actually deployed military power. The third element is the political psychology, culture and behaviour of its ruling elites who have been charged not only by foreign but also by some German historians and political scientists with lack of a sense of proportion and realism and a tendency to pursue unlimited goals. Germans have been characterized and perceived as unstable, restless and obsessed with an acute and morbid anxiety (*angst*) bordering at times on hysteria.[1] Whatever truth there is in these observations and assessments, combined with the fact of Germany's geopolitical location, they have had and still continue to have an influence on other countries' attitudes to the question of Germany's future role in Europe. In the words of a distinguished American scholar, 'because of its geography Germany's instability was an immediate threat to Europe. Modern Germany was born encircled.'[2]

Little wonder then that the division of Germany from 1945 to the present, whether intended or not, was regarded by many Europeans as a tolerable solution of the German 'problem' at least for the foreseeable future. Though the German Reich had been divided in 1945 into separate zones of occupation to be administered by the USA, the UK, France and the USSR, it was to be treated as an economic whole and governed as an entity by a Four Power Council composed in the first instance of the military governors of the individual zones. This body was to prepare plans for an eventual unified Germany after the completion of a process of denazification, demilitarization and democratization. Given the differences in ideology, political and social systems and foreign policy and strategic interest between the western powers and the Soviet Union, the successful and harmonious implementation of these directives would have been nothing short of miraculous. However the responsibility for the inauguration of the 'cold war' is allocated, once it began it was almost inevitable that it should reach a climax and new intensity in a struggle over Germany. 'The cold war began with a deliberate Soviet decision to divide Europe and in reacting the western powers took a deliberate decision to divide Germany in two.'[3]

From the end of 1947 Germany was progressively divided; economically (Marshall Aid 1947/48), politically and constitutionally (the almost simultaneous establishment of the Federal Republic of Germany (FRG) in the western zones and of the German Democratic Republic (GDR) in the eastern zone September/October 1949; then the integration of each state into the western political, economic and military bloc (ECSC, NATO, WEU and the EC) and the eastern bloc (CMEA and the Warsaw Pact) respectively between 1952 and 1958. What role did a divided Germany perform in the bipolar balance in Europe? It is an axiom that neither the western powers nor the Soviet Union was prepared to contemplate or accept a unified Germany under the control of or allied with the other. Furthermore the former were additionally opposed to a neutral or neutralized united Germany (a stance supported to date by successive West German governments), which would be an arena of continual conflict between rival blocs. In the words of John Foster Dulles, US Secretary of State, 1953–59, 'a Germany which was left in a position of neutrality in the centre of Europe would be under the irresistible temptation to play one against the other and that this would dangerous for the west, dangerous for the Soviets and – for the Germans.'[4] Thus, the division of Germany into two states each anchored in the contending alliances, however repugnant to and unfortunate for the Germans themselves, was in the circumstances probably the only way that a fairly stable equilibrium could be achieved and maintained and a 'cold war' prevented from becoming a 'hot' one. An unlimited superpower struggle for the mastery of Germany would very likely have led to a military confrontation of some sort which could have escalated to the massive nuclear exchange that most feared. Essentially the problem, at least from 1950 to 1988, has been how to manage the division of Germany without prejudicing the stability, peace and security of Europe. To many for much of the time it seemed a very precarious stability in view of the potentially explosive forces of national and political discontent which erupted periodically in East Berlin and the GDR in 1953, Poland and Hungary in 1956 and Czechoslovakia in 1968. Yet paradoxically in one sense in the case of Germany the most stable element was the underlying instability of the GDR. After 1953 a serious revolt there was thought to pose such a threat to the peace of Europe, and later in the 1970s and 1980s to *détente*, that no one was tempted to push any crisis beyond a certain point. Though the western powers and the Soviet Union waged a diplomatic and propaganda war over Germany, they were at the same time involuntary partners in so far as they were both anxious to prevent Germany from becoming a theatre of actual military struggle.[5] Indeed it could be suggested that divided Germany provided the conditions and the incentive for the development of a range of conflict management procedures which remained more or less in place irrespective of the ebb and flow of 'cold war' and *détente*. These procedures were most in evidence with regard to the status of and access to West Berlin, which was subject to informal procedures and tacit rules up to 1971 and after that year by formal arrangements under the Four Power 'Quadripartite Agreement' (on Berlin) of September 1971. Other examples of a more recent date are the Confidence Building and Security measures introduced by the Helsinki Final Act of 1975 and further extended and reinforced in the Stockholm CBM conference of September 1986, and on a bilateral level intra-German trade arrangements. During 'cold war' and *détente* both adversaries were engaged in a competition to win German hearts and minds. The western powers offered rhetorical support for the right of the German people to self-determination. So did the Soviet Union at first but since the middle of the 1950s its advocacy became less enthusiastic and from the late 1950s it became conspicuously silent about the idea of German reunification. Moreover, the four victor powers of 1945 still retained some of their residual rights and responsibilities in respect of Germany as a whole and the city of Berlin under the Potsdam Agreement of August 1945. United States policy in Europe has been described as 'double containment', 'the containment of the Soviet Union at arms length, and of West Germany with an embrace'.[6] West Germany's economic reconstruction within the constraints of OECD, its rearmament within the framework of NATO and WEU, and the development of NATO into an integrated military organization were logical consequences of this policy. It was General Ismay, the first Secretary General of NATO, who said that the purpose of the alliance was 'to keep the Americans in, the Russians out and the Germans down'. The special position or singularity of the FRG in the western alliance is exemplified by the retention of the legal rights and responsibilities of the four Potsdam powers, the complete subordation of the West German armed forces, the *Bundeswehr*, to the control of NATO Supreme Allied Commander Europe, and its renunciation of the possession and manufacture of weapons of mass destruction in the Western European Union Treaty. Correspondingly control over the GDR provided the Soviet Union with leverage to be used to try to influence the behaviour of the FRG. The more importance the latter attached to its relations with East Germany, as was the case after 1974, the more the scope offered to Moscow for pressure on Bonn. On the other hand, closer co-operation between the two Germanys to a certain extend fuelled suspicion in the Kremlin that the GDR might be seduced by the siren voices from across the Elbe offering financial and economic inducements in return perhaps for some closer form of association between the two states. However, when the rigid attitude of the GDR, under Ullbricht's leadership, to the *rapprochement* with the FRG following Brandt's *Ostpolitik* initiative, and specifically to the Four Power Quadripartite Agreement in 1971 persisted, the Kremlin quickly brought pressure to bear on the Socialist Unity Party of the GDR to bring about Ullbricht's replacement by the more flexible and congenial Honecker. It is perhaps of some significance that the Soviet Union has tended to base its right to deploy troops in the GDR on the grounds of its rights as a victor rather than on a voluntary agreement with the government in East Berlin.

The emergence of the FRG as the foremost European economic power by the 1960s, and a world economic and monetary power by the end of the 1970s (formally recognized by the invitation to Chancellor Schmidt to participate in the world economic summit meeting at Guadeloupe in 1979), enabled it to play an increasing, and possibly at times decisive, role in the European Community's discussions and plans for further integration. It also provided it with prestige and influence in Eastern Europe and its value as a source of credit and investment enhanced its importance in the eyes of the Soviet Union. But it was less successful in converting its economic power into political leverage in the issue areas of security and arms control. This discrepancy was the basis for Brandt's reported description of West Germany as 'an economic giant and a political dwarf'. One can point to two reasons at least for this discrepancy. First, the FRG's strategic vulnerability to potential conventional force attack on the central front made it dependent on US extended nuclear deterrence, the credibility of American administrations and the cohesion of NATO. This dependency severely restricted the FRG's choice of foreign policy and defence options. It made successive Bonn cabinets inordinately sensitive to every shift in Washington's strategic doctrine, objective and policy. However, during periods of superpower *détente* the FRG's freedom of diplomatic manoeuvre was marginally augmented. Even then West German leaders were sometimes uneasy lest US–Soviet *rapprochement* might be achieved and deepened at the expense of German interests.[7] Second, the moral burden of the Nazi past weighed heavily on the reputation of Germans and inhibited the FRG from asserting its legitimate national interests with the vigour, robustness and persistence of other European states for fear of arousing the suspicions, hostilities and fears of allies and adversaries alike. Increasingly, some West Germans began to feel that the FRG should behave like any other normal West European state without being suspected of entertaining ulterior designs and covert ambitions. To some extent Brandt's *Ostpolitik* initiative in October 1969 was a gesture of independence on the part of the Social Democratic/Free Democrat coalition government, since the representatives of the three western allied powers the USA, the UK and France, were informed of the new policy only *after* the Chancellor's statement to the *Bundestag*.[8] During Helmut Schmidt's chancellorship there were considerable differences between Bonn and Washington on international economic and monetary issues and what responses should be made by the west towards the USSR's invasion of Afghanistan and and later towards Marshall Jaruzelski's imposition of martial law in Poland. The reluctant assent of Chancellor Kohl's cabinet to the scrapping of Pershing IA missiles, deployed in Germany and tipped with US controlled nuclear warheads, in order to secure Soviet acceptance of the double-zero agreement on INF (Intermediate Range Nuclear Forces) proposed by the Reagan administration, indicated the FRG's limited influence at that time in the security and arms control issue area once the US government had made up its mind. However, the resistence of Kohl and his foreign minister Hans-Dietrich Genscher in particular to Anglo–American pressure for the early modernization of short range nuclear forces (SRNF) located on West German territory, which was backed by an impressive consensus from the SPD to the right wing of the Christian Democrat and Christian Social parties, indicated that there was a point beyond which the West German leaders would not be pushed. There were divergences on strategic interests between the FRG and the USA expressed in a conflict between two competing aphorisms; 'the shorter the range the deader the Germans' and 'the longer the range the deader the Americans'.[9] The divergences sprang from their very different geostrategic situations. The Germans were both fearful that the Americans would not use their nuclear capability to deter an attack in Europe and that they would use them in defence of US interests outside Europe and involve Europeans in war. They also feared that the USA would like to limit a nuclear war to European territory (indeed especially to German territory), and that their Western European allies, in opposing the withdrawal of short-range nuclear weapons and urging their modernization, were similarly determined to keep German territory as a *glacis*.[10] It could be suggested that were the Soviet direct military threat to Western Europe and therefore to Western Germany to recede or be perceived to have receded, the FRG's relative capacity to convert its economic power into political leverage would be appreciably increased, but whether it would be expanded enough to satisfy the expectations of Germans in West and East Germany, created by the liberation of Eastern Europe, remained to be seen.

The scope and speed of events in East Germany took most West German politicians, academics and commentators and almost everyone outside Germany by surprise. Even those who had considered *Ostpolitik* as a preliminary overture to a gradual process of reunification did not foresee these events. Brandt's original *Ostpolitik* initiative in 1969 had been based on three premises; first, the need to recognize the *status quo* of a divided Europe and Germany in order to re-establish relations with the states of Eastern Europe and improve relations with the Soviet Union; second, to bring the FRG into alignment with the *détente* postures and policies of its allies and thus banish the danger of diplomatic isolation; and third, in the view of some of Brandt's advisers, eventually to change the *status quo* in Europe and Germany through recognizing it, (*Wandel durch Annäherung*, change through *rapprochement*). The primary aim of successive Bonn governments since that of Brandt has been to improve the quality of life of fellow Germans on the other side of the border in East Germany and maintain a tolerable relationship of coexistence between the two German states. However, the Kohl/Genscher government has also placed emphasis on 'keeping the "German question" open', insisting anew on the right of Germans to self-determination. However, there was a broad consensus between government and opposition in Bonn that reunification was not an operative goal of West German foreign policy in the short or medium term. There was also agreement that no attempt should be made deliberately to de-stabilize the GDR. Despite the GDR government's introduction of a policy of *Abgrenzung* (demarcation) designed to counter any weakening of the loyalty of East German citizens which might result from the consequences of *Ostpolitik*, GDR/FRG relations ranged from near normal to almost cordial under Chancellor Schmidt and did not deteriorate under his successor Kohl. Indeed, during the height of the crisis over the deployment of intermediate nuclear forces 1982–85, intra-German relations constituted almost an autonomous zone of *détente* insulated from the tension between their super-power patrons and protectors.

There were some in West Germany who had come to the conclusion that the two communities in West and East Germany had now moved so far apart as to become almost two separate nation states.[11] In retrospect it may be that most of us, Germans and non-Germans alike, overestimated both the legitimacy and stability of the GDR regime. The retreat of communism before popular forces in Poland and Hungary undermined and discredited Marxism-Leninism, which formed the primary source of legitimacy as far as the members of the East German ruling SED party were concerned. The party ideologists had sought to develop a separate national identity for the GDR and an additional source of legitimacy for the majority of its citizens by cultivating a rather spurious kind of neo-Prussianism, based on the virtues of duty, discipline and hard work. As for the mass of citizens, their passive loyalty to the state was seemingly related to its economic performance and the social welfare system.[12]

Bonn's initial response to the exodus of East Germans to West Germany through Hungary was cautious. It sought to discourage the outflow because its continuation could both seriously destabilize the GDR and impose an onerous burden on West German welfare and administrative services. The breaching of the Berlin Wall and the lifting of restrictions on travel between East Berlin and West Berlin was as dramatic a watershed as the original erection of the wall in August 1961. The continued exodus, though at a reduced rate, changed the government's strategy. On 28 November Chancellor Kohl presented his Ten Point Plan for reunification to the *Bundestag*. It proposed, first intensified scientific, technological and environmental cooperation; second, the development of confederal structures and after free elections in the GDR, the setting up of common organs for political consultation and harmonization; and third, progress towards federation in a form which would fit into the future architecture of Europe.[13] Some German commentators described the proposals as a bold assertion of independence by Kohl since apparently the FRG's allies were not consulted in advance. It was also seen as an indication that the Chancellor no longer intended to limit his aim 'to the alleviation of the consequences of the division of Germany ... but to overcome that division'.[14] Nevertheless, prudent caution still characterized the general attitude of the government. Most official and semi-official opinion still seemed anxious that the process of association should be gradual. From late December 1989 it became clear that the federal government in Bonn and the reformist government in East Berlin under the moderate Hans Modrow were being faced with forces over which they had limited control. Most crucial was the continuing exodus of East Germans, an haemorrhage of professional and skilled people which had already damaged the industry and public services of the GDR. Second, was the further erosion of the credibility of the regime and third the growing demand for *einig Deutschland*.

On 7 February this year the Bonn government decided to promote urgent negotiations with Prime Minister Modrow for a currency union between the FRG and GDR. A new interdepartmental committee on German 'unity with representatives from seven key ministries in Bonn was set up to formulate West German policy.[15] It appeared that the Chancellor had changed tack and was deliberately trying to speed up the process. It was certainly the impression created abroad. But it is most likely that the most important reason responsible for the apparent decision in Bonn to accelerate discussions about currency union was the widespread belief that the GDR's political and economic stability and credibility was approaching crisis level. With the setting of East German elections for 18 March domestic party political calculations became a factor in Kohl's *Deutschlandpolitik*. Indeed, considering the dominant role played by West German party leaders, organization and election material, East and West Germany could already be said to constitute in a way parts of one overarching party political system. Chancellor Kohl's rather ambiguously worded promise to East German voters of a one to one exchange between Deutschmarks and Ostmarks was without doubt one of the key factors responsible for the victory of the centre–right Alliance for Germany coalition, composed of the CDU, German Social Union and Democratic Awakening. Since the election the complications, difficulties and implications involved in establishing a currency between the two German states were being given greater weight. The federal government seemed to be anxious to slow down the process of unification to some extent and reassure its allies and fellow members of the EC that its commitments to NATO and the Community remained as strong as before.

Now that German reunification is no longer a distant prospect the ambivalence which has always existed below the surface in the attitudes of other countries has emerged once more. It was significant in its way that the representatives of the Four 'Potsdam' Powers in Berlin met as a body shortly after the breaching of the wall to discuss the situation and how it affected the regime set up in the Quadripartite Agreement of 1971. They had not met for many years. The Soviet government was apparently concerned about the possible erosion of four-power status and rights in respect of the city of Berlin.[16] Theo Sommer, co-editor in chief of *Die Zeit*, expressed the views of many of his fellow-citizens when he commented that the 'division of Germany has had deeper reasons than east/west confrontation and that the protecting powers turn out to be like controlling powers'.[17] The FRG's western allies have committed themselves to support the right of the German people to self-determination in general and, in Article 7 of the 23 October 1954 Paris Protocol to the General Treaty of 26 May 1952 on relations between the FRG and the Three Powers, specifically to the reunification of Germany. Of course, at the time they did not expect to be called upon to honour the obligation in the foreseeable future. Perhaps one might suggest that they were not too unhappy with the *status quo*. This ambivalence is aptly expressed in the much quoted words of Francois Mauriac: 'I am so fond of

Germany that I rejoice in the idea that there are two of them.'[18] British leaders and media, and French and Italian politicians to a somewhat lesser extent, have emphasized the obstacles in the path of reunification. These attitudes have led to considerable irritation in some quarters in West Germany which has even found expression in newspapers supporting the government such as *Die Welt am Sonntag*, 'Germans have a second class right of self-determination but 45 years of inferiority are enough.'[19] Statements that reunification 'is not on the international agenda' or that it can only be achieved over five to ten years have all too readily given Germans the impression that others want to delay or halt the process. Fears expressed in the west that Germans might be tempted to downplay their NATO obligations evoked the retort from Rudolf Augstein, editor of *Der Spiegel*, 'No one should argue, as happens at the moment, that the West Germans must, if you please observe their obligations in NATO, in the EC, but that their western allies should not honour their treaties with the West Germans.'[20] It is not surprising that the apprehensions and fears of East Europeans, particularly the Poles, are even greater, as their reactions to Chancellor Kohl's reluctance to give a categorical recognition of the German–Polish border indicate. In the first phase of the popular movement in East Germany Gorbachev was very negative on the prospect and desirability of a unified Germany, dismissing it as 'historically unrealistic', but during the visit of Chancellor Kohl to Moscow in early February and since, he has accepted its inevitability. It is important to record that most German political leaders understand the reservations of their fellow Europeans.[21] Behind this ambivalence is a concern that a unified Germany will become even more dominant economically on the European continent. It would also be the second most populous country. In the last ten to 15 years the FRG has become the third largest economy in the world in terms of GDP, the second largest exporter of manufactured goods and the possessor of the largest trade surplus. The Deutschmark is the third most important currency. The FRG represents 24 per cent of the GDP of the EC and 20 per cent of its population. Its trade with Eastern Europe is greater than that of any other western nation, although it represents a very small proportion of its total trade. The present population of the FRG is just about 61 million or so, but that includes a considerable number of guest workers. What additional increment in GDP and population will East Germany contribute to a unified state? The initial GDP of a unified Germany would be no more than ten per cent higher than the FRG's. Unification would increase Germany's share of the European Community's GDP to 24 per cent and to 29 per cent if the productivity of East German workers were to reach West German levels.[22] The population of a unified Germany will be between 78 and 79 million. The population of the GDR is now below 17 million, less than that of North Rhine/Westphalia. To get near an accurate picture of Germany's relative population in the next decade or two, it is necessary to bear in mind the future demographic trends. The present low birth rate and the age structure in the FRG at least suggest on today's projections a progressive decline in population in the coming decades, so that according to some estimates the total population of Germany will have declined to about 73 million by the year 2000 and about 61 million by 2030, while the population of the UK and France is likely to be about 62 million each and that of Italy about 60 million by 2000.[23] The FRG accounts at present for 20 per cent of the total population of the EC; the share of a unified Germany would rise to 22.7 per cent.[24] These figures help to put the prospective economic power and size of a reunified Germany in perspective. Moreover, a united Germany, like the FRG, will be inextricably involved in a complex web of economic, monetary and trade interdependence which will impose its own tangible and intangible constraints upon Germany's exercise of economic power.

The Eastern European revolution of 1989/90 has confronted us with the oldest and most critical problem in modern European history, that is, how to balance Germany's national interests against the claims of European security and stability. What is to be united Germany's status and role in what President Bush and Chancellor Kohl have referred to as the 'architecture of Europe' as well as its role in the present or any future security system? More precisely and immediately, is Germany to continue to remain a member of NATO or be accorded a neutral or neutralized status of some kind? Among the many factors which need to be considered and evaluated is to what extent NATO itself will remain relevant in the Europe and particularly in terms of the central Europe which may finally emerge from the upheavals and political transformations of the last few months. Much will depend on whether the Soviet polity itself remains intact or shrinks to its Russian ethnic core. Even so the residual largely ethnic Russian state would still be large in territorial terms and population, and would probably still remain a major European power and a nuclear superpower, even though it would probably be deficient for some time in the economic and technological attributes of superpower status. Few would dare predict with confidence whether the new central and eastern Europe will be a region of political stability or an arena of ethnic tension and potential conflict. For that reason, many would strongly argue that it would be unwise and premature to dismantle the alliances which have helped to preserve peace and security in Europe. Indeed, it is now almost becoming the fashion to defend the continuation of NATO and the Warsaw Pact as together constituting an essential element of European order in a potentially unstable world, particularly now that a united Germany is about to reappear on the European scene. This event will affect not only the great powers of the west and east but also all the medium and small states. Two issues are involved: how, and by whom is the future of Germany to be resolved, and should the unified Germany remain in NATO?

The procedure for dealing with the definitive status of a reunified Germany, its boundaries and its security role, was agreed by the USA, the UK, France, the USSR, the FRG and the GDR at the meeting of foreign ministers of NATO and the Warsaw Pact in February 1990. This procedure is now known as the *two plus four* formula Having worked out the form which unification should take and the modalities for achieving it, the governments of the FRG and GDR would meet the four 'Potsdam' powers. There are a number of issues which although technically procedural have substantive implications. The first is the status of the Two plus Four deliberations. It is reported that President Bush and Chancellor Kohl agreed at their Camp David meeting in February that the two plus four group would hold discussions, not negotiations, and that a CSCE summit scheduled for November this year would merely receive and note the result.[25] Second, however, at some stage the four powers are expected to dismantle the four power regime in respect of Germany as a whole and Berlin, which would involve the abolition of their residual powers, rights and responsibilities, which were partly confirmed or regulated by the Quadripartite Agreement on Berlin 1971, which presumably would be abrogated. These steps would complete the process of restoring Germany to full sovereignty subject only to those limitations which as a member of the European Community it shares with its fellow members. Third, the question of Germany's borders will come up, but the only controversy likely to arise, concerns the German–Polish border along the Oder–Neisse. Unfortunately FRG relations with Poland were adversely affected by what was regarded as Chancellor Kohl's rather unimaginative and insensitive handling of the issue.

The future security role of a united Germany is the issue which is likely to present problems. However, there is so far a basic agreement between the US, British and French governments that a unified Germany must remain in NATO, and the government of the FRG broadly supports that view,[26] although there are differences of emphasis between the CDU/CSU and the Free Democrats. The case for continued membership of a united Germany in NATO is twofold. First, accepting the view that NATO has at least been and may still be a key factor in the maintenance of the security of Western Europe and the peace and stability of Europe as a whole, then the role of the FRG has indeed been vitally important. Without West German armed forces, territory and strategic location, even the present limited option of using conventional forces for as long as possible before resort to nuclear weapons, an essential element of NATO flexible response strategy, would not be viable. It is further argued that the continued presence of US forces in Western Europe and its commitment to its defence would be unlikely to survive Germany's departure from the alliance, and the American nuclear guarantee would be decoupled from Europe. Second and less strongly articulated was the claim that NATO was and still is an essential vehicle for containing Germany. For its own sake no less than for the sake of its neighbours and other European nations, a united Germany should be firmly anchored in the western alliance, which would reinforce other constraints and encourage self-restraint on the part of the Germans themselves. To some extent, if the USA is the leader of the western alliance, Germany is its lynch pin. The symbiotic relationship between them is well portrayed by Hanrieder in his perceptive analysis of German foreign policy, (*Germany, America, Europe:* p. 62):

Any fundamental change in NATO would reopen the issue of how to contain the Federal Republic within the alliance and within Europe. There persists a solid consensus that because the Soviets present at least a latent threat to the security of western Europe, an alliance with the USA is indispensable. Equally important there is a consensus that an alliance with the USA is indispensable to making the Federal Republic of Germany's contribution to European security politically acceptable both to the Germans and to Germany's allies.

Seen from the perspective of the German 'question' the political function of the western alliance is no less important, perhaps indeed more important than the military one. I now turn to the Soviet attitude towards the prospect of German reunification.

Once the Soviet Union had accepted, however grudgingly, the inevitability of reunification it was assumed that it would insist on some form of neutral or neutralized status for Germany. Although it was mentioned initially for the most part Soviet spokesmen have preferred an indirect or oblique allusion to the matter. Thus, Soviet foreign minister Shevardnadze, on his visit to NATO and the EC in Brussels in December last year, after voicing some reservations about German reunification, asked a number of pointed rhetorical questions. How would a united Germany fit in to the existing military structure? Then he almost answered his own question by intimating that no one could really expect the GDR to change its status while that of the FRG remained unaltered. The latest Soviet position was recorded in an interview given by Shevardnadze and in his talks with British foreign minister Douglas Hurd in April; a united Germany should simultaneously be a member of NATO and the Warsaw Pact.[27] Since then Gorbachev has referred to the need for 'a strategic balance of power' between NATO and the Warsaw Pact forces as the basis of security in Europe and of a new and stable inter-state system. Clearly German membership of NATO would be incompatible with this Soviet concept of strategic balance. The western powers seem to believe that Moscow will ultimately accept that the close integration of a unified Germany within NATO and the EC is the most effective way of ensuring that it does not become a threat to the security of the Soviet Union or other eastern European countries.

Compromise proposals designed to reassure the USSR concerning the security implications of German reunification have been developed, originating reportedly in the planning department of the West German foreign ministry. While Germany would remain in NATO, the operational control of Supreme Allied Commander Europe would not be extended to the German–Polish border. US and other non-German forces would not be deployed in East Germany and Soviet forces and bases would be permitted to remain in East Germany at least for an interim period.[28] Bonn's desire to meet and placate Soviet anxieties was further demonstrated by its willingness to refrain from deploying the *Bundeswehr* on East German territory. These proposals are in sense a triumph of ingenuity over logic, but they could provide an interim arrangement pending future agreement between the the western powers, the Soviet–Union and other European countries on an alternative security system. At the present time the positions of the western powers and the Soviet Union on the security status and role of a unified Germany seem to be incompatible. Although Moscow has apparently retreated from its previous insistence on a neutral or neutralized Germany,[29] it is clear that it continues to be opposed to NATO membership for the reunified state. It seems that the western powers are convinced that eventually the Soviet Union will give way and accept a NATO Germany not only as inevitable but as the most effective method of ensuring that an economically powerful and dynamic unified Germany does not become a threat to its neighbours in Eastern Europe. However in view of Gorbachev's recent application of economic sanctions against Lithuania, it would be unwise to assume that he would or could afford to accept what would appear to be a diplomatic defeat. The USSR has legitimate reasons for concern about the consequences of the emergence of a unified Germany in a central and Eastern Europe where the latent propensity to instability and ethnic conflict could quickly manifest itself in the wake of the withdrawal of its forces from Czechoslovakia and Hungary within one year or two, the erosion of the cohesion of the Warsaw Pact and the probability of the disintegration of CMEA. The Soviet government is likely to seek if not demand a *quid pro quo* for any concession it may be compelled to make on this issue. The deployment of the twenty division strong Group Soviet Forces Germany (GSFG) in East Germany provides some opportunity for leverage but only of a negative kind. *The Times* of 20 April 1990 reported that the western powers were so confident that German membership of NATO was in the bag that they would refuse to discuss the matter within the forum provided by the Two plus Four Group, thus depriving the Soviets of a veto over the substance and timing of reunification. Whether they could make it stick is quite another matter. Possibly the USA, UK and France hope that their expressed willingness to discuss transitional arrangements (along the lines of the 'compromise formula' described earlier) particularly the provision for continued temporary deployment of Soviet military forces in East Germany, would secure reluctant Soviet assent to continued German membership of NATO. The Soviets do have some other cards to play. First, there are suggestions they will seek substantial limitations on the size of German armed forces in the Conventional Forces Europe (CFE) negotiations in Vienna; second they could refuse to surrender their rights and responsibilities as one of the 'Potsdam' powers; third, of doubtful legality or usefulness as an means of pressurs, would be to object to the constitutional procedure proposed by the West German government for achieving unification. In fact, *The Guardian* reported on 30 April that the Soviet ambassador in East Berlin had handed an unofficial note to the GDR Prime Minister, de Maiziere, expressing reservations about the projected application of Article 23 of the West German constitution (the Bonn Basic Law) to speed up the unification process and declaring that the Soviet Union would wish to have a say in the way Germany was to be unified.

If western/Soviet deadlock on this security issue were not resolved it might conceivably hold up the final stage of German reunification. This is the point where German public opinion might come into play, particularly if the west and the Soviet Union began to blame each other for the delay in abandoning the residual rights and responsibilities of the four powers over Germany as a whole and Berlin. The government parties in Bonn, the CDU/CSU and FDP, support membership of NATO for the united Germany. The GDR government, a coalition of the centre-right *Allianz für Deutschland* (Alliance for Germany) and the SPD, however, are committed in their coalition agreement to Germany remaining in NATO for a transitional period as long as the NATO alliance abandons its strategy of nuclear deterrence and first strike capability. Adherence to this position creates problems for the negotiations for reunification between the governments of the FRG and GDR, and eventually for the western powers. Also, the SPD defence spokesman Karsten Voigt and Egon Bahr, one of the architects of *Ostpolitik*, have both advocated Germany's membership of NATO, but only on condition that nuclear weapons are removed from German territory.[30] Oscar Lafontaine very likely to be the SPD's Chancellor candidate in the West German election in December this year, favours the withdrawal of both US and Soviet forces from German territory. German membership of NATO and the conditions attached to it might well become one of the issues in the election at a very sensitive stage in the four power talks. While it is doubtful whether reunification could be blocked if the four powers were to fail to resolve their differences, it might be held up. This might cause irritation, resentment and even bitterness among East and West Germans, were expectations of a swift conclusion of the process of unification to be disappointed. A columnist of the *Süddeutsche Zeitung* warned the western powers against conveying the impression that the maintenance of NATO was an end in itself.[31] *The Sunday Times* reported that the Britain Prime Minister, Mrs Thatcher, at the Bermuda summit meeting with President Bush, had insisted that the external consequences of German reunification be negotiated *before* the two Germanys become one. This could increase the disquiet of many Germans with all four powers. It will require diplomatic skill, understanding and statesmanship on the part of all to manage the transition from two German states to a unified Germany without damaging West/Soviet relations.

For many in Europe the EC is no less important to the security, stability and well-being of Europe than NATO: A unified Germany will continue to be a member of the Community, firmly anchored in the political and economic mechanism of Brussels and in the liberal democratic value system of Western Europe. The processes and institutions of the EC have provided the FRG and will continue to provide united Germany in the future with an environment within which to exercise power and influence with responsibility. It provides an opportunity for leadership to a Germany whose major constituent, the FRG, has had over 40 years experience of democratic constitutional politics. Both Chancellor Kohl and Foreign Minister Genscher, anxious to reassure their EC colleagues that reunification will not turn Germany's face away from Western Europe towards Eastern Europe, have repeatedly declared that their aim is a united Germany in a more deeply integrated Community. There has been some concern, particularly in France, that preoccupation with the task of establishing German Monetary Union would so absorb the energy, time and thought of German officials and ministers involved as to lead the government to give less attention and commitment to European Economic and Monetary Union. Kohl has however urged more rapid progress on EMU. It is significant that on 19 April he joined with President Mitterand in a call for swift advance towards European political union, which would involve greater powers for the European Parliament.[32]

Throughout the history of the European Communities the FRG, under successive chancellors, from Konrad Adenauer through Willy Brandt to Helmut Kohl, has shared responsibility for major policy decisions and initiatives which have led to further European integration and extension of Community membership. It was once said that the division of Germany would only be overcome when the division of Europe had ended. A unified Germany is about to take its place among the great nations of Europe. This time it is a Germany with over 40 years of democratic parliamentary experience, with an impressive record of international cooperation and a succession of leaders with a deserved reputation for moderation. A unified Germany restored to its position in the centre of Europe may yet share in leading a concerted effort to integrate the historic nations of central and eastern Europe into the European Community. Germany's political predicament of being both pressured from and attracted by west and east would be perhaps resolved

University College, Aberystwyth,
University of Wales

NOTES

1. For further studies and discussion of German political leadership and political behaviour, see: Ludwig Dehio, 'Germany and the epoch of world wars', in Hans Kohn, Ed., *German History: Some new German Views*. London. Allen & Unwin, 1954. Immanuel Geiss, *German Foreign Policy 1871–1914*; London, Routledge & Kegan Paul, 1976. K. Hildebrand, *The Foreign Policy of the Third Reich*, London,

Batsford, 1973; William Carr, *Hitler: a study in Politics and Personality*, London, Edward Arnold, 1978; L. Barzini, 'The Mutable Germans', in his *The Impossible Europeans*. Weidenfeld & Nicolson, 1983; Arnulf Baring, *Unser neuer Grössenwahn: Deutschland zwischen Ost und West*, Stuttgart, Deutsche Verlagsanstalt, 1989; the latter warns his fellow countrymen against succumbing once more to the temptation of overestimating their power.

2. David Calleo, *The German Question Reconsidered: Germany and the World Order, 1870 to the present*, Cambridge, Cambridge University Press, 1978, p. 206.
3. Philip Windsor, *German Reunification*, London, Elek Books, 1969, p. 23.
4. Cited by Gerald Freund, *Germany between Two Worlds*, New York, Harcourt Brace, 1961, p. 126. This view was shared most strongly by Konrad Adenauer, first Chancellor of the Federal Republic, who described past German policies of playing the west against Russia and *vice versa* as *Schaukelpolitik* (see-saw policy) For a study of Adenauer's policy see Hans-Peter Schwarz, 'Adenauer's *Ostpolitik*, in Wolfram F Hanrieder, Ed., *West German Foreign Policy 1949–1979*, Boulder Co., Westview Press, 1980.
5. For an interesting slant on the cold war, see Gordon A Craig and Alexander L George, 'The Cold War as an International System' in their *Force and Statecraft: Diplomatic Problems of our Time*. Oxford, OUP, 1983, pp. 114–31.
6. Wolfram F Hanrieder, *German, America, Europe: Forty years of German Foreign Policy*, New Haven and London, Yale University Press, 1989, p. 6
7. Adenauer was always preoccupied with the fear of West-Soviet *rapprochement* which would bypass legitimate German interests. To quote Schwarz, 'Adenauer's *Ostpolitik*', op. cit., p. 131, 'Just as Bismarck had his "cauchemar des alliances" . . . so Adenauer had his Potsdam complex, a fear that the four powers would settle their differences – and the German eagle would get plucked of its last feathers.'
8. Brandt had earlier declared to a group of American correspondents, 'I will not be the chancellor of a defeated Germany but a liberated Germany.' David Binder, *The other German: Willy Brandt's life and times*. Washington cited in Werner Link, 'Aussen- und Deutschlandpolitik' in der Ära Brandts 1969–74, in Karl Dietrich Bracher, W. Jäger, W. Link; *Geschichte der Bundesrepublik Deutschland, Band 5/1 Republik in Wandel 1969–74*. Stuttgart, Deutsche Verlagsanstalt, 1986: For Brandt's *Ostpolitik* see also Arnulf Baring, *Macht-Wechsel: Die Ära Brandt-Scheel*. Stuttgart, Deutsche Verlagsanstalt, 1982; Günter Schmid, *Entscheidung in Bonn: Die Entstehung der Ost- und Deutschlandpolitik 1969/70*. Köln, Verlag Wissenschaft und Politik, 1979.
9. Christopher Layne, 'Superpower Disengagement', *Foreign Policy*, No. 77, Winter 1989/90, p. 23.
10. Wolfram F Hanrieder, *Germany, America, Europe*, op. cit. p. 120.
11. See Gebhard Schweigler, *National consciousness in a divided Germany*. London, Beverly Hills, Sage publications, Vol. 15 1975; also his 'German questions or the Shrinking of Germany,' in F. Stephen Larrabee, Ed., *The Two German States and European Security*. New York, St Martin's Press, 1989. For other views see: Peter Christian Ludz, *Die DDR zwischen Ost und West von 1961 bis 1976*. München, Beck Verlag, 1977. Eberhard Schulz, 'Berlin, the German question and the future of Europe', in K. Dyson, Ed., *European detente: Case Studies of the Politics of East/West relations*. London. Pinter, 1986. Ronald Asmus, 'The GDR and the German Nation: sole heir of socialist sibling?' *International Affairs*, Vol. 60, no. 3, Summer 1984.
12. See the interesting chapter on 'Legitimation in the German Democratic Republic', by Martin McCauley in Paul G. Lewis, Ed., *Eastern Europe: Political crisis and legitimation*; London & Sydney. Croom Helm, 1984, for the specific reference. p 63.
13. Official Report of Chancellor Kohl speech in the *German Tribune* no. 1398, 10 Dec. 1989, p. 3. See also comment on speech by Konrad Feldmeyer in the *Frankfurter*

Allgemeine Zeitung, 30 Nov. 1989.
14. Feldmeyer, op. cit.
15. *The Financial Times*, 8 Feb. 1990.
16. The mayors of west Berlin and east Berlin bypassed the four powers in dicussing water, effluent and traffic problems in the city, and the Bonn government established regular flights between Frankfurt and Leipzig without consulting any of the four powers. See Josef Joffe in the *Suddeutsche Zeitung*, 10 Dec. 1989.
17. Theo Sommer, *Die Zeit*, 15 Dec. 1989.
18. Quoted by Renata Fritsch-Bournazel in 'The French view', in Edwina Moreton, Ed., *Germany between East and West*. Cambridge, Cambridge University Press (in association with the Royal Institute of International Affairs), 1987, p. 76.
19. Hubert Kremp, *Die Welt am Sonntag*, 17 Dec. 1989
20. Rudolf Augstein, 'Sagen was ist.' *Der Spiegel* no. 47/1989 20 Nov. 1989.
21. Former chancellor Helmut Schmidt is reported to have remarked that 'in the eyes of others the division of Germany is today part of the European balance of power that secures peace.' Theo Sommer remarked in *Die Zeit*, 'Reunification may be a dream to us but it would only be a nightmare to most of our neighbours. They are aware that the reassociation of the two German states would mean the largest possible distortion of the East/West balance –' *Die Zeit*, 15 Aug. 1986.
22. Cited by John Roper 'Germany and the EC', *World Today*, no. 15 March 1990.
23. Eberhard Schulz, *Die deutsche Nation in Europa: Internationale und historische Dimensionen*; Bonn, Europa Union Verlag (Schriften des Forschungsinstituts der Deutschen Gesellschaft für Auswärtige Politik) 1982, p. 119.
24. John Roper, op.cit.
25. Claus Gennrich, *Frankfurter Allgemeine Zeitung*, 26 Feb. 1990.
26. In an interview with the *Financial Times*, 2 April 1990, Chancellor Kohl stated 'Germany's adhesion to the western alliance cannot be bargained away. NATO is not first of all a military alliance but a community of like minded states'. The latter emphasis on the political rather than the military aspect may be a pointer to the direction in thinking in which Bonn is moving.
27. Reports from Moscow and Bonn, *The Guardian*, 12 April 1990, p. 22. See also comment by Hella Pick, *The Guardian*, 13 April 1990, p 23.
28. For detailed report see 'Bizarres Szenario' in *Der Spiegel*, Vol. 44 no. 7, 12 Feb. 1990, pp. 22–3.
29. Ibid.
30. *The Guardian*, 19 April 1990.
31. Manfred Holken, *Suddeutsche Zeitung*, 21 Feb. 1990.
32. *The Independent*, 20 April 1990.

European Integration and the End of the Cold War

PIERRE-HENRI LAURENT

> The success of this great European
> experiment, perhaps more than any other
> factor, has caused eastern Europeans to
> recognize that people as well as nations
> cooperate more productively when they are
> free to choose.
>
> Secretary of State James Baker,
> Berlin, 12 December 1989

> When our brothers on the other side of the
> Iron Curtain look at us, they do not see our
> material prosperity and our relative economic
> efficiency alone, they do not merely see the
> way we live; they see that twelve sovereign
> countries have joined together in a community
> based on the rule of law and that the
> smallest country has its say like the others.
>
> President Jacques Delors
> Strasbourg, 17 January 1990

A new era has dawned in the world in the last year. The unexpected revolutionary events of 1989–90 in Eastern Europe and the Soviet Union have impacted swiftly and deeply on the entire post-World War II international system. Beyond the meaning of these historic changes for the superpower relations, these happenings which constitute the beginning of the end of the post-Yalta world have their most substantial consequences in west-west ties (read European–American) and intra-European relations.

This article asserts two major points-one concerning the causes behind the recent turbulence and the other on the major implications for European integration, given the 1989–90 developments. In the first case, the historical perspective suggests that the significant primacy of Western European integration achievements in the eighties in part fostered the massive peaceful uprisings in the east. Although an undeniable basic cause of the eastern upheavals has been the Gorbachevian acceleration of history when he released the bonds with which his predecessors confined the eastern bloc, there has been a spillover effect into the communist states from the European Community (EC) building victories in both the economic and political realms. What the eastern revolutionaries moved to accomplish in this last year was linking up to the political and economic traditions of the west from which they had been cut off for over 40 years. In particular, the Soviet bloc member states viewed the march of the Community to a more dynamic, assertive and independent role in the new global order. In the second proposal, an argument is made that there remains an even stronger necessity to move to a more enhanced and powerful role for the EC in the 'rush to freedom and capitalism' nineties in order to achieve a stable and peaceful restructuring of the rapidly transforming European centre piece of the international state system. The disruption, or even slowdown, of the EC march toward those bold goals cannot cast a shadow over the Community's future for long or the energy and will of the Twelve will fragment and disintegrate. If the job of addressing the 1989 problems consumes the EC, the creation of a Europe in depth *and* scope will be deflected and seriously impaired.

Project '92 as the Backdrop to 1989

The resuscitated take-off of the EC in the last decade has been a central historical process in that this second integration *relance* has moved from 'Eurogloom' to 'Europhoria' to a Western Europe assuming a key role in the world. The Community became the functional equivalent of a superpower. An enormous momentum to complete the unification process within the EC has emerged in the Single European Act (SEA) and the mid-decade White Paper. This unprecedented exercise of liberalization was the result of a concerted European response to the Japanese and American challenges in the seventies which urged the Community to relaunch its effort to complete its creation of a true Western European economy of scale. Resurgent Europe with a single market of over 325 million people gained the attention and adherence of member states, governments, and the general populace. This further uniting of Europe via the construction of a great European market and thus turning it into a real global actor was the intention behind not just the completion of the internal market by 1992 but the political commitments to augment Community institutional powers and ultimately build a genuine European foreign policy. Even the security realm was to feel the impact of this new European identity and organizational prowess with projected alterations of the Euro-American military alliance framework.[1]

This accelerated progress in Western European integration has centred on the rededication to the economic and political aims of the original architects of the Treaties of Rome. The emergence of Project 92 was also, however, a great leap forward, meant to address the contemporary circumstances of the seventies and early eighties, in effect unblocking the multiple impasses that had both stalled EC integration and threatened European global trade competitiveness as the century came to an end. The burst of initiatives of the then ten member countries that emanated from Brussels between 1979 and 1984 was the result of a new awareness in the EC Commission and national governments. At its heart, this breakthrough was stimulated and driven by the Commission and a co-operative band of influential, politically active and far-sighted industrial and technological elites who were subsequently joined by the Common Market state leaders. What was at first a limited set of high-priority action programmes such as ESPRIT which deal with fostering greater transfrontier research and development efforts in the information technology areas became, through the efforts of Commissioner Etienne Davignon and several prominent industry vested interest groups like the Roundtable of Industrialists, a much more far-ranging set of measures to stimulate Europe trade power via transnational co-ordination, co-operation and joint venturing.[2] Beginning with the EC Council meeting at Fontainebleu in 1984 and throughout the Milan EC summit of 1986, a vast complex intrastate bargaining process evolved among the Ten (and eventually Spain and Portugal *en route* to Community enlargement). This explicit requirement to gain the backing of the national governments was a monumental achievement of the Community in that it required commitments to both the 1992 market completion objectives and the associated institutional reforms aimed at log-jam breaking voting changes. The deadlock and paralysis of more than a decade was ended with the consensus to assault Project 92.[3]

The 1992 proclamation was from the start more important as a concept and even symbol than as a target date. The meaning and significance of the reasserted dedication to the idea of European unification under the leadership of Commission President Jacques Delors included both immediate and widespread recognition and acknowledgment of this pathbreaking goal in the west but it was also felt in the Communist world. The impact of '92 in the east was reflected in the late eighties with various Soviet and Eastern European responses. Both Gorbachev's *perestroika* and Comecon future designs began to include intensified attempts to draw the east closer to the west. There is now little doubt that among both the elites and general publics of the communist states there emerged a new consciousness concerning the vibrancy and vitality of EC integration. What Secretary of State James Baker was to proclaim in his Berlin December 1989 speech was well documented; the EC role and 1992 became indirect motivaters of 1989 events.[4]

The attractiveness and appeal of the increasingly democratic experience in the western part of the continent in terms of political and economic change helped to propel the outbursts in the six eastern states. Within the 1992 idea and the swift primary success of the project between 1986 and 1989, a western model of growing economic prosperity and capitalist market economy triumphs was perceived in the east along with the liberal parliamentary and democratic infrastructure of the EC and its member states. Certainly the economic failures of the east and the still rigid control of these command economies by Moscow contributed to their alienation, but the 'pull factor' of integration dynamism in the west was a catalyst for revolution in the east. The rise of a lean and successful European competitor for global markets and the explosions in the communist countries were inextricably linked. The sentiment and wish to share in the western prosperity and democracy were evident first in the mid-1989 Polish and Hungarian calls for multiparty government and free market economies that quickly spread to the GDR, Czechoslovakia and eventually even Bulgaria and Rumania. Although Soviet bloc policy under Gorbachev appeared to sanction some changes in these directions by 1989, the eastern countries' gaze had been substantially driven toward the EC integration activities. If the bloc could break the shackles that bound them to the Soviet Union, the result could include some degree of participation in the further economic and political rewards of western integration.

European Integration in the Post-Wall Era

The intersection of Eastern European bloc decay and collapse and Western European quickened integration and unity in 1989–90 have posed formidable challenges for the EC. As Walter Russell Mead has put it, 'the Europe of 1989 has overtaken the Europe of 1992.'[5] What was to be Western Europe as the major pillar of the new international order with all its newfound strength of size, consensus and potential has now to be contemplated in the mostly changed context of post-Soviet Central and Eastern Europe and a diminished superpower Russia.

If the need is to recast Europe anew, then the pivotal challenge with all the opportunities, both dangerous and alluring, appears to be one that, to a large extent, will be decided by the Europeans themselves. The urgent agenda item has become German reunification and, quickly coming upon centre stage, the reconstruction of the eastern economies within a governance system based on multiparty politics. The reunification of the German people and a politically reconstituted Europe now go hand in hand. The Federal Republic's new-found exercise of power, as the prime motor of the EC *relance* and nexus of continued economic growth, has been thrust quickly into the commanding limelight of international politics. Between November 1989 and the March 18, 1990 elections in the GDR, the German destiny question (*Schicksalfrage*) moved at a blinding speed through *Vertragsgemeinschaft* to *Wiedervereingung* and finally to the full merger into one Germany. This overthrow of hegemonic communism in the GDR and the press for a new united Germany has suddenly further empowered Bonn.

Creating a unified Germany with some eighty million citizens, however, recasts the EC balance of power in addition to presenting novel problems for the Community. The imminent reunion in central

Europe became inevitable as 1990 began, when not just the euphoria of the revolutionary rush of events threw Germans into each other's arms but the prospects of forging a broader base to a 'European economic space' was viewed as both necessary and pragmatically possible.

The near total collapse of the ideological confrontation that powered the cold war and its division of Europe has necessitated a reassessment exercise about the EC future. By 1990, the daunting Community job was completing the unified market and simultaneously discovering ways that would address and not alienate their eastern cousins. This connection between increased solidarity in Western Europe and support for the success of economic and democratic reform in Eastern Europe was at the heart of what President Delors indicated would be the new EC mission of the nineties.[6]

To Germany's western neighbors who had to deal with the new 'German problem' the issues were twofold.[7] First, the emergence of a superpowerful enlarged Germany meant new diplomatic and political arrangements were required among the EC states that called for delicate bargaining. Second, there was the economic cost factor in the east for Bonn and her partners which was to be addressed alongside the sizable financial costs of Project 92 into the twenty-first century. Neither of these changes would be accomplished easily, quickly, alone or without serious repercussions and costs to the EC states and to their attainment of the new Europe. The name of the game and even many of its rules had been altered in one striking historic moment.

The reunion of Germany had become the highest priority project for all Europeans and the superpowers. For the EC members, the question was whether integration and reunification (with its attached economic/financial tasks) were reasonable parallel goals in the severe stresses of the nineties. The obstacles to the implementation of the SEA were multiplied immensely in that there was no alternative on the New Germany issue. The unstoppable force of 'people power' that rejected the artificial dividing line originally forced on them by the war's end demanded immediate attention. The obligatory need to devise a new structure of relationships -political, security, and economic -within which first the East Germans and then the former satellite states might affiliate, associate (under Article 238) and eventually participate as an integrated whole became irrestible for Bonn and therefore to her partners.

Within weeks of the Berlin Wall collapse, the new mission was unavoidable -how to unite Germany. The economic dimension of that challenge, given the shambles of the GDR economy, became suddenly a vexing paramount issue. The cost demands for Western Europe, not only Bonn, were astronomical and inevitably impinged severely on the integrationist task of the Twelve. This cost factor (in the trillions of dollars) was revised upward nearly each week in early 1990, resulting in the fear in some western capitals that the eastern economic problems would easily and fully preoccupy the west for the foreseeable future. The enormity of helping the east with its dizzying array of allied issues become in fact a complex and potentially dangerous set of problems alongside renegotiating and rewriting the continent's security arrangements. At minimum, the new legitimate economic financial expectations of the east vastly complicated the attainment of the SEA goals.

The greatest apprehension among Bonn's EC partners concerned the potential derailment of 'Europe Without Borders' and all its monetary/currency, institutional revisions and foreign policy constructions. The formation of one colossal European state and the seizure of apparently brilliant economic chances in East Germany by Bonn appeared to its western friends as dampening and diverting the West Germans from the '92 package. One particular example of conflict between EC and German programs centred on the EC central bank plans (with the ecu as the common currency) which could fade away in terms of its allure, once the D-Mark became the united German currency.

A more universal threat was the spread of nationalism. If 1989 was to lead to the rebirth of a great German phoenix that provoked an all-consuming European national self-assertion climate, no New Europe would emerge but rather a greater Germany and a patchwork of squabbling nations. This might mean, as Charles Krauthammer has written, that 1989 derailed a process by which Europe was hoping 'to make itself safe from itself' within the formation of a new European community.[8] The potential primacy of reactive nationalism, if it did take root and flourish, would arrest Europe's great integration exercise. If the ambitions and demanding internal market plans were hindered by the German unity movement with all of its connected routes to stable democracies and market economies for the east, then it might be argued that the EC thrust might not be regenerated.

One immediate sign of this EC worry was the speed with which the Schengen accords were shelved after the Berlin Wall opened. This pact of the five core 'Europeans' (France, Germany, Belgium, the Netherlands and Luxembourg) agreed to abolish all border controls and let people flow freely. Behind the agreement was a Delors/Mitterand attempt to show the other EC members that further integration was possible, possibly even to be speeded up, and perhaps even to suggest that the fast-track integrationists would go on ahead without the slower and more reluctant states such as Great Britain. This setback suffered by the Community could be followed by other retreats or even passivity by the EC in 1990. The crucial area which many in Brussels saw threatened by the German problem was the monetary union component of Project 92. Bonn's commitment to a German monetary union would doubtlessly entail difficult and costly decisions and almost certainly some inflationary times that might result in side-tracking the 'European' monetary project. If a recession in Europe were added to the considerations along with these eastern distractions, the entire '92 plan would be blocked. The most negative EC scenario was a Germany unable to dovetail both reunification and integration.

Some observers saw the results of the March 18 elections in the GDR as another disadvantage for the EC. The unexpected victory of the centre–right alliance for Germany with its advocacy of quick unification was viewed as a headlong dash by the impatient East Germans which further diminished a slower pace that was more compatible with Germany's enduring role as a motor of European integration. The dramatically shortened timetable for German togeth-erness as urged by a mesmerized Chancellor Kohl suggested an *Anschluss* power-play rather than a measured tread to unity, therefore minimizing the beneficial aspects which a more multilateral economic diplomacy might develop.

Divergence within the EC developed over Chancellor Kohl's new *Ostpolitik*. The smaller and weaker economies of the Community fringe (Ireland, Portugal, and Greece) became anxious about Germany's willingness and capability to continue financing their less developed regions. Reallocating regional development funds from the EC poorer states to Eastern Europe looked like a distinct possibility that the Federal Republic might choose. Another worry centred in France and the Benelux nations revolved around the overall slowdown of integration and was reflected in both Dutch and Belgian resistance to the quick reunification path and rapid Community admission of East Germany.

The issue of European future unity was even further blurred when one considered the dilemma of Paris and London as the other weighty members of the EC. The difficulties of constructing or resurrecting an Anglo-French *entente* as a significant counterweight to control the pacing and substance of a new powerhouse German state could be partially overcome with the Genscher 'Two plus Four' formula that allowed the British and French along with the two superpowers the right of approval or modification of the two Germanies' reunification plan. Yet, the Mitterand–Thatcher differences about the EC goals, let alone the means by which they would move, were considerable. Some observers interpreted the Thatcher actions during the 1989–90 events as not only foot-dragging, but grasping at the opportunity to deflect the integration process. The turmoil of the east pressed the EC to the limit to resolve its incongruities that stood as barriers to Community progress.

For some in the EC, the new times suggested the need to chart a path with a much looser pattern of integration. These problem-solvers pointed to a much more variegated process of combining or pooling national power represented by the 'variable geometry' or 'dual track' approach.[9] They argued that further progress might only be possible if one devised separate speeds for the divergent New Europe economies, particularly when one introduced the potential associate or affiliated members-to-be of the east, i.e., Austria, Poland, Hungary, and even Turkey. This thesis did not lack some basic merit, but the Brussels direction under Delors resisted this 'watering down' integration methodology as flawed and unacceptable. The Delors 'concentric circles' concept hinged on incremental, step-by-step, and in-unison progression for the Twelve, first to fulfil all of the 1992 objectives *before* the EC folded in the EFTA group and finally and lastly then brought in the former eastern bloc.

There developed serious criticisms about Brussels warding off or delaying initiatives from the east about enlargement commitments. Nevertheless, Brussels continued to accentuate gaining a more clear-cut agreement from the Twelve together on all pertinent matters, and not dividing the Community. The Delors strategy was to push for an intergovernmental conference of the EC by the end of 1990 that would consider a dramatic acceleration to political union which forced Great Britain to move with the other eleven. Even if Mrs Thatcher were not to be in the driver's seat at that point, the evidence was straightforward that the Delors-led EC would attempt with effective statecraft to keep the cohesiveness of the past, and in fact labour to widen and deepen the Common Market as a unit.[10]

The massive economic recovery problems of the east, with its stagnant growth, decrepit infrastructure, low investment, and high debt, interjected the important issue of timing. The uncharted waters of conversion from communist to market economy would require considerable time. The speed of the political revolution of separation in the east had been blinding in a historical sense, with ten years for Poland, ten months for Hungary, ten weeks for the GDR and ten days for Czechoslovakia and Rumania. The more cumbersome and complex economic rebuilding process if it allowed the EC integration process to continue and alleviated the pressures from Bonn members would necessitate the involvement of the United States as an active participant in the critical economic endeavors. In many western circles, it became evident that American interests in a reconstituted, stable, peaceful, and democratic Europe would ultimately drive Washington to engage in aid, trade, and investment policies of meaningful size for the eastern states, and possibly the Soviet Union.

The pro-EC views of President Bush that emerged in 1989 and the initial American posture during the 1989–90 crises as signalled in the Baker Berlin speech were certainly welcomed in European capitals, but they were not followed with economic commitments of any scale. This reluctance was based on American desires to see the security matters associated with bloc disintegration dealt with first. It was also related to the huge international debt and foreign trade deficit of the US and the Bush 'read my lips' promise on taxes which limited any American financing of Eastern Europe. In an era of intense competition for Washington's more limited resources, the prospects of Europe did not, for a series of reasons, appear bright. The point remained, however, that the need for Washington to collaborate with the EC in the gigantic task of economic reconstruction would become unavoidable if either western integration was to continue or the eastern states' democratic and market conversion was to succeed.[11]

A more vigorous American involvement was certainly one way around the medium-term financing problems that the Community faced with the former communist nations. In contrast to Japan, which has ploughed ahead into the east with various large-scale involvements, Washington appeared to be constrained by both policy and legislation (Jackson-Varik Amendment). The Group of 24 meetings in the spring of 1990 have illustrated the American hesitancy to assume an active and primary role on the emergent democracies and even more so the Soviet Union itself. The small packages of American aid for Eastern Europe and the continued restrictions and barriers to private American investments indicated Washington was extremely wary about economic participation with the EC in forming elaborate and liberal assistance projects. The resultant negative impact this might have on US and world trade did not appear to impress Washington. A group of significant queries about American policy arose. If the Community turned inward, absorbed by its eastern periphery problems, the consequences nullified what President Bush proclaimed in May 1989 at Boston University when he drew a tight linkage between EC and US fortunes.[12] If American interests and policies were halting or pulled back, American competitiveness would be reduced even further. If a stable and peaceful New Europe was the goal, larger US engagement in all aspects of order building was mandatory.

Integration, Reunification, and Security

The most obvious consequence of the post-Wall occurrences has been the fact that Europe has become the subject of contemporary global politics and no longer the mere object. The two original superpowers will now be required to interact closely with the more potent European actors, most critically the Germans and the Community. The initial Western European lead in the composition and management of the novel components of a new system building will highlight Bonn and then the New Germany but increasingly will depend on German relations with the EC partners.

Europe's ability to surmount the new thorny problems will revolve around three core questions related to German reunification. The process first must address any lingering scepticism about an expansive and threatening new German nationalism or a 'Fourth Reich'. Reassurance from central Europe on Germany's continued commitment to the short- and long-term EC course of enhanced economic and political integration must be part of the nation formation work and the refurbished linkages between East and West Europe. In the second place, the EC must open a fully collaborative diplomatic avenue with the six of Comecon on the nature of new connections, including a timetable for eventual membership in the Community. Brussels must commence the design with concrete procedures that include enlargement and avoid the development of what Jim Hoaglund calls a 'quasi-colonial relationship' with 'mansions in the west and slums in the east'.[13] The origination of the European Bank of Reconstruction and Development (BERD) to aid the east was an important sign in that this February 1990 EC initiative resulted in a multilateral structure to co-ordinate the multiple ventures. However, those same meetings sadly reflected American doubts about following the European lead. Third and lastly, the EC needs to co-ordinate the integration of Moscow and Washington into this entire reorganization scheme. The Soviets will insist on participation in the economic formulations for central Europe and should not be given such a role for diplomatic and security reasons alone. Gorbachev's goals of *perestroika* and the revamping of the Soviet economy toward some market economy directions should be incorporated into EC plans which, hopefully, gain a broad-based positive American reception. Again, American reluctance about any new Russian aid and their low-level contributions to the former bloc economies did not bode well for the concerted approach.

The mammoth assignment for the EC leaders will be devising the best architecture for the new 'New Europe' while still keeping and deepening its own homogeneity and forward unity thrust. Having embarked on the internal market completion and particularly the crucial central bank and common currency process, the Twelve face the peril inherent in a headlong sprint into, and engrossment with, German unity and the economic conversion of the near basket cases in the east.

If, as Jacques Delors insists, the EC should be the economic and political core around which Europe should now begin to coalesce, many on the continent believe that the EC agenda must continue to be emphasized. A major indicator of the EC capability to sustain the integration momentum will be the commencement on 1 July 1990 of the European Monetary Union (EMU). Given the proposed abolishment of the GDR currency and adoption of a unified currency on that same day, some pundits have already claimed that the new German priorities will be demonstrated as driving the new European construction, particularly if Brussels is unable to complete its EMU deadlines.

When the security concerns about the NATO and Warsaw Pact are inserted into the reconfiguration task, the EC dilemmas are greatly compounded. In the security dimension of transforming Europe, the US cannot and will not be irrelevant. If American policy states that there will be life for NATO after the cold war, it must be nevertheless acknowledge again that the game cannot be played by the old rules anymore. With the collapse of the communist alliance, a larger Europe contemplates the power conferred on it with both German unity and closer east-west economic ties. For many, the potential menace of a new German nationalism will be a more central concern within the EC than any aggressive Soviet and Warsaw Pact inclinations. Even if the reports of the cold war demise have been exaggerated or if an economically destabilized eastern bloc becomes a dangerous geopolitical factor, the western prospects, mainly for the Twelve, are nevertheless basically the same. An indispensable prerequisite in the early nineties is negotiating a security consensus agreement.

Washington and their western allies do not have a concerted outlook in this domain. There is much ambivalence in Europe about the Baker 'New Atlanticism' that links Europe integration and transatlantic partnership. More concretely, differences exist concerning even the NATO role in unified Germany, with a mounting minority, particularly in the German left, supporting a drawback position for NATO in a neutralized *Mitteleuropa* and others proclaiming the validity of a pan-European defence identity and institution. One perception on the continent at least concerns the possible creation of an EC with a military function or at minimum a revamped WEU.[14]

While American policy seems to be to continue with a NATO nexus, there must be an appreciation that the European search for a post-Yalta era security identity now insists on the primacy of its own choices. The Year of Europe may have finally arrived some 17 years after Henry Kissinger called for it, but it does not follow that the superpowers will be without influence. German reunification and the follow-up instrumentation for the security and economic reformation of Europe will necessitate the approbation of the major World War II allies. This will, in part, be accomplished via the '2–4' Genscher formula, the most outstanding illustration of sagacious European diplomacy since the Wall tumbled down. The rhythm and timing of that merger has been controlled in the first phase by the central Europeans, but the longer range, more complex questions of post-reunification will see that heartland core of European dominance fall away to a wider multilateral diplomacy.

The broad context of a Helsinki II appears to be one vehicle for reaching agreement on the security portion of the Europe of the nineties. The proposal for the convening by the end of 1990 of the 35 nations of the Conference on Security and Co-operation in Europe (CSCE) has gained strength throughout Europe. This pan-European security approach, which has the basic merit of keeping the two giant powers in the game, is being advocated with increasing intensity in Paris, Brussels, among Social Democratic Germans and in the Soviet Union in addition to the middling and smaller European states. The hopes for a '2+4+35' outcome would see a year's end Paris congress to ratify the 'Two plus four' reunification and security agreement and possibly get a multilateral accord to the longer-range responsibilities in terms of a division of labour on the entire economic transformation. All of this, as of springtime 1990, still requires a serious alteration in the Washington position in that the Bush administration has expressed its dislike of the Helsinki milieu. American insistence on the continuing centrality of a restructured NATO may be translated into a 'Two plus Four' (informally giving Polish and smaller NATO states consultative approval) that is set in stone on the German issue.

In that case, not only the economic reconstruction and conversion of the former communist states will be put aside or left to be settled in an *ad hoc* fashion by the Europeans, but the arms reduction talks and solution of Vienna and Geneva will be left to move on their own (and slower) momentum.

From the Community point of view, the Helsinki model after the '2–4' process is attractive in that it could produce widespread legitimacy for a comprehensive post-cold war settlement *plus* set the stage in a more favourable and beneficial atmosphere for further Common Market development. Then, if the '2+4+35' road map does succeed, the Twelve should have the energy and time to work on 1992 and after. Helsinki II might even create the specific economic and financial collaboration and burden-sharing patterns plus the roles of assistance, specifically from the US, that release the EC at an earlier date to return to the integrationist goals.

Conclusions

The almost entirely non-violent whirlwind of change that swept over 1989 Europe was the end result of not just Soviet impotence but the rising economic prowess and political attractiveness of the Community in the eighties. Importantly, the rush to and through revolution came not just without US involvement but with Washington cast in the reactor role. Alongside the ideological and economic disintegration of Soviet power was a clearcut diminution of American capacity to exercise its influence and power in this European metamorphosis. The more marginal and eroded roles of the superpowers have produced a new backdrop for the Europeans which they have long sought but that now place greater responsibility along with more power on them and the complicated multilateral bargaining of the future. Russia and America will not be detached from influential inputs, but Europe will be, in essence, the arbiter of its fate.

Western Europe's augmented self-determination and striving for unity that propelled it through the eighties has now to address the unavoidable consequences of the ferment and change from the east. The thesis that reunited Germany as a political and economic superpower should be firmly anchored in the EC in every way possible has wide Community following. The diplomatic means to reach that objective have yet to emerge. There have already been some EC setbacks and others may be inevitable, given primarily the German obsession with their newest *Ostpolitik*. But there need not be a contradiction between European integration and German unity if the will of the leadership prevails and the new German nation is solidly embedded in an economically and politically cohesive and united Community. The central fact remains that the EC cannot be blown off its course by all the excitement of the cold war termination. In fact, maintaining momentum on '92 is not enough; there should be no letup in the critical domains of movement toward political union and foreign policy coordination. For it is in these developments behind the market unification program, 'the profound political process and ideological momentum', as Leigh Bruce maintains,[15] that the work to strengthen the EC legitimacy and authority through institutional development and reform will be achieved. It is certainly noteworthy at this point to note that the greatest EC progress has often been the result of responding to crisis.

The contemporary global power diffusion so aptly described by Joseph Nye continues in the aftershocks over the 1989 revolutions.[16] In the redistribution of power and new balance of power that evolves from the European changes, Germany and the EC appear to come out winners. But the task of Community will only become more difficult in this new era, for if the Twelve are to become the fourth superpower, they must not only sustain the integration impetus of the eighties but accept the new political and economic power role in European affairs which the end of the cold war has thrust on them.

Tufts University

NOTES

1. Reinhardt Rummel (ed.), *West European Security Policy: Asserting European Priorities* (Boulder: Westview Press, 1990), in particular the Rummel articles and those of Roy Ginsberg and David Allen/Michael Smith. See also Max Weisglas, 'Europe on its way', European Cultural Foundation, The Hague, 1989, and Jacques Delors, 'Programme for the Commission for 1989' *Bulletin of the European Communities*, Supplement Feb. 1989.
2. Pierre-Henri Laurent, 'The European Technology Community, the Meeting of the Elites and the Creation of the Internal Market', *Il Politico*, no. 3 (1987), pp. 168–81 and 'The Road to 1992: The Politics of the New Eurotech Relance', in M. Steinberg (ed.), *1992: Technological Challenges to European Unity* (London: J. Pinter, 1990).

Bogdan Denitch, *The End of the Cold War: European Unity, Socialism and the Shift in Global Power* (Minneapolis: University of Minnesota Press, 1990) argues the integration ramifications in the east, with emphasis on social policy implications for the Community.

3. Wayne, Sandholtz and John Zysman, '1992: Recasting the European Bargain', *World Politics*, XLII no. 1 (Oct. 1989) pp. 95–128.

4. James Baker, 'A New Europe, A New Atlanticism: Architecture for a New Era', *United States Department of State, Bureau of Public Affairs*, Current Policy no. 1233.

5. Walter Russell Mead, 'The United States and the New Europe', *World Policy Journal*, VII, no. 1 (Winter 1989–90), pp. 35–70.

6. Jacques Delors, 'Address to the European Parliament', Strasbourg, Jan. 17, 1990. Publication of the European Communities.

7. Anne-Marie Burley, 'The Once and Future German Question', *Foreign Affairs*, vol. 68, no. 5 (1989–90) pp. 63–83; see also Stanley Hoffmann,' A Plan for the New Europe,' *New York Review of Books*, Jan. 18, 1990.

8. Charles Krauthammer, 'The Real German Danger', *New Republic*, March 26, 1990.

9. Jeffrey Harrop, *The Political Economy of Integration in the European Community* (Brookfield, Vt.; Gower Publishing, 1989), pp. 188–92.

10. Anthony Harley, 'Europe After the Wall', *Encounter*, Jan.–Feb. 1990.

11. See Jeanne J. Kirkpatrick, 'Beyond the Cold War', *Foreign Affairs* vol. 69, no. 1 (1989–90), pp. 1–16.

12. New York Times, May 20, 1989.

13. Jim Hoagland, 'Europe's Destiny', *Foreign Affairs* vol. 69, no 1 (1989–90), pp. 33–50.

14. Alfred Cahen, *Western European Union (WEU) and NATO: Strengthening the Second Pillar of the Alliance*, (Washington: The Atlantic Council, Jan. 1990)

15. Leigh Bruce, 'Europe's Locomotive', *Foreign Policy*, no. 78 (spring 1990), pp. 68–90.

16. Joseph Nye, *Bound to Lead: The Changing Nature of American Power* (New York: Basic Books, 1990).

The Military Aftermath of the Cold War

IAN CLARK

The hallmark of the cold war was its system of military security which legitimized the partition of Europe, the dismemberment of Germany and the presence of the armed forces of the two superpowers in central Europe. Security came to be institutionalized in the military alliances of NATO and the Warsaw Pact which, analysts can now clearly see, brought dividends in terms of predictability and stability whatever the human costs of such a security structure. The price that had to be paid for this was the considerable militarization of European life, not only in the sense of the armed confrontation along the central front, but also in the wider sense that European security was predominantly approached from a military perspective, centred upon the balance between the two blocs.

It follows that the beginning of the end of the cold war brings with it two sets of consequences. Most immediately, it has led to a loosening of the alliance system and considerable uncertainty about the overarching frameworks of European security. Additionally, however, it has brought to the foreground the many non-military aspects of European security that had been marginalized by the institutional arrangements of the cold war. Whereas the discussion of European security has for four decades proceeded in terms of the conventional balance of forces and the tenets of nuclear deterrence, it is now generally appreciated that non-military aspects of security – and particularly those concerning economic management and development, political legitimacy, and nationalist representation – constitute the substructures on which any future system of security must be based.

Such a readjustment, and potentially a reversion to a more historical European balance-of-power situation complete with nationalistic divisions, brings with it also the prospect of a return to 'historical' levels of defence spending. Levels sustained by some NATO members, and certainly by the USSR, since 1945 have been well in excess of inter-war rates of expenditure. As against this, however, there are also predictions that force reductions, at least in the short term, will cost rather than save money as forces are relocated, especially when this is coupled with new expenditure on verification of arms agreements.

The present diplomatic task is therefore the dual one of managing the existing military-dominated framework during the period of transition and then adapting it to a new format to meet the emergent conditions of the more complex social, political and economic pattern that will be necessary to sustain European security in the longer term. This article concentrates on the former problem of post-cold war security, which, in its military dimension, is really a set of four inter-related issues. The first three are the future role of the military pacts, the status of Germany at their core, and the process of disarmament which was already under way at Vienna before the revolutions in Eastern Europe occurred but which has been given a new dynamic as a consequence of them. Fourthly, these military problems can be fully analysed only within emerging European political and economic fabrics, such as the EEC, which inescapably take on a wider security function as guarantors against destabilization in the rapidly changing European landscape.

The Future of the Alliances

NATO

The tasks confronting the alliance are multifold. It must delineate for itself a central purpose appropriate to the new political conditions and devise military strategies which are in keeping with them and which are likely to find endorsement amongst member publics, expectant with promises about peace dividends and persuaded that the traditional threat from the east has now been all but dissipated. Specifically, it has to face immense problems about the future of German membership.

The emerging consensus seems to be that NATO must increasingly take on the appurtenances of a 'political' organization. Although always part of NATO philosophy, as exemplified in the Harmel report, the track of political dialogue has largely been overshadowed by NATO's military preoccupations. It is now widely suggested that this balance must change and that NATO must increasingly devote its energies to negotiation, particularly in the arms control field.

This may well be valid and realizable as a general objective but it does not address some of the specific obstacles which must inevitably arise. Amongst the more difficult of these are likely to be the following.

Firstly there are the many issues raised by the future status of Germany. Short of the specific agenda raised by German unification, however, it seems clear that Bonn's voice within NATO councils is even now a more powerful one which will have a major influence on debates about military strategy, particularly as it affects Eastern Europe in general but Eastern Germany in particular, and on the stationing of foreign forces on West German soil when their nuisance value has grown in inverse proportion to the decline in their reassurance value. Accordingly NATO's character is likely to change as a reflection of the Federal Republic's heightened stature within it. How this might be reconciled with the objective, of necessity expressed *sotto voce*, of using NATO politically as an instrument to monitor Bonn's security behaviour is anyone's guess and contains within it considerable potential for acrimony amongst the allies. An example can already be found in Bonn's ability to assert its preferences, with the blessing of Washington, in the adoption of the 'Two plus Four' formula for the consideration of German unity, a formula which firmly places the 'two' first and leaves many interested parties out of the subsequent parley amongst the 'four'.

A related issue is that of the future role of France. It stands to reason that an alliance which is more overtly political in nature, and de-emphasizes the integrated military structure, and which in any case is less likely to have such a large American military presence, should be one with which France can more readily identify. Hence, there is need to foster those already emerging conditions which would permit a wholehearted French commitment to NATO[1]. As several professional analysts have commented, 'we also believe that the special status of France in the alliance has to be reviewed, in light of the emergence of a more politicized NATO and a new Europe'.[2] It may, of course, be difficult to persuade France that NATO is worth the candle until a new role for the organization is more clearly articulated but there can be no doubt that the traditional basis of French defence policy has been substantially eroded by recent developments.

On the more narrowly military front, several questions remain. How viable will those twin elements of NATO doctrine – forward defence and flexible response – remain into the longer term future and can they be reconciled with a changing image? It is unthinkable that a more political NATO could operate without some military guidance because how else would it have a strategy to direct its arms control initiatives? At the same time, it can scarcely present itself as a credible political instrument while dragging with it those very items of military baggage which might prejudice negotiations on the future status of Germany (forward defence) and cloud the political atmosphere with the new Eastern Europe (theatre nuclear elements of flexible response). In any case, the parameters of strategy are likely to be determined by the outcome of events in Germany and the course of arms control and disarmament, both of which have developed a semi-autonomous momentum of their own.

As NATO searches for a new *raison d'être*, there are suggestions that the decline of the traditional threat from within Europe will be replaced by regionally more diverse challenges to western interests and that NATO must increasingly redefine its security role on a global basis. It is a moot point, however, whether an Atlantic alliance is really the best structure for such an undertaking, given that historically the relationship between the United States and its European allies has been severely tested whenever 'out-of-area' issues have confronted the organisation.

Warsaw Pact

There is nonetheless an impressive commitment to the future of NATO and its paramount problem is how to adapt: the Warsaw Pact's problem is much more fundamental and is whether it will survive. The omens are not presently favourable. As the pressures for Soviet withdrawal of forces from Eastern Europe intensify, so does the military infrastructure of the Pact seem out-moded and, given that the Pact embodied a Soviet political strategy (control of Eastern Europe) which has now been abandoned, its very rationale has largely been lost.

It is possible to discern a residual security function for the Pact, in terms of a military guarantee against German revisionism, which might hold some appeal in Poland and Czechoslovakia. However, this interest is likely to be more than outweighed by the negative political image which the Pact retains. It is difficult to see how the successor regimes of Eastern Europe can maintain their political credibility if they continue to adhere to an instrument which symbolizes that very dominance by externally-supported communist regimes against which the revolutions have been directed.

Status of Germany

The shape and function of the existing alliances is intimately inter-woven with the final outcome of events in Germany. As the likelihood at the moment is of a speedy movement to full unification of the country, within a relatively short time frame, the military implications of this need to be assessed.

There would seem to be various possible scenarios which will be reviewed in ascending order of likelihood of realization: unification with a continuing Soviet military presence; neutrality; German mem-bership of NATO but withdrawal from the integrated military structure; full German participation in NATO but a special demili-tarized status for what is currently East Germany.

The first option can scarcely be treated seriously as more than a transitional arrangement. Evidently the Soviet Union has a continuing security interest and, insofar as it still intends to maintain some forces in Eastern Europe over the next decade, needs to have some location to deploy these. The pressures to withdraw from Poland, Czechoslovakia and Hungary are currently leading to agreements and it will eventually be unsustainable to have forces in Germany cut off logistically from the USSR. In any case, it is not to be imagined that the government of a unified Germany, of whatever political complexion, would tolerate a long-term Soviet presence on its soil. Accordingly, we can confidently expect a phased withdrawal of Soviet forces from East Germany with such presence as remains in the medium term being viewed only as part of a transitional regime, rather than as a permanent feature of the situation.

Thus far, the Soviet position has moved significantly from one which refused to countenance the possibility of German unity to one which accepts its inevitability. However, in terms of negotiating strategy, Mr Gorbachev is evidently pressing for a unified Germany which is neutral rather than one which would embrace the east in NATO and so neutrality is the second possible outcome. It is easy to see that the other alternatives would be difficult for the Soviet Union to accept. As ex-Prime Minister James Callaghan has written, 'a united Germany which opted for membership of NATO would upset the present balance, because potentially it would advance the front line of NATO right up to the Polish border. It would probably be unwise for NATO to do this . . .'[3]. From the Federal Republic's point of view, there is equally need to avoid the impression of such an outcome as it would merely reinforce Soviet resistance to unification in any form. Not surprisingly FRG Foreign Minister Genscher has spoken out emphatically in a newspaper interview against the insistence that East German membership of NATO should be a condition of reunification: 'Anyone who wants to extend NATO borders to the Oder and Neisse . . . is slamming the door on a united Germany'.[4] However, reports indicate that Poland and Hungary have expressed misgivings about the idea of a neutral Germany and it certainly remains the mainstream western intention to persuade Gorbachev that such an outcome is not in Soviet best interests either. Perhaps he already accepts this logic but has to play the neutrality card as it is the only real leverage available to ensure a resolution of the German question which takes account of Soviet security interests.

The third option is adoption of the French model as reflected in recent reports: 'There is a growing belief among NATO governments that the West German government may be ready to leave its integrated military command as part of security arrangements for a progressively reunited Germany designed to reassure the Soviet Union . . .'.[5] Such a fallback position might have some attractions for the Soviet Union. However, it would offer no safeguard against a future German decision to re-integrate. From the NATO point of view, such proposals will be strongly resisted as a German defection, even if only partial, would seriously undermine a military apparatus already caught off balance by the pace of events.

The fourth possibility is that of a special demilitarized status for East Germany: 'The Bonn government's view as set out by Mr Hans-Dietrich Genscher . . . is that a reunified Germany should remain part of NATO but that the area taken up by East Germany could be demilitarized'.[6] Reports suggest that this outcome has been widely canvassed within NATO: 'West German, US and other allied officials said Thursday that the most likely military status of a future Germany would involve a largely demilitarized zone in the territory that is now East Germany'.[7] This issue brought into the open a difference of opinion within West Germany between Foreign Minister Genscher and Defence Minister Stoltenberg, the latter suggesting that Bundeswehr troops operating outside NATO could be deployed in Eastern Germany. This provoked denials by Genscher, attuned to the sensitivities of the matter, and was only resolved by an agreed statement, imposed by Kohl, which settled the matter largely in favour of Genscher's stance[8].

It may, of course, be that the final outcome is the much more radical one of the elimination of the two alliances and their replacement by some form of pan-European security structure. Ken Booth, for example, has argued that the 'bipolar *status quo* is the structure least able to cope with German reunification; this fundamental problem can only be accommodated in a looser structure of complex economic interdependence and an embryonic common security system'[9]. This may prove to be so but all predictions about the capacity of the German issue to be resolved within the contours of the existing bloc system have so far been confounded. Even if events do edge the issue away from the present alliance framework, John Roper is probably correct in arguing that this is unlikely within the next five years[10].

Arms Control and Conventional Disarmament

The third dimension of future security brings together elements of the former two and interacts closely with them, both in form and in substance. The present CFE negotiations are pact-to-pact and their survival in this form is naturally, therefore, contingent on the future of the pacts themselves. Likewise, it is possible to discern distinct, competing and overlapping functions for the disarmament talks. These may be seen as: reducing forces by imposing ceilings on overall levels; inhibiting future reductions by presenting agreed levels as floors; using a multilateral forum to restrain unilateral reductions; using negotiations (from the Soviet perspective) to achieve concessions for reductions that will in any case be imposed by East European pressures; to avoid (from the US perspective) legitimizing a residual Soviet presence; to accelerate (from the East European perspective) the process of Soviet withdrawal. Moreover, a reduction in quantity of weaponry should not be confused with reductions in quality as the negotiators seek to ensure that the oldest equipment alone is removed and the newer recycled to friends. 'For the less well-off NATO countries', it has been cynically observed, 'disarmament would become a means of modernizing their forces'.[11]

Initial negotiating positions in the Vienna CFE talks aimed at reducing superpower manpower in Europe to 275,000 on each side. However, this target was overtaken by events as the Soviet Union was faced with the new situation in Eastern Europe and the United States responded to the diminished threat from the Warsaw Pact. Soon there were repeated calls for this figure to be lowered. Sam Nunn, for instance, called for troop reductions to 200–250,000. 'His argument, however, that the US ceiling of 275,000 troops "validates" a higher Soviet military presence than either President Gorbachev or the East Europeans want is something which some US officials already seem willing to accept . . .'[12]. In the face of these demands, President Bush moved swiftly to take the initiative and in his State of the Union address declared the new US goal of reductions to 195,000 each but with the USA permitted to retain an additional 30,000 troops in the UK, Italy, Turkey and Greece. On 13 February, at the Ottawa meeting of NATO and Pact foreign ministers, agreement on these levels was broadly reached but there remains every possibility that even these figures will be lowered in future negotiations.

The dynamic for these proposals is coming in large part from Eastern European demands for unilateral Soviet withdrawals from their territory. Czechoslovakia's President Havel reached agreement on 26 February 1990 for the removal of all 73,000 Soviet troops by July 1991. This has been accompanied by similar efforts by other Pact members. Leaders in Poland and Hungary, in which the Soviet Union currently has some 40,000 and 65,000 troops respectively, set deadlines for Soviet troops to leave their countries over the next two years,[13] even if it is possible to imagine some retention of Soviet forces in Poland until such time as the issue of a reunified Germany's borders is fully resolved to Polish satisfaction.

In the face of these developments, the US administration has been confronted by a dilemma. On the one hand, it has not wished to erode the western negotiating position at Vienna by an uncontrolled disarmament process and has had to take account of allied anxiety, expressed most notably by Mrs Thatcher, not to weaken NATO's defences too precipitately. On the other hand, a CFE agreement would be counterproductive if it tried to sanction a larger Soviet presence than would be there in its absence, and especially so if this was in the face of Eastern European opposition. This was former Defense Secretary James R. Schlesinger's message to the Senate Armed Services Committee: 'It would be worse than ironical if the CFE negotiations were to result in legitimating the long-term presence of Soviet forces in Eastern Europe that might otherwise be withdrawn in the absence of such negotiations . . . It would be far worse if the nations of Eastern Europe were to hold the United States or NATO responsible for the continued presence in their countries of Soviet forces'.[14]

The momentum for disarmament does not operate exclusively on the Soviet side. In framing its proposals, the USA has also had to take into account scarcely veiled intentions by some NATO members to reduce or withdraw their contingents. As Frank Gaffney observed with considerable frustration, 'by threatening a precipitous dismantling of NATO forces . . . the Belgians' announcement of their desire to withdraw their forces from Germany is giving the Soviets back their negotiating position at CFE'.[15] In any case, it can scarcely be imagined that NATO can retain its present rationale for deployment of large numbers of allied forces in the central region in the face of long-term Soviet withdrawal of its troops. Accordingly, while the disappearance of the threat of large-scale attack against NATO with minimal warning time is welcome, it brings with it the need for major rethinking of NATO's own force dispositions.

Ultimately, it must also be recognized that the extent of the reduction of conventional forces in Europe will be related to the creation of conditions of mutually perceived security. At the moment, the tide of events is favourable to the west and Gorbachev's domestic problems have eroded his international bargaining position. All the more does this place the onus of responsible statesmanship on the west. As Lawrence Freedman has argued, it is not in the west's long-term security interests to create an 'illegitimate' security structure which would encourage revisionism from a stronger Soviet Union in the future[16].

The other closely related aspect of arms control which will impinge directly upon NATO's future military options is the vexed question of short-range nuclear forces. As the third category left behind by the 1987 INF agreement, short-range forces had already created alliance strain in early 1989, well before the momentous events at the end of the year. In response to the acrimony emerging between Britain and the Federal Republic over a Lance follow-on, and the related issue of short-range negotiations, President Bush sought to defuse the tension at the NATO summit in May by his initiative on conventional forces. The compromise struck in the Comprehensive Concept had various elements to it: nuclear forces, if not 'modernized', would be kept up to date where necessary; the question of deployment of a Lance successor would be postponed until 1992; once implementation of a CFE agreement was under way, negotiations for a *partial* reduction of short-range nuclear forces could be entered into. Thus was created the linkage between the timetable of the conventional and putative nuclear arms control discussions.[17]

Much has changed since this compromise was reached. A Federal Republic that was already coy about short-range weapons will most assuredly not now countenance them as they can reach only the emerging democracies in Eastern Europe. This must surely undermine any future NATO decision to deploy these weapons and spur the demand for a withdrawal of existing systems. Hence, it seems most unlikely that new deployments will occur in the present political climate. In short, NATO will have to assess this issue as part of a larger and painstaking review of its military posture that, in a sense, can scarcely be begun until the new security architecture has more clearly emerged. While the pressures for denuclearization will grow, there will undoubtedly also remain a solid stratum of official opinion, particularly in Britain and France, which is committed to a nuclear deterrent because of a lack of faith in purely conventional deterrence. Francois Heisbourg is perhaps correct in seeing the probability of *European* nuclear deterrents assuming a greater role in the new context and his preference is for an Anglo-French partnership: '. . . a much smaller number of theatre nuclear weapons will be required in a post-CFE Europe devoid of massive troop concentrations and where conventional forces are numerically equal: instead of some 4000 tactical nuclear weapons, NATO could then probably make do with fewer than 1000 . . . logic dictates that France and Britain should develop an airborne missile jointly to reach beyond Eastern Europe'.[18] Such a venture may be encouraged by the difficulty which the French government is likely to face in sustaining a rationale for its Hades programme, given the range of that missile.

Not only does Heisbourg see such a development as desirable. He also thinks it now more likely, given revised American attitudes to its own nuclear strategy and the emphasis which the Bush administration now places on European collaboration: 'The British and French governments now seem to have the blessing of the Americans for their efforts to try and develop a new arsenal of European nuclear weapons, starting perhaps with a joint, short range, air launched missile . . .'[19]. Whether or not this will prove possible will very much depend on the role played in European security by the various economic, political and security organizations which are now likely to be called upon to be more assertive in their presence.

The Security Architecture

The past five years have witnessed a burgeoning of interest in the future of the European pillar within the NATO alliance. Much of the activity associated with this revival has been symbolic and rhetorical and the record of concrete achievement remains relatively humble. However, in an area that had been self-consciously exorcized from the European political debate for most of the preceding three decades, such symbolism is not without its own importance. There is broad agreement on the factors which have encouraged the new wave of Europeanism within the alliance.[20] Additionally, there is widespread recognition of the major themes – and difficulties – which are associated with such an endeavour.

There remains also deep uncertainty as to whether improvements in the superpower relationship, and prospects for a diminished American security role in Europe, are integrative or disintegrative as far as European defence efforts are concerned. It might logically be contended that recent shifts in Soviet policy, coupled with a successful detente with the United States, provide a more favourable security environment in which creative evolution might be risked and a European identity more vigorously presented. Alternatively, the sceptics have speculated that declining concerns about security in Europe are more likely to erode the will to European defence collaboration and to remove the necessary political incentive to work towards this goal.[21] Likewise, opinions vary as to whether a diminished American presence will foster European cooperation or simply permit old antagonisms to come to the surface. This latter thought was evidently on Sir Geoffrey Howe's mind when he wrote the following words of caution:

> For frankness' sake I have to add that the most likely result of withdrawing the American 'prop' might well not be to spur the Europeans to stand on their own two feet and multiply their own defence efforts. It could be more likely to make them question whether their own commitments to each other were still worth the sacrifices involved.[22]

There are three bodies which are likely to feature prominently in the emergence of new security structures in Europe: the European Community, the Conference on Security and Co-operation in Europe, and the Western European Union. Institutions are means to ends rather than ends in themselves and yet they can become, as they have done since 1984, matters of considerable preoccupation. The question of appropriate institutions could not be avoided because their very proliferation, and variable if overlapping memberships, reflected the mixed character of 'Europe'. Accordingly, European and NATO diplomacy has since the mid-1980s been engaged in a delicate exercise of institutional adaptation and development the final results of which remain far from clear.

Under the heading of 'general purpose' security organizations, there has been the reactivation of the Western European Union since 1984. This has sat in slightly uncomfortable juxtaposition to the specifically 'NATO' branches of the pillar, such as the Eurogroup, but also to the 'functionally specialist' organizations such as the Independent European Programme Group, which has operated since 1976 but has itself become somewhat more active during the past decade. The fact that these institutions are jostling for position in the security field with European Political Co-operation, and potentially with the European

Community as it moves towards 1992, adds to the complexity of the institutional scene and adds force to calls for some reorganization and rationalization.[23] Unhappily, such efforts have been stymied because each institution has offered competing attractions as to composition of membership, national purposes and differing conceptions of the pillar.

EC and the 1992 Process

At one level, the principal questions pertaining to the EC at the moment centre on the future of Germany. This is so in a dual sense: the future of the EC itself is bound up with the course of German development and, to some, the EC is a necessary safeguard to future German unification. On the former, in crude terms, the fear has been that interest in unification, and perhaps the economic opportunities presented by other revolutions in Eastern Europe, might sidetrack Bonn from its present commitments to European integration and lead it to prefer 'broadening' to 'deepening' at the present juncture. If this were so, it would diminish any potential security role that the EC might play. On the other hand, many commentators have stressed the importance of a deepened EC as part of the fabric which would make German unity both possible and less awesome. Not surprisingly, proposals for the reinvigoration of the EC were President Mitterand's reflex response to the fall of the Berlin wall. Likewise, this seems to have emerged as part of the US administration's policy which sees the EC as fundamental to the management of orderly change.

The future of the WEU and of European defence institutions more generally is bound up with the role which the EC may come to play in the defence sphere. Indeed, to some extent the present profile of the WEU reflects the present inability of the EC to function on defence matters – a consequence both of the EC's 'civilian' ethos and of its 'neutralist' members. Had this not been so, the EC, rather than the WEU, would have been the logical expression of a European defence interest. As Alfred Cahen, formerly Secretary-General of the WEU, has remarked 'It is in the European Political Co-operation of the Twelve, and not in a reactivated WEU, that a European security dimension should have developed'.[24]

It is, of course, true that incremental change permitting some role in security matters has been taking place and is embodied in both European Political Co-operation and in the Single European Act, under the provisions of the latter's Article 30, paragraphs 2 and 6. Suggestions for an augmented EC defence role have been revived more recently. The Spanish foreign minister, Mr Francisco Fernandez Ordonez, speaking after Spain's assumption of the presidency of the EC Council of Ministers, suggested that it may be necessary to consider removing the defence restrictions contained in Article 30[25].

Such calls have found considerable academic support from various analysts who, albeit for varying reasons, believe that a genuinely European defence pillar can emerge only under the auspices of the EC. For some, the central dynamic of this process will come from the EC's concern with European industry, especially in the high technology sphere where the distinction between military–civil uses is most difficult to sustain.[26] For others, it will be the legitimizing function of the EC which will be most necessary: as the late Jonathan Alford commented, 'it is hard to imagine any effective and durable European defence cooperation taking place without the sustained political endorsement of the Community'.[27] However, the role of the EC in the dialogue about the future of Eastern Europe scarcely makes this an opportune time for it to stress a security function that traditionally reflects a bloc antagonism. Nor can the EC further the cause of pan-European economic integration by dwelling on security matters. Accordingly, it might be preferable to see these tasks performed by the WEU, even if it suffers from the handicap of a more restricted membership. This is certainly the view of the President of the WEU Assembly, Charles Goerens: 'It is time . . . to recognise that Western European Union is by treaty, and until further notice, Eastern Europe's correct interlocutor for the security and disarmament aspects of the intra-European dialogue. The Community cannot at one and the same time open towards the East, whatever the form of this opening, and have the ambition of substituting itself for WEU in the East-West dialogue on security'.[28]

CSCE

It is inevitable that a body that already has a proven track record in east-west dialogue is going to play a substantial part in creating the new security structure in Europe. Without doubt, the CSCE, which gave rise to the Helsinki accords and, indirectly, the Stockholm agreements on confidence building, will feature prominently as a forum for the transition to the new Europe. Professor O'Neil is surely correct in his claim that 'while the decline of the Warsaw Pact signifies that less and less can be gained through bloc-to-bloc negotiations, the regenerated independence of the states of Eastern Europe stands to strengthen the CSCE yet further'.[29] It can also confidently be predicted that CSCE will be the forum in which the new arrangements for unified Germany are given formal sanction and perhaps 'supervised' to some degree.

What is less clear is just how fundamental a security role can be performed within the CSCE ambit. Some experienced diplomats have portrayed it as an embryonic collective security structure, perhaps sustaining its own peace-keeping force.[30] As a legitimizing body for overseeing transition, it is certain to be irreplaceable: whether it has the cohesion and common interests to become itself a 'collective security organization' is much more doubtful and the suggestion is greeted with scepticism on the part of security analysts who tend to prefer the continuation of the Atlantic alliance in some form rather than the complete disappearance of the present security structures.

WEU

The WEU has become a focus of some European pillar aspirations. As it includes all key European members of the alliance, especially France, as it has a specific brief for defence matters, and as its council now regularly brings together defence as well as foreign Ministers, it is regarded by many as a convenient forum for co-ordinating European concerns and positions. From this perspective, it matters little that the motivations for its revitalization were national and various, it serving the French interest of guarding against German disaffection, and the German interest of enhancing its partnership with France within a multilateral setting: what mattered was that this was a forum in which European NATO might do meaningful defence business. The record has fallen short of such promise but it would be premature to dismiss the longer-term impact of this institution, especially at a time when its membership has expanded (Spain and Portugal) and its treaty basis is being reviewed. In the longer term, there will need to be clearer redefinition of WEU's relationship to the EC. Indeed, the former's Secretary-General has argued that one of WEU's tasks at present is to serve as a kind of surrogate for the EC in defence matters and, in these terms, might well be merged into the Community structure in the future if the EC manages to grapple with the issues of European defence.[31]

Meanwhile the current Secretary-General, Willem van Eekelen, has proposed a WEU role to surmount the problems of German unification and its membership of NATO. According to this scenario, Germany would remain a full member of NATO but present Warsaw Pact and NATO forces deployed in Germany would be replaced by a WEU 'Euro-Army', although 'linked to NATO's command structure'. In this scheme, US forces would not be a part of these multinational units.[32] Not the least difficulty facing this proposal would be the gathering of support for it from such as the British government which could scarcely be expected to be enthusiastic about any 'Euro-Army' concept, however pro-NATO in inspiration.

The role of the WEU is symbolic because, better than any other institution, it straddles the twin roles of European construction and of Atlanticism, portraying itself as the genuinely European pillar which makes the Atlantic alliance stronger. At present, the post-cold-war transition is being managed in the expectation that these roles are not simply compatible but more than ever necessary: the US endorses Europeanism because it is the best way of coping with Eastern Europe, taking the heat out of the German question and permitting the US to reduce its defence commitments. One wonders, however, whether much of the present thinking is not too conservative or, at least, too optimistic. Ultimately, the military consequences of the end of the cold war will be closely associated with the extent of European integration, including in the security sphere, and the manner in which the superpowers respond to this. Whether the magic formula can be found which will overcome potential points of dissension remains to be seen. Will Germany remain enthusiastic about any form of European integration that is implicitly designed to constrain her? Will the Europeans find Atlanticism as attractive when the threat from the east has diminished? Can the West Europeans find the will to take their integration further if the risk is that of the greater alienation of the Eastern Europeans? Once the Americans begin their process of military withdrawal from Europe, will they be able to establish a new political consensus about how much is enough? Pierre Hassner is less persuaded than some by many of the comfortable assumptions on which is based the optimistic view of a triumphant Atlanticism enduring into the indefinite future: 'I tend to think that the dynamics go the other way and that the priorities will not be in keeping this happy European unity and Atlantic alliance together'.[33] If this scepticism is justified, the military implications of the end of the cold war may be much more far-reaching than we can presently envisage.

Selwyn College, Cambridge

NOTES

1. For general background, see G.L. Williams, *Coming in From the Cold: The Evolution of French Defence Policy* (Occasional paper 42, Institute for European Defence and Strategic Studies: London, 1989).
2. J. Eberle, K. Kaiser and D. Moisi, *International Herald Tribune*, 22 Dec. 1989.
3. *The Times*, 5 Jan. 1990.
4. *The Financial Times*, 30 Jan. 1990.
5. *The Guardian*, 2 Feb. 1990.
6. *The Financial Times*, 2 Feb. 1990.
7. *International Herald Tribune*, 2 Feb. 1990.
8. See *The Independent*, 19 Feb. 1990, *The Wall Street Journal*, 20 Feb. 1990 and *The Times*, 20 Feb. 1990.
9. K. Booth, 'Steps towards stable peace in Europe: a theory and practice of coexistence', *International Affairs*, Jan. 1990, p. 25.
10. 'Europe and the Future of Germany – a British View', *The World Today*, March 1990, p. 48.
11. *The Financial Times*, 17 Jan. 1990.
12. *The Financial Times*, 2 Jan. 1990.
13. *International Herald Tribune*, 19 Jan. 1990.
14. *International Herald Tribune*, 6 Feb. 1990.
15. *The Sunday Telegraph*, 28 Jan. 1990.
16. *The Independent*, 22 Feb. 1990.
17. *A Comprehensive Concept of Arms Control and Disarmament* (NATO Information Service: Brussels, 1989), especially p. 11.
18. *The Independent*, 28 Dec. 1989.
19. J. Palmer, *The Guardian*, 3 Jan. 1990.
20. For representative analyses, see J. Alford & K. Hunt (eds.), *Europe in the Western Alliance; Towards a European Defence Entity* (Macmillan: London, 1988), Part 1, and Ian Gambles, *Prospects for West European Security Co-operation* (Adelphi Paper No 244, IISS: London, 1989). Also, H. Sonnenfeld and C. Bertram, contributions in *The Changing Strategic Landscape* (Adelphi Paper No. 235, IISS: London, 1989). Some see the genesis of the problem in NATO's own success in producing security, e.g. J. Joffe, *The Limited Partnership: Europe, the United States, and the Burdens of Alliance* (Ballinger: Cambridge, 1987), p. xxiii.
21. A view expressed in L. Freedman, 'Managing Alliances', *Foreign Policy* (Summer 1988), p. 85.
22. Sir Geoffrey Howe, 'The European Pillar', *Foreign Affairs* (Winter 1984/5), p. 33.
23. T. Taylor, 'Alternative Structures for European Defence Co-operation' in K. Kaiser &

J. Roper (eds.), *British-German Defence Co-operation* (Jane's: London, 1988)
24. A Cahen, *The Western European Union and NATO* (Brassey's: London, 1989), pp 15–16.
25. *The Times*, 18 Jan. 1989.
26. See e.g., T. Taylor, 'A European Defence Entity: European Institutions and Defence' in Alford and Hunt, op. cit., p. 202–3; J. C. Rallo, *Defending Europe in the 1990s: The New Divide of High Technology* (Pinter: London, 1986).
27. J. Alford, 'Introduction', in Alford & Hunt, op. cit., pp. 8–9.
28. *Letter from the Assembly* (Western European Union) No 4, Jan. 1990, p. 1.
29. R O'Neill, *The Times*, 22 Jan. 1990.
30. Sir Nicholas Henderson, *The Daily Telegraph*, 13 Feb. 1990.
31. Speech in Paris on 7 Feb. 1989, *Europe*, 8 Feb. 1989. For an earlier expression of the same view, see *Atlantic News*, No. 1805, 27 March 1986.
32. *The Wall Street Journal*, 23 Feb. 1990.
33. Transcript of BBC broadcast, 8 Feb. 1990.

The United Nations

ALAN JAMES

The United Nations is a body which can easily evoke strong emotions. Among publics, this is perhaps most clearly seen in the hopes which are periodically aroused that the UN is about to usher in a better world. After all, the UN Charter starts off with the ringing declaration that the organization is intended 'to save succeeding generations from the scourge of war'.[1] It is not surprising that some take this at face value, and imagine the UN to have the ability to achieve this end independently of the sovereign states who are the components of both the world's political structure and the UN. All that is needed, it often seems to be implied, is a requisite amount of effort and determination on the part of 'the UN', and 'peace' will be not just around the corner but present in the here and now.

Not unnaturally, the failure of this a-political vision tends to produce disenchantment. And sometimes, maybe but not necessarily for reasons connected with this, publics swing in the opposite direction. Now the UN is seen as an organization full of mischief and even malice, and therefore one which should be viewed with grave suspicion. Instead of a body whose face is automatically turned towards the light, it is characterized, almost, as the abode of darkness. The United States public, with what some might see as typical volatility, provides illustrations of both these phenomena, the first of them echoing the enthusiasm for the League of Nations which was to be found in Britain between the two world wars.

It might be thought that governments would be immune from such attitudes, because of their presumed political literacy. This, it could be supposed, would lead them to take a cool view of the UN, seeing it as an arena available for manipulation rather than as a notional person marching determinedly (indeed, pre-determinedly) in this direction or that. But not so, or at least apparently not so. For, perhaps on account of the UN's wide-ranging agenda and the distance at which it usually stands from the immediate concerns of its member states, the organization can easily trigger official responses of a distinctly emotional sort. And the lather into which states sometimes get about the UN can be of both the hot and cold varieties. On the one hand, but only when there is a close identification between national positions and those taken by the UN, the organization is sometimes represented as in natural occupation of the moral high ground. On the other, and often when a state is in the minority at New York, the UN may be officially pictured as malignly biased against that state. In the UN's early years the United States tended to adopt the first approach, and in the 1980s the latter. Under de Gaulle in the 1960s, France had little but contempt for the organization.

One must, of course, not be over-swift to assume that in their public statements states always express the whole truth and nothing but the truth about their private attitudes. But even when account has been taken of the opportunities which the UN offers for both rhetoric and relaxed generalities, it does seem that states sometimes adopt genuine feelings of an overall kind about the UN, whether of optimism or pessimism, warmth or hostility. This may not be unconnected with two considerations. Firstly, that, as has been suggested, the nature and role of the UN is such that it is more likely to elicit emotion and generalized feeling than many other international issues. And secondly, that states are, after all, run by flesh and blood individuals who do not always put their prejudices, hopes, and sensitivities on one side when making foreign policy.

The UN and the 'End of the Cold War'

A notable instance of this phenomenon is to be found in the marked revival of official (and unofficial) interest in and expectations of the UN in consequence of the remarkable developments in Soviet foreign policy over the past five (Gorbachev) years. More particularly, it has been widely thought that, at last, the organization might play a leading role in the maintenance of international peace and security. It has not been supposed that it is likely to do so exactly on the basis of the tough and hierarchical prospectus which was provided in 1945, which envisaged that the great powers, in their capacity as permanent members of the UN Security Council, would organize 'such action by air, sea, and land forces as may be necessary'[2] to repel aggression. But it has been anticipated that by some less costly but little specified means the UN will belatedly inherit its birthright.

Much of the impetus for this broad scenario comes not just from the changed international context but also from the linked professions of support for the world organization which have been made by the Soviet Union. Initially, and notably, these appeared in a veritable 'road to Damascus' article by Mr Gorbachev which appeared in *Pravda* and *Izvestia* on 17 September 1987 (although at the time his 'conversion' was not widely remarked upon in the west). In it he called for a 'comprehensive system of international security . . . [which] could function . . . within the framework of the United Nations'.[3] Thus the UN, 'the main universal security body', was looked to for 'extensive international verification of compliance with agreements to lessen international tension and limit armaments and for monitoring the military situation in conflict areas'.[4] In this connection, 'we are arriving at the conclusion that wider use should be made of . . . United Nations Military Observers and United Nations peace-keeping forces'.[5] There followed calls for cooperation within the framework of the UN for uprooting terrorism, the alleviation of the developing world's debt, the protection of the global environment, the creation of a world space organization, and – a huge turnabout – the statement that 'one should not forget the capacities of the International Court'.[6] The article concluded with promises of Soviet assistance in overcoming the UN's financial difficulties and – another noteworthy recantation – with the injunction that 'all states should give [the UN Secretary-General] the maximum of support'.[7]

If Soviet policy had stopped at the level of assurance and exhortation, it would have not have given overmuch encouragement to those who were open to the possibility of or even looking for a revived UN. But the 17 September article, and other ensuing announcements of a like kind (notably Mr Gorbachev's speech at the UN General Assembly on 7 December 1988), were accompanied by deeds which were deemed to represent real achievement. Even before the article, the Soviet Union had said that it would start to pay its share of the costly UN peace-keeping force in Lebanon, and had begun to behave co-operatively at the UN in certain other financial respects.[8] And over the next couple of years it made a very positive contribution in the discussions and negotiations which resulted in, relatively speaking, an upsurge of UN peacekeeping activity.

Thus, there were established, always with superpower consent, the UN Good Offices Mission in Afghanistan and Pakistan (UNGOMAP), the UN Iran–Iraq Military Observer Group (UNIIMOG), the UN Angola Verification Mission (UNAVEM), the UN Transition Assistance Group (UNTAG) in Namibia, and the UN Observer Group in Central America (ONUCA – the acronym deriving from the Spanish rendering of the group's name). Moreover, one of these bodies (UNGOMAP) was entrusted, among other things, with checking on the departure of Soviet troops from Afghanistan – the first occasion on which a major power had whole-heartedly consented to such an invigilation. And another (UNAVEM) had the task of verifying the departure of Soviet proxy troops (Cubans) from Angola.[9]

It should also be noticed that in the 1980s China gradually changed its position on UN peacekeeping in a number of important respects. Hitherto it had stood conspicuously aloof from all questions concerning this matter, including the bills. But in 1981 it began to pay for some existing operations, and in 1986 promised to pay all the sums it had withheld from the UN's regular budgetary assessments since 1971.[10] Two years later it quietly joined the UN's Special Committee on Peace-keeping Operations, on which the other four permanent Security Council members already sat, as well as almost all the other leading members of the UN. In this way the committee of 33 became the Committee of 34.[11]

These eastern initiatives and attitudes have contributed to some very up-beat comments about the UN's possible role in relation to peace and security. The Special Peace-keeping Committee put in a very positive report to the UN General Assembly in mid-1989, listing 61 'Proposals on Peace-Keeping' and recommending a variety of measures which might encourage the use of that device.[12] The foreign ministers of the five permanent members of the Security Council, after meeting with the UN Secretary-General in September 1989, agreed that 'at the present time of positive change in the international political climate from confrontation to relaxation and interaction among states, the United Nations has an important role to play'. They went on to express their 'satisfaction at the improved working

relations within the Council and with the Secretary-General', and
their 'determination to work together and in co-operation with the
Secretary-General for the prevention and resolution of international
conflicts'.[13] In an address to the General Assembly in November
1989, no less hard-nosed a person than the British prime minister
spoke of the thaw in east–west relations having 'brought the promise
of a new dawn, of new hope'.[14] And in the same month the altered
east–west climate was symbolized by an Assembly resolution adopted
by consensus which called on all states to co-operate more closely in
the spirit of the UN Charter.[15] The significance of this resolution,
however, lay not in so much in its content as in its sponsors – the Soviet
Union and the United States. It was the first time in the Assembly's
44-year history that they had come together in this way.

The Nature of the UN

In all probability, the very positive approach to the UN which is
now current expresses genuine feelings that the organization offers
a number of desirable opportunities. It does not follow, however,
that they are directly and continuously translatable into successes,
so that the world is thereby about to become and remain a much
safer place. Accordingly, it ought not to be assumed that the UN's
overall prospects have been greatly improved in consequence of recent
developments in east–west relations. Few would deny that the cold
war has ended, in the sense that the super powers no longer see each
other as necessarily at odds in virtually every important respect. But
that is not to say that the UN's day has fully come.

One reason for caution stems from the possibility that political
upsets in the Soviet Union or even the United States could result in
a check or a reversal to the recent ameliorative process. Another,
quite separate reason, which will be focused on here, stems from
the nature of the UN. There are certain limited respects in which
it may be seen as more than the sum of its parts, and having an
independent life of its own.[16] But those respects are very limited.
For essentially the UN is a gathering of sovereign states, and what
it can do is therefore circumscribed by the extent of the common
ground which exists between them. Moreover, that common ground
will vary from case to case, and also from one period to another.

Even an individual state will sometimes change its posture on this issue or that, in response to changes in its internal circumstances, the international environment, its conception of that environment, or of what its interests dictate. In this light, an organization of 160 such states is likely to have considerable difficulty in plotting a steady and coherent international course – or even any recognizable course at all which goes beyond rhetoric and generalities.

This situation is a reflection of the basic fact that each member of the UN tries to use its membership to further its own interests. States have not joined out of respect for the 'UN idea', or with a view to creating a stronger organization by transferring some of their powers to it. Rather, they are in the UN for what they can get out of it. Of course, some states may see it as in their interests to increase the deference which is paid to the opinions of the UN – as expressed, particularly, in the resolutions of its General Assembly. This is likely to be much more true of the weaker than of the stronger members, and there are many more of the former than the latter. But even the weaker states show little sign of wanting to endow the UN with any general authority. What they are interested in is very much a selective (and probably variable) legitimacy. The stronger members, on the other hand, being in the minority, are not at all concerned to foster such a development. For them the UN certainly has its uses. But those uses chiefly relate to the UN as a diplomatic meeting place and as an occasional tool.

The Soviet Union and the UN

In this light, it is not hard to understand the relatively accommodating face which the Soviet Union has shown at the UN in recent years. She has more or less ditched the ideological prism through which she used to view the political world, and is much concerned about her internal economic difficulties – and, latterly, her nationalities problem. More than ever, therefore, she is interested, broadly speaking, in international stability, and in good relations with other states. The UN offers many possibilities of working towards the last-mentioned end and some opportunities to help in achieving the former. It is also a forum in which the Soviets can generally advertise their changed political values.

These points find graphic illustration in the ways in which the Soviet Union has contributed towards the use, in the late 1980s, of UN peacekeeping as a stabilizing mechanism. So far as the Gulf War between Iran and Iraq was concerned, which had been dragging on since 1980, she did not display great urgency in trying to bring it to an end. But in that respect the Soviet Union was not differentiated from the other major powers. All of them saw some merit in these two potentially troublesome states being kept out of other mischief. More particularly, all the nearby powers (the Soviet Union being the nearest, having a long border with Iran) felt very uneasy at the thought of a possible Iranian victory, for fear that that state's thoughts might then turn to the further external celebration of its Islamic revolution. Thus it was not until 1987 that the Security Council got around to demanding a cease fire, and a further year before the weakening Iran agreed to one. Once that point had been reached, however, the Soviet Union was in full support of the idea that the cease fire should be watched over by a UN Observer Group (UNIIMOG) Together with the United States she provided transport for the mounting of the operation, and airlifted some returning Canadian UNIIMOG personnel free of charge.[17]

In the case of the war in Afghanistan, the Soviet Union was a direct participant, having sent in about 100,000 troops at the end of the 1970s in an effort to bolster the country's ailing left-wing regime. It proved an exceedingly ill-judged venture. The Afghan army more or less disintegrated, and Soviet troops were harried at many points by the Mujahidin – the numerous but far-from-united opponents of the Soviet presence and her puppet Afghan government. To make matters worse, the Soviets went down to resounding annual defeats at the UN as the General Assembly called, in effect, for a Soviet withdrawal.

With the advent of Mr Gorbachev the Soviet Union engaged in serious (UN-sponsored) talk about withdrawal. Eventually, in 1988, a series of agreements were reached: Afghanistan and Pakistan (whither most of the five million Afghan refugees had gone, and where the Mujahidin had a safe rear base) agreed not to interfere in each other's affairs; the superpowers also agreed to keep out; and the Soviet Union was to withdraw her troops over a nine-month period. A UN Good Offices Mission in Afghanistan and Pakistan (UNGOMAP) was also set up.[18] It was understood, although not explicitly set out, that UNGOMAP's military officers were to check on the Soviet withdrawal. This they did, with full co-operation from the departing Soviets,[19] who were anxious to show to a widely-sceptical world that they were honouring their promise. In this way UN peace-keeping gave significant help in extricating the Soviet Union from an embarrassing situation, and in winding-up a major international trouble spot. But the success of the operation was, of course, entirely dependent on the Soviet willingness to go.

UN peace-keeping also featured in an indirect Soviet withdrawal – from Angola. In the mid-1970s Cuba, with Soviet financial and logistical support, sent about 20,000 troops to Angola to assist the left-wing claimant to that formerly-Portuguese territory. This move, too, was very far from a success, for although the left came out formally on top, civil war continued, with increasing numbers of Cubans being required to prop up the government. Its chief challengers were receiving support from South Africa and the United States, and in the discussions which went on throughout the 1980s about South African withdrawal from neighbouring Namibia, that issue and the situation in Angola became inextricably linked. For South Africa said that it would only depart from Namibia if Cuba did likewise in respect of Angola.

On balance, and in the disengaging Gorbachev context, this came to look to the Soviet Union like a good deal. For although the Angolan government would be weakened by the loss of the Cuban connection, South Africa would no longer be on hand in Namibia to provide cross-border assistance to its opponents. Furthermore, the Soviet Union would be relieved of a costly embarrassment, and it could be fairly confidently expected that the government of an independent Namibia would be sympathetic towards and valuable for the Soviet Union. After much intensive negotiation the deal was therefore struck, and at the end of 1988 the Security Council established a Verification Mission (UNAVEM) to check on the phased withdrawal of Cuban forces from Angola over a two-and-a-half year period. Cuba made no difficulty about this arrangement or over its implementation, and at the end of October 1989 UNAVEM reported that about 25,000 Cubans had already left Angola.[20]

Meanwhile, the Soviet Union was cooperating fully in the plans for the independence of Namibia. This was strikingly signified by the fact

that it, together with the United States, was given observer status in
the joint commission which was set up in December 1988 to serve as
a forum for discussion and for the resolution of any problems which
arose regarding the linked activities in Angola and Namibia.[21] The
commission's members were Angola, Cuba, and South Africa, and its
meetings were held on a rotational basis in each of these countries. It
was indeed a sign of the changing times to have United States officials
going to Cuba, and Soviet officials going to South Africa, all in a
warmly co-operative spirit.

The UN's Transition Assistance Group (UNTAG) in Namibia came
into being on 1 April 1989 with the task of watching over the last
days of the South African regime and, in particular, of ensuring that
a constituent assembly was freely and fairly elected. It was a large,
complex, and multi-layered peacekeeping operation – and almost
came off the rails before it had started. For also on 1 April more
than 1,000 armed members of the body which had been leading the
fight against South Africa's presence in Namibia allegedly crossed
into the territory from Angola. This event threatened the basis on
which the whole peace process rested, and the UN Secretary-General
agreed that South Africa might quash the infiltration. This was done,
but not without considerable casualties. At the diplomatic level the
joint commission was called into urgent session, and the crisis was
quite quickly patched up. None of the commission's members tried
to make political capital out of the episode – in marked contrast to
what might have been expected to happen only a relatively short while
before. Thereafter events in Namibia proceeded fairly smoothly, and
the elections of November 1989 were given the UN's imprimatur.[22]
They, together with the whole UNTAG operation, were seen on all
sides as a great success, and on 21 March 1990 the sovereign state
of Namibia came into existence. In this way an issue which had been
the focal point of much international tension was defused, along with
another such issue focused on a neighbouring state. In respect of both
developments the Soviet Union played a positive and valuable role.

The Soviet Union's wish to encourage the winding up of situations
which are causing international aggravation, particularly those which
in one way or another involve both herself and the United States,
is also to be seen with regard to Central America. Here too, the
device of UN peace-keeping has been turned to for assistance in

achieving the desired result. The problem in this area arises out of civil conflict in Nicaragua, but also extends to some other issues in the region. The coming to power of the left-wing Sandinista regime in Nicaragua in 1979 heralded the start of a ten-year effort to unseat it by its right-wing Contra opponents. Many of the Contras were based in neighbouring Honduras, and received huge amounts of aid from the United States. Nicaragua, on the other hand, received a certain amount of support from the Soviet Union. In the late 1980s, however, the Soviets joined the other Central American states in pressing for a settlement to the increasingly costly war.

These efforts gave rise early in 1989, and against the wishes of the United States (who judged that the timetable was too precipitous), to an agreement that the Honduras-based Contras should be disbanded, that Nicaragua should institute certain democratic reforms, and that elections should be held there not later than February 1990. The attempt to implement this programme encountered a number of difficulties, not least because the Contras themselves were not a party to it. But in November 1989 an observer group (ONUCA) was set up by the UN Security Council[23] to check on the termination of Central American support for irregular forces and insurrectionist movements and also on the ending of the use of Central American territory for attacks on neighbouring states. Following the surprise defeat of the Sandinistas in the elections, the Security Council added an infantry battalion to ONUCA in March 1990 to enable it to supervise the disbandment of the Contras.[24] How smoothly this whole peace process goes remains to be seen. But what is clear is that here, as elsewhere, no obstacles are being presented by the Soviet Union to the use of the stabilizing peacekeeping device. On the contrary, that state must be given a not insubstantial part of the credit for the marked increase in the UN's activity in this field.

The Outlook

On the (widespread) assumption that stability is better than instability, and co-operation better than conflict, all the developments which have just been discussed must be accounted a considerable gain. But it must be remembered that they are not the outcome of 'the UN' taking itself firmly in hand or of any similar intra-organizational mechanism. Rather, they are a reflection, very largely, of the Soviet Union's changed assessment of its interests, of the fact that the United States has seen the issues in question in much the same light, and of the further fact that this superpower alliance has been able to win the support of the Security Council for its peace-keeping proposals. It may well be that this favourable conjunction of circumstances will repeat itself in respect of other problems. But it cannot be assumed that it will do so, let alone that that will now invariably be the case. In the future, as in the past, the UN will be able to contemplate an operational role in matters of peace and security only to the extent to which the major powers are able to agree. And their agreement will be the outcome of case-by-case calculations, based on individual perceptions of interest, and not of the application of some general, UN-oriented, principle.

Two further points must also be kept closely in mind. The first is that there are limits to the influence of the major powers, even when they display a firmly united front. At bottom, situations can only be stabilized when the parties to them are so inclined, or can be persuaded to adopt that inclination. Equally, peacekeeping operations can only be mounted with a prospect of success if all the parties are willing to act co-operatively, or are persuadable in that direction. Almost by definition, however, disputants are of a belligerent rather than a conciliatory frame of mind. And states often look askance at the prospect of a peace-keeping presence, particularly on their own soil.[25] It is by no means an easy task to induce a change of mind on these often-connected matters, not even for the major powers acting in unison.

An example of their limited influence is provided by the problem of the former Spanish colony of Western Sahara, which has been occupied by Morocco since the late 1970s but is claimed by the indigenous (but Algerian-backed) Polisario movement. In 1988, after lengthy negotiations, the UN came up with a plan for its solution which involved a large peace-keeping operation. It was given a fair wind by the Security Council,[26] but as of the end of March 1990 the parties have not been able to agree on the details of its implementation. Another such example is provided by Cambodia, from which in 1989, after an 11-year sojourn, Vietnam withdrew the large army which had been supporting the more or less puppet government. Discussions were then held about how the process of internal reconciliation might be advanced with the UN's peacekeeping help, but to no avail on account of local disagreement. In January 1990 the five permanent members of the Security Council endorsed an ambitious plan providing for the UN's administration of the country for a year, during which time elections would be held to determine a new government.[27] But as yet the internal contestants have been unable to agree on the matter. Until they do, and notwithstanding the support of the major powers for the plan, the UN will be unable to act.

The second point which must be kept in mind when considering the UN's possible role in a post cold war context is that this context is by no means necessarily one of super-power amity. It does not follow that because the Soviet Union and the United States no longer see each other in nothing but the worst light, they are always going to fall into each other's arms. Certainly, the opportunities for fruitful co-operation will be much greater than heretofore, and the UN can be expected to benefit accordingly (although it must not be assumed that that cooperation will automatically be channelled through the UN). Of that there is already an appreciable amount of evidence.

But the fact remains that these two states will continue to have distinct and often incompatible interests; that they will frequently find themselves in competition for influence in certain quarters; that they will each have friends and clients to support whose behaviour may offend the other; and that they will sometimes find it appropriate to make claims upon or about the other which will be found objectionable. In other words, the situation will be one of what might be called 'traditional' great power rivalry. Almost all observers find that a great deal more acceptable than rivalry of a rigidly hostile and ideologically-bound sort. But it is rivalry nonetheless – and will find reflection in the international forum which is called the United Nations. One relatively small instance of this occurred at the start of 1990, when UNGOMAP's mandate was about to run out. The United States would have been glad to see the operation wound up, as now it was largely a means whereby the Afghanistan Government could obtain publicity for its complaints about Pakistani (and American) interference in allegedly internal Afghan affairs. By the same token the Soviet Union wanted an extension of six months.

After some squabbling a compromise extension of just two months was agreed.[28]

Neither this kind of occurrence nor larger conflicts of interest are going to be eradicated by tinkering with the UN's structure (which, in any event, can only be altered with the approval of the five permanent members of the Security Council). Nor are any such changes likely to increase the likelihood of the UN being used as a co-operative mechanism. The present institutional set-up is entirely adequate for the needs of a society of sovereign states – and that, emphatically, is the kind of society which both currently exists and shows every sign of continuing for a long while. The general temperature of superpower relations may change from time to time, of which recent developments are a notable instance – one showing that in international relations a warming effect is widely seen as a wholesome. As a body which reflects the condition of the state system, the UN has benefited from these events. But the basic system remains the same, so that diplomacy and statecraft will continue to be employed for national ends. In consequence, one does well to be cautious in face of suggestions that the UN is now operating and will continue to operate on a new and higher level of inter-state relationships. None of the evidence in support of that claim is at all persuasive. One can feel more sanguine about the short and even mid-term avoidance of Armageddon. But the world is very far from the verge of the millenium.

Department of International Relations,
University of Keele

NOTES

1. UN Charter, Preamble.
2. UN Charter, Article 42.
3. 'Gorbachev – Article' (London: Novosti Press Agency, 17 September 1987), pp. 1, 6.
4. Ibid., pp. 8 and 12
5. Ibid., p. 12.
6. Ibid., p. 20.
7. Ibid., p. 22.
8. See Alan James, 'The Security Council: Paying for Peacekeeping', in D.P. Forsythe (ed.), *The United Nations in the World Political Economy. Essays in Honour of Leon Gordenker* (London: Macmillan, 1989), p. 24 and note 30
9. See Alan James, *Peacekeeping in International Politics* (London: Macmillan, for the International Institute for Strategic Studies, 1990), for case studies of each of these

operations.
10. See work cited in note 8 above, p. 25.
11. The Committee was expanded by General Assembly resolution 43/59 of 6 December 1988.
12. See UN document no. A/44/301, Report of the Special Committee on Peace-keeping Operations, 9 June 1989.
13. UN document no. S/20880, 3 Oct. 1989.
14. UN document no. A/44/PV.48, 13 Nov. 1989
15. Resolution 44/21 of 15 Nov. 1989
16. See Alan James, 'International Institutions: Independent Actors?', in A. Shlaim (ed.), *International Organisations in World Politics Yearbook 1975* (London: Croom Helm, 1976)
17. See UN document no. A/43/696, 10 Oct. 1988
18. See UN documents nos. S/19834, S/19835, and S/19836, 26 April 1988. It was not until six months later that the Security Council passed a resolution confirming UNGOMAP's establishment: resolution 622 (1988) of 31 Oct. 1988
19. See UN document no. S/20465, 15 Feb. 1989
20. See UN document no. S/20955, 9 Nov. 1989
21. See *Namibian Independence and Cuban Troop Withdrawal* (Pretoria: Department of Foreign Affairs, Republic of South Africa, 1989), Appendix 9.
22. See UN document no. S/20967, 14 Nov. 1989.
23. See UN document no. S/20979, 21 Nov. 1989.
24. See UN Information Centre, London: *News Summary*, 20 March 1990.
25. See Alan James, 'International Peacekeeping: the Disputants' View', *Political Studies*, Vol. XXXVIII, No. 2 (July 1990).
26. Resolution 621 (1988) of 20 Sept. 1988.
27. See UN Information Centre, London: *News Summary*, 18 Jan. 1990.
28. Resolution 647 (1990) of 11 Jan. 1990.

The End of the Cold War and the International System

R. J. VINCENT

The 'Cold War' was a shorthand phrase widely used to describe the pattern of relations between the superpowers (and the blocs they led) prevailing during the four decades following the second world war. Its appeal lay in its calling attention to a suspicion that, but for certain powerful constraints, the pattern would disintegrate into 'hot' war. This suspicion, derived partly from the idea that when the number of great powers in a system is reduced to two, war between them is more likely because there is no third force to hold the balance. And it derived in more significant part from the ideological hostility between the powers. When their ordinary rivalry as great powers was compounded by the disposition of both of them to take domestic politics as as much the arena for the contest as international politics, their open conflict might seem the inevitable result.

Thus bipolarity and ideological incompatibility were the mutually reinforcing elements of the cold war. Here states really were like gladiators having their swords drawn and their eyes fixed on a single opponent (and his gang). And as Ian Clark stressed in his chapter on the military aftermath of the cold war, the hallmark of the period was the system of military security showing itself most obviously in the two armed camps adjacent to each other in Europe. Add to this the continuing sense of crisis (spawning the cold war sub-discipline of 'crisis-management'), moderated only slightly in periods of detente, and this completes the pattern of the cold war.

What held it in place? What were the powerful constraining factors? The acquisition of nuclear weapons by both sides, producing the doctrine of mutual nuclear deterrence, is conventionally taken as the chief agent producing the 'long peace' in Europe which came to be a description, from another point of view, or in a different mood, of the same phenomenon of the cold war. And nuclear weapons conspired with the reduction of the number of great powers to two to produce, counter-intuitively, the 'stability of a bipolar world'.[1]

It is salutary, if not mandatory, in a special issue on the end of the cold war to reflect on its beginning, and Geoffrey Warner's chapter produced not one origin but several in terms both of time and of place: the end of the nineteenth century, 1917, 1939, 1942, 1945–47; Germany, Eastern Europe, south east Europe, the far east. And if the story of origins is plural we might expect too more than one account of the conclusion of the cold war. But there might be some symmetry between origins and conclusion in point of explanation. Thus the 'orthodox version' in the west on the origins of the cold war, namely that 'they started it' (by for example communizing Eastern Europe) might be expected to produce an explanation at its end which had to do with the change in 'their' objectives and instruments.[2] Equally, a revisionist account of the origins of the cold war, namely that 'we started it' (by for example seeking to keep the trade door open right up to and beyond the frontiers of the Soviet Union) might be expected to produce an explanation at its end which had to do with the long-term success of this strategy. And a post-revisionist account of the origins of the cold war, namely that its origins were complex and interactive, might be expected to produce an explanation of its end which went beyond a 'they lost no we won' discussion. This special issue has not plotted this symmetry but there are examples in it of all three patterns of thought.

I

The idea given greatest credence in this special issue is that, if the cold war was a war, they lost. The Soviet Union, *le grand absent*, as Geoffrey Warner reminded us, from the historiography of the cold war, was also absent from its victory celebrations despite the political virtuosity of an enterprising Soviet president seeking to turn defeat into victory. The most uncompromising statement of this view in this special issue was that of Gerald Segal, who not only has the Soviet Union losing, but acquiescing tacitly in this outcome. And many contributors show how the loss was sustained on various sectors of

the economic front – Western Europe being a demoralizing neighbour
to Eastern Europe in this regard (Bennett Kovrig), even being partly
responsible for the Eastern European revolution in 1989 (Pierre-Henri
Laurent), and the secular economic decline of the Soviet Union being
so grim and apparently irreversible as to render the country unable
substantially to benefit from the Soviet end of the peace dividend
derived from the saving in military expenditure (Christopher Mark
Davis). Looked at from an American point of view, one of the chief
ironies of the end of the cold war might be, as John A. Thompson
points out, the approximate fulfilment of the Kennan strategy despite
its author's recantation. Kennan's doctrine of containment envisaged
the damming up of Soviet expansionist tendencies until in the fullness
of time internal decay rotted an unviable system.[3] It may be argued
that the rotting process is now complete.

The triumphalism of a western victory as opposed to a Soviet
self-defeat has been less vaunted in this special issue, though there
have been whiffs of it from time to time. Of course, it could be
said, especially if the zero-sum logic of the cold war is accepted,
that an eastern defeat is a western victory and vice versa. And if
Eastern Europe now, and perhaps the Soviet Union tomorrow, opt
for the market and liberal democracy, this certainly looks like a
victory as well as a defeat. If, further, we take with the revisionists
the rhetoric of democracy to be a disguise for the reality of capitalist
expansion, then the *we* began it (and won it) school has some
plausibility.

But part of the ending of the cold war is the termination of thought
in these cowboy categories. And the complexities of the German
question dealt with here by Ieuan John, connected to the broader
questions of the future of the alliances, of conventional and nuclear
arms control in Europe and elsewhere, and of what has come to be
called the architecture of security in Europe and outside, are not
susceptible to zero-sum analysis.

II

Amidst the flux it is difficult to identify the decisive changes which are
going to shape the international system into the twenty-first century.
What can be said, however, is that the changes nodded at piously over

the last two decades have now unmistakably occurred: bipolarity is
now for most purposes a thing of the past; the ideological contest once
lying at the centre of world politics can no longer locate that centre;
world politics defined in terms of a first, second and third category
according to fundamental economic orientation now have an archaic
ring.

The bipolarity now consigned in substantial part to history has been
sent there not by the arrival of new powers (as has been tiresomely
reiterated over the last two or three decades) but by the near-collapse
of an old one. If a position as a pole is determined by strategic,
economic, and ideological attractiveness then the Soviet Union has
only a third of a claim to that status. The direction of change in
this regard might not be back from a bipolar to a multipolar world
but onto a world in which only one power has all-round attraction
and multipolarity is a game played in the second division. The
hegemon whose declining relative power has preoccupied it since
its defeat in Vietnam might turn out to have a new lease of life.
Neither Germany, nor Japan, the new super powers in the making,
can yet claim attractiveness beyond the economic component of
power. In this regard, those who would discern the shape of the
new international system might continue to study imperial political
ordering as fruitfully as the multipolar politics of balance of power.
The idea that we now live in a post-hegemonial international order
may turn out to be premature.[4]

The end of the ideological contest between east and west does
not mean the end of ideology, however much the reporting of that
death might have been exaggerated. The world, in this regard, was
already authentically multipolar long before 1989, not only because
of the tenacity of alternative universalistic ideologies like Islam, but
also because of the plurality of nationalisms made legitimate by
the United Nations doctrine of national self-determination. In this
respect, the new shape of the international system looks like the
very old nationalist shape but now relatively unconstrained by the
export of doctrines associated with the nationalist experience of the
superpowers (the Soviet Union because it no longer commands respect
as a model, the United States because it no longer needs to counter
the Soviet model).

The distinction related to ideology, between first, second and third worlds, terms of art in the theory and practice of post 1945 politics is now more than ever a blurry one. The post-war 'architecture' depended very heavily on it. You were either western or eastern or very self-consciously neither. If one of the poles collapses there is a loss of role-definition for the other pole, and no even-handed policy of non-alignment available to a third world following a strategy of equidistance from each pole.

All this can be exaggerated. 'It ain't over till it's over', Uri Ra'anan suspiciously reminded us, suggesting that a prudent respect for the Soviet Union's continuing military might might be a better policy for the west than a wholesale abandonment of the cautiousness of the cold war. In this respect, global politics remain bipolar even if only by virtue of inertia or by courtesy. In the same way the obliteration of a particular kind of 'left' in world politics may be neither once and for all nor applicable everywhere. And with regard to the third world, the great watershed in world society between the haves and the have-nots remains whatever the peculiar ideological beliefs of those powers who currently happen to find themselves at the top of the greasy pole.

This is a reminder of an important continuity in world politics. Whatever new shape global political arrangements take they are likely to be mediated by power and the differential between those who have it and those who do not. The idea that the break-up of a coalition and of a habit of thought associated with it will lead necessarily to a new enlightenment is a mistaken one, as Alan James pointed out in pouring a bucket of cold water over renewed enthusiasm for the United Nations. What is more nearly necessary is the ordering of world politics according to the interests of those most involved in them, the great powers who are also the great responsibles. Who are the great powers? The United States alone for some purposes (to do for example with the provision of collective economic goods); the United States and the Soviet Union still for others (to do for example with nuclear arms control); for others the United States, Japan and the European community (to do for example with trade regimes); for others the regional top dogs (to do for example with local order). The break up of a particular pattern of power does not in short overturn a world patterned by power.

III

It may be that when the international historians of the twenty-first century seek to characterize the post-Second World War era they will treat the cold war as the unfinished business of the hot war, and will celebrate or lament the reunification of Germany within a wider security system as the true end of a phase of world politics beginning with Hitler's coming to power in 1933. They may also remember, writing like Richard Langhorne in this collection, the historical precedents that might have been useful if the history that actually unfolded was to have been different. Thus, conscious as the 1945 peacemakers were of the mistakes made in 1919, they themselves could make no provision for the failure of the great powers to attach themselves jointly and severally to the purposes of the United Nations. Some nineteenth century ad hoccery along the lines of the concert system might here have made a difference.

The reason it was not possible for the great powers to act in this way may have been the coincidence at the pinnacle of world politics of two powers accustomed to seeing international politics as an extension of their domestic orders, so that what has been called the 'diplomacy of principle'[5] from the American side confronted great Russian moralism combined with the superior creed of communism. This combination of exclusive superiorities inhibited diplomatic flexibility and it may be that the end of the cold war will bring with it a refreshing appreciation on the part of both superpowers of their ordinariness as great powers dealing with dilemmas that have been faced by others before and will confront others after their own period of greatness has passed.

If ordinary powers produce ordinary politics these are not necessarily, in the international arena, the politics of peace. For one of the features of the cold war was its exaggeration of what is in international politics ordinary – the international anarchy, the disposition to over-insure militarily against the possibility of a future danger (thus bringing on the very danger the policy sought to avoid), the distrust of everyone including one's 'friends', and the search for the stick concealed in the olive branch. But also ordinary in international politics is the cooperative routine of diplomacy allowing the overlap of separate interests to produce defensible agreements which are not overwhelmed by ideologists of any colour. The end of the cold war might produce ordinary international politics of both these descriptions, but the expectation of surprise is also part of the pattern of international politics, and the pundits will be on the look out for the next cold war.

The London School of Economics and Political Science

NOTES

1. Kenneth N. Waltz, 'The Stability of a Bipolar World', *Daedalus*, vol. 93 (Summer 1964).
2. The terms here are well established in the historiography of the cold war. See, for example, J. L. Gaddis, 'The emerging post revisionist synthesis on the origins of the Cold War', *Diplomatic History*, vol. 7, no. 3 pp.171–90.
3. See X, 'The Sources of Soviet Conduct', *Foreign Affairs*, July 1947, reprinted in George F. Kennan, *American Diplomacy 1900–1950* (New York, 1952).
4. This is a theme of Susan Strange's. See, for example, *States and Markets* (London, 1988).
5. See Bruce Kuniholm, 'The Origins of the First Cold War' in R. Crockatt and S. Smith, *The Cold War: Past and Present* (London, 1987)

A Chronology of the Cold War

ERIK GOLDSTEIN

1944

21 July	Poland: a Committee of National Liberation established at Lublin under Soviet auspices
9 September	Bulgaria: a Fatherland Front established under Soviet auspices
20 December	Hungary: a Provisional Government established under Soviet auspices
31 December	Poland: the Committee of National Liberation declares itself the Provisional Government. Recognised by Soviet Union

1945

11 January	Soviet army captures Warsaw
4–11 February	Yalta Conference
6 March	Romania: a Communist dominated government formed led by Petru Groza
12 March	Soviet Union transfers Northern Transylvania from Hungary to Romania
12 April	United States: death of President Franklin Roosevelt, succeeded by Harry Truman
13 April	Soviet army captures Vienna
21 April	Soviet Union and Polish provisional Government sign twenty-year Treaty of Mutual Assistance
7–8 May	Surrender of Germany
29 June	Czechoslovakia cedes Ruthenia to Soviet Union
17 July	Potsdam Conference
26 July-2 August	Great Britain: Churchill government defeated. Clement Attlee becomes prime minister
6 August	First atomic bomb dropped on Hiroshima
14 August	Surrender of Japan
4 November	Hungarian Elections. Smallholders' Party wins majority (245 of 409 seats)
18 November	Bulgaria: communist-controlled elections

1946

9 February	Stalin's 'Two Camp' speech
12 February	George Kennan's 'Long Telegram' despatched
16 March	Churchill's 'Iron Curtain' speech, Fulton Missouri
8 September	Bulgaria abolishes monarchy and Republic of Bulgaria established
19 November	Romania: communist-controlled elections
2 December	Anglo-American agreement to economically merge their zones

1947

	of occupation in Germany (bizonia)
19 January	Poland: communist controlled elections
1 February	Hungary: republic proclaimed replacing notional monarchy
10 February	Peace treaties signed with Finland, Italy, Bulgaria, Hungary, and Romania
4 March	Anglo-French Fifty Year Treaty of Alliance
12 March	Truman Doctrine announced
5 June	Marshall Plan announced
July	United States: article 'The Sources of Soviet Conduct' by X (i.e. George Kennan) appears
31 August	Hungary: semi-communist-controlled elections give majority to Communist led coalition (271 of 411 seats)
4 December	Bulgaria alters name to People's Republic of Bulgaria
5 October	Cominform (Communist Information Bureau) founded
30 December	Romania: abdication of King Michael and establishment of the People's Republic of Romania

1948

25 February	Communist coup in Czechoslovakia
10 March	Czechoslovakia: death of Jan Massaryk
17 March	Brussels Treaty (Western Union) for collective defence (Britain, France, Belgium, Netherlands, Luxemburg)
11 June	US Senate passes 'Vandenberg Resolution'
18 June	Currency reform implemented in American, British, and French zones of Germany
24 June	Berlin Blockade begins
28 June	Yugoslavia expelled from Cominform
1 July	Berlin Airlift begins
3 November	United States: President Truman (Democrat) re-elected

1949

22 January	COMECON (or CMEA, the Council for Mutual Economic Assistance) established
4 April	North Atlantic (NATO) Treaty signed (Belgium, Canada, Denmark, France, Great Britain, Iceland, Italy, Luxemburg, Netherlands, Norway, Portugal, United States)

8 May	German Federal Republic (West Germany) established
9 May	Berlin Blockade lifted
25 September	Soviet Union: announces test of first atomic bomb
1 October	People's Republic of China established
7 October	German Democratic Republic (East Germany) established

1950

7 April	United States: NSC-68 produced
25 June	Korean War begins
17 October	Protocol signed admitting Greece and Turkey to NATO
28 November	East Germany and Poland accept Oder–Neisse Line as frontier

1951

| 25 October | Great Britain: Winston Churchill (Conservative) wins general election, replacing Attlee government (Labour) |

1952

| 3 October | Great Britain tests first atomic weapon |
| 4 November | United States: Dwight Eisenhower (Republican) elected President |

1953

5 March	Soviet Union: Stalin dies, Georgi Malenkov becomes Premier (6 Mar.)
23 July	Panmunjon armistice ends Korean War
20 August	Soviet Union: announces test of first hydrogen bomb
September	Soviet Union: Nikita Khrushchev becomes first Secretary of the Communist Party
23 December	Soviet Union: execution of L.P. Beria

1954

| 6–8 September | SEATO (Southeast Asia Treaty Organisation) established |

1955

8 February	Soviet Union: Malenkov resigns as Soviet Premier, succeeded by Marshal Bulganin
5 April	Great Britain: Churchill resigns as Prime Minister, succeeded by Anthony Eden
5 May	West Germany joins NATO
7 May	Soviet Union cancels friendship treaties with Britain and France
14 May	Warsaw Pact signed (Soviet Union, Albania, Bulgaria, Cze-

choslovakia, East Germany, Hungary, Poland, and Romania)

15 May	Austrian State Treaty (Britain, France, Soviet Union, United States, and Austria). Effective 27 July
18–23 July	Geneva Conference (Eisenhower, Bulganin, Khrushchev, Eden, Faure)

1956

26 January	Soviet Union returns Porkkala naval base to Finland
25 February	Khrushchev's 'Secret Speech' denouncing Stalin to the 20th Congress of the Communist Party of the Soviet Union
16 April	Dissolution of the Cominform announced
28–30 June	Poland: riots in Poznan
19 October	Soviet Union and Japan resume diplomatic relations
21 October	Poland: 'Spring in October' Revolution. Gomulka becomes First Secretary
24 October	Hungarian Revolution begins
1 November	Hungary proclaims neutrality and leaves Warsaw Pact
4 November	Soviet suppression of Hungarian Revolution. Janos Kadar installed as leader

1957

10 January	Great Britain: Harold Macmillan replaces Eden as Prime Minister
15 January	Soviet Union: Andrei Gromyko becomes Foreign Minister
25 March	Treaty of Rome establishing European Economic Community (effective 1 Jan. 1958)
3 July	Soviet Union: Malenkov, Molotov, Kaganovich, and Shepilov removed from Soviet Communist Central Committee
4 October	Soviet Union launches Sputnik

1958

27 March	Soviet Union: Khrushchev becomes premier replacing Bulganin, remaining Communist Party First Secretary
17 June	Former Hungarian reform leader, Imre Nagy, executed

1959

1 January	Cuba: Fidel Castro overthrows Batista government
15 & 25–27 September	Washington-Camp David summit conference (Eisenhower, Khrushchev)

1960

1 May	United States U-2 reconnaissance airplane shot down over

	Soviet Union
16–19 May	Paris summit conference (Eisenhower, Khrushchev, Macmillan, De Gaulle)
9 November	United States: John Kennedy (Democrat) elected president

1961

3–4 June	Vienna summit conference (Kennedy, Khrushchev)
13 August	Construction of Berlin Wall begins
31 October	Soviet Union: Stalin's body removed from Lenin Mausoleum
10 December	Albanian–Soviet split

1962

16–28 October	Cuban Missile Crisis

1963

20 June	American–Soviet agreement to establish a 'hotline'
25 July	Nuclear Test Ban Treaty initialled (Britain, Soviet Union, United States), signed 5 August
31 August	United States-Soviet 'hotline' becomes operative
18 October	Great Britain: Macmillan resigns as Prime Minister, succeeded by Alec Douglas-Home
22 November	United States: assassination of President Kennedy, succeeded by Lyndon Johnson

1964

15 October	Soviet Union: Khrushchev deposed, and replaced by Leonid Brezhnev as First Secretary, and Aleksei Kosygin as Premier
16 October	Great Britain: Harold Wilson (Labour) becomes Prime Minister China tests first atomic bomb
3 November	United States: Johnson wins election as President

1965

7 February	First attacks on North Vietnam by United States
9 December	Soviet Union: Nikolai Podgorny elected President

1966

10–14 February	Soviet Union: 23rd Congress of the Communist Party of the Soviet Union, retores use of title General Secretary instead of First Secretary
10 March	France announces withdrawal from NATO integrated military structure

1968

5 January	Czechoslovakia: Alexander Dubcek becomes First Secretary of the Communist Party, replacing Antonin Novotny who remains President
23 January	Pueblo incident. North Korea seizes United States naval ship
30 March	Czechoslovakia: General Ludvik Svoboda replaces Novotny as President
1 July	Nuclear Non-proliferation treaty signed
15 July	Brezhnev Doctrine announced
21 August	Soviet invasion (with Poland, Hungary, Bulgaria, and East Germany) of Czechoslovakia
5 November	United States: Richard Nixon (Republican) elected President

1969

17 April	Czechoslovakia: Gustav Husak replaces Dubcek as First Secretary of the Communist Party.

1970

19 March	Erfurt meeting of West German Chancellor Brandt and East German premier Stoph. The beginning of German *Ostpolitik*
26 March	Four-Power talks on Berlin
16 April	Opening of the SALT (Strategic Arms Limitations) talks in Vienna
19 June	Great Britain: Edward Heath (Conservative) becomes Prime Minister
18 November	German–Polish Treaty of Reconciliation initialled (signed 7 December)
15–19 December	Rioting in Polish cities, particularly Gdansk
20 December	Poland: Edward Gierek replaces Gomulka as First Secretary of the Communist Party

1972

22–30 May	Moscow Summit Conference (Nixon, Brezhnev)
26 May	SALT interim agreement signed in Moscow
3 June	Four Power Agreement on Berlin
21 November	SALT II talks open in Geneva
21 December	Basic Treaty signed between West and East Germany

1973

19–24 June	Washington summit conference (Nixon, Brezhnev)
3 July	Opening of CSCE (Conference on Security and Co-operation in

Europe) in Helsinki

30 October — Opening of MBFR (Mutual and Balanced Force Reductions) talks in Vienna

1974

4 March — Great Britain: Harold Wilson (Labour) becomes Prime Minister

27 June — Moscow summit conference (Nixon, Brezhnev)

3 July–9 August United States: resignation of President Nixon, succeeded by Gerald Ford.

23–24 November Vladivostok summit conference (Ford, Brezhnev)

1975

27 May — Czechoslovakia: President Svoboda removed and replaced by Gustav Husak (29 May), who remains first secretary of the communist party

1 August — Helsinki Final Act signed at end of CSCE talks

1976

5 April — Great Britain: James Callaghan (Labour) becomes Prime Minister

2 November — United States: Jimmy Carter (Democrat) elected President.

1977

24 May — Soviet Union: Podgorny removed as President

4 October — CSCE follow-up meeting opens at Belgrade (met until 9 March 1978)

16 June — Soviet Union: Brezhnev elected President

1979

18 June — SALT II treaty signed (not ratified by US Senate) at Vienna summit conference (Carter, Brezhnev)

4 May — Great Britain: Margaret Thatcher (Conservative) becomes Prime Minister

27 December — Soviet invasion of Afghanistan

1980

4 May — Yugoslavia: death of President Tito

14 August — Poland: strikes, particularly at Lenin shipyard in Gdansk led by Lech Walesa

31 August — Poland: Gdansk Agreements provide official recognition of the independent trade union, Solidarity

23 October	Soviet Union: Kosygin replaced as premier by Nikolai Tikhonov
4 November	United States: Ronald Reagan (Republican) elected president
11 November	CSCE follow-up meeting opens at Madrid

1981

11 February	Poland: Gen. Wojciech Jaruzelski replaces Giereck as Premier
13 May	Attempted assasination of Pope John Paul II
18 October	Poland: Gen. Jaruzelski replaces Stanislaw Kania as First Secretary of Communist Party (Polish United Workers' Party), remaining as Premier
30 November	INF (Intermediate-range Nuclear Forces) talks open in Geneva
10 December	Spain joins NATO (effective 30 May 1982)
13 December	Poland: martial law imposed

1982

30 June	Opening of START (Strategic Arms Reduction Talks) in Geneva
10 November	Soviet Union: death of President Brezhnev
12 November	Soviet Union: Yuri Andropov becomes General Secretary of Communist Party

1983

22 July	Poland: martial law lifted
16 June	Soviet Union: Andropov elected President
1 September	Soviet Union shoots down Korean Air Lines flight 007

1984

9 February	Soviet Union: death of President Andropov
13 February	Soviet Union: Konstantin Chernenko elected General Secretary of Communist Party
11 April	Soviet Union: Chernenko elected President

1985

10 March	Soviet Union: death of President Chernenko.
11 March	Soviet Union: Mikhail Gorbachev becomes General Secretary of the Communist Party of the Soviet Union
2 July	Soviet Union: Gromyko elected President, replaced as Foreign Minister by Edvard Shevardnadze
27 September	Soviet Union: Tikhonov replaced as premier by Nikolai Ryzhkov
12 November	Poland: Gen. Jaruzelski resigns as premier and becomes President (Chairman of the State Council).
19–21 November	Geneva summit conference (Reagan, Gorbachev)

1986

11–12 October	Reykjavik summit conference (Reagan, Gorbachev)

1987

8–10 December	Washington summit conference (Reagan, Gorbachev)
8 December	INF Treaty signed
17 December	Czechoslovakia: Milos Jakes succeeds Gustav Husak as General Secretary of the Communist Party

1988

8 February	Gorbachev announces Soviet intention to withdraw its military forces from Afghanistan
18 February	Soviet Union: Boris Yeltsin removed from Politburo
14 April	Geneva Accords on Afghanistan signed. The Soviet Union to withdraw half its forces by 15 August 1988, and the remainder by 15 February 1989
22 May	Hungary: Karoly Grosz succeeds Kadar as General Secretary of the Communist Party
29 May–2 June	Moscow Summit between President Reagan and General Secretary Gorbachev
1 October	Soviet Union: Gorbachev becomes President, replacing Andrey Gromyko
10 October	Czechoslovaka: resignation of Premier Lubomir Strougal, replaced by Ladislav Adamec (11 October)
8 November	United States: George Bush (Republican) elected President
23 November	Hungary: Miklos Nemeth becomes Premier, replacing Grosz who had become Communist Party General-Secretary

1989

11 January	Hungarian parliament allows independent parties
15 February	Soviet Union completes military withdrawal from Afghanistan
26 March	Soviet elections for new Congress of Peoples Deputies. Many Senior officials and military candidates lose to independents.
17 April	Poland: the trade union, Solidarity, is legalised
25 April	Gorbachev removes 110 officials from the Central Committee
2 May	Hungary begins to dismatle barbed-wire barriers on Austrian frontier.
3–4 June	Chinese government uses armed forces to surpress pro-Democracy movement.
4 June	Poland: Solidarity wins majority in parliamentary elections
16 June	Hungary: Imre Nagy ceremonially reburied
19 July	Poland: Gen. Jaruzelski elected President

25 July	Poland: President Jaruzelski invites Solidarity to join a coalition government
24 August	Poland: Tadeuz Mazowiecki becomes first non-Communist Premier since World War II.
10 September	Hungary: allows East German refugees to cross into Austria. Eventually 180,000 East Germans flee to West
7 October	Hungarian Communist Party dissolves itself, becoming the Hungarian Socialist Party
17 October	Hungarian parliament adopts new constitution guaranteeing multiparty elections
18 October	East Germany: Erich Honecker resigns and is replaced by Egon Krenz
23 October	Hungary adopts new constitution and alters name to the Republic of Hungary
25 October	Gorbachev renounces the Brezhnev Doctrine
3 November	Czechoslovakia opens borders for transit of East German refugees
7 November	East Germany: Premier Willy Stoph resigns, replaced by Hans Modrow
10 November	East German government begins to dismantle Berlin Wall
	Bulgaria: Todor Zhikov resigns as Secretary-General of Communist Party (held since 1954) and as President, succeeded by Petur Mladenov as Secretary-General of the Communist Party.
17 November	Bulgaria: Mladenov elected President.
20 November	Czechoslovakia: mass protests in Prague's Wenceslaus Square.
24 November	Czechoslovakia: Communist Party leadership resigns, including General Secretary Miklos Jakes who is replaced by Karel Urbanek
28 November	West German chancellor Kohl calls for German federation.
1 December	Gorbachev meets Pope John Paul II.
	East German parliament ends Communist Party's special status.
1–3 December	Malta summit conference (Gorbachev, Bush). Gorbachev states that 'the characteristics of the Cold War should be abandoned'
3 December	East Germany: resignation of entire Communist Politburo, including Krenz as party leader
6 December	East Germany: Egon Krenz resigns as head of state, replaced by Manfred Gerlach
7 December	Lithuanian parliament abolishes Communist Party's special status
	Czechoslovakia: resignation of communist-led government of Ladislav Adamec and new government formed by Marian Calfa (10 December)
8 December	East Germany: Gregor Gysi elected chairman of Communist Party.
10 December	Czechoslovakia: non-Communist government takes power. President Gustav Husak resigns
17 December	East Germany: communist party changes name from Socialist

Unity Party of Germany (SED) to Socialist Unity Party of Germany-Party of Democratic Socialism (SED-PDS)

22 December	Romania: Nicolae Ceaucescu overthrown, replaced with a National Salvation Council, and subsequently executed.
23 December	Brandenburg Gate reopened in Berlin
28 December	Latvian parliament abolishes Communist Party's special status
	Czechoslovak parliament elects Alexander Dubcek chairman
29 December	Czechoslovakia: Vaclav Havel elected President of and Dubcek elected speaker of federal assembly
30 December	Poland alters name to Republic of Poland

1990

15 January	Bulgaria: national assembly abolishes Communist Party's special status
28 January	Poland: communist party renamed Party of Social Democracy of the Polish Republic
2 February	Bulgaria: Alexsandr Lilov replaces Mladenov as chairman of the Communist Party.
3 February	Bulgaria: Andrey Lukanov appointed Premier replacing Georgei Atanasov
4 February	East Germany: communist party renamed Party of Democratic Socialism (PDS), previously renamed on 17 December 1989
23 February	Estonian Supreme Soviet abolishes 'leading role' of the Communist Party
11 March	Lithuania declared independence from the Soviet Union. Name altered to Lithuanian Republic and Vytautas Landsbergis elected President.
13 March	Soviet Union: Congress of People's Deputies abolishes 'leading role' of the Communist Party
14 March	Gorbachev elected first executive President of Soviet Union
18 March	East Germany: Christian Democratic Union led Alliance for Germany wins election
29 March	Czechoslovakia alters name to Czechoslovak Federative Republic in the Czech lands and the Czecho-Slovak Republic in Slovakia
3 April	Bulgaria: Mladenov elected President, resigning as Secretary-General of Communist Party, which is renamed Bulgarian Socialist Party
4 May	Latvian parliament votes for independence
20 May	Romania: Ion Iliescu elected President and National Salvation Front wins majority.
29 May	Soviet Union: Boris Yeltsin elected President of the RSFSR.
30 May–3 June	Washington summit (Gorbachev, Bush). First state visit by a Soviet leader to the United States

NOTES ON CONTRIBUTORS

David Armstrong is co-editor of *Diplomacy & Statecraft* and a member of the Graduate School of International Studies, University of Birmingham, of which he was founder and first Director. He has published books and articles on East Asian international relations and international organisation. He is currently completing a book on the revolutionary state in international society.

Ian Clark is Assistant Director of Studies in International Relations, University of Cambridge and, a Fellow of Selwyn College. His most recent publications are *Waging War* (OUP, 1988), *The Hierarchy of States* (CUP, 1989) and (with N.J. Wheeler) *The British Origins of Nuclear Strategy 1945–55* (OUP, 1989).

Christopher M. Davis is lecturer in Soviet Studies at the Centre for Russian and East European Studies at the University of Birmingham. He is the author of numerous articles on the Soviet economy and its defence sector, and is the co-editor of *Models of Disequilibrium and Shortage in Centrally Planned Economics* (1989).

Erik Goldstein is co-editor of *Diplomacy & Statecraft* and Senior Lecturer in International History and Director of the Graduate School of International Studies at the University of Birmingham. He is the author of *Winning the Peace: British Diplomatic Strategy, Peace Planning and the Paris Peace Conference, 1916–1920* (OUP, 1991).

Alan James is Head of the Department of International Relations at the University of Keele, having previously been Reader in International Relations at the London School of Economics. He has published widely on the United Nations and his more recent work is *Peacekeeping in International Politics* (London, Macmillan, for the International Institute of Strategic Studies).

Ieuan G. John is Emeritus Professor, University College of Wales, Aberystwyth, where he was formerly Woodrow Wilson Professor in International Politics. More recent publications include: Editor and contributor,. *EEC policy towards Eastern Europe*, (Saxon House, 1975); 'Cooperation among socialist states; CMEA and the Warsaw Pact', in *European Cooperation Today*, edited by K. Twitchet, (Europa Press, 1981); and articles on West Germany and the European Community.

Bennett Kovrig is professor and former chairman of political science at the University of Toronto. In 1987–88 he served as director of research and analysis at Radio Free Europe. He is the author of *The Myth of Liberation: East-Central Europe in U.S. Diplomacy and Politics since 1941* (Baltimore, 1973), *Communism in Hungary from Kun to Kadar* (Stanford, 1979), and *Sphere of Influence: America's Dilemmas in Eastern Europe* (forthcoming 1990).

Richard Langhorne is Director of the Centre of International Studies at the University of Cambridge and a fellow of St. John's College. He is the author of *The Collapse and the Concert of Europe* (1981) and editor of *Diplomacy and Intelligence during the Second World War* (1985).

Pierre-Henri Laurent is Professor of History at Tufts University. He has contributed to various journals on contemporary European diplomacy and to *International Fascism* (1979), *The Reshaping of Europe* (1984), *The United States and the European Community* (1988), and *Technology Challenges and Opportunities of United Europe* (1990) among others. He is an Executive Committee member of the European Community Studies Association

Uri Ra'anan is University Professor and Director of the Institute for the Study of Conflict, Ideology and Policy at Boston University, and Fellow of the Russian Research Center at Harvard University. He is the author of numerous books on Soviet affairs, including the recently published *Inside the Apparat* and *The Soviet Empire and the Challenge of Nuclear and Democratic Movements*.

Gerald Segal is a Research Fellow at the Royal Institute of International Affairs, Reader in International Relations at Bristol University, and Editor of *The Pacific Review*. His publications include authorship of *The Great Power Triangle* (Macmillan, 1982) *Defending China* (OUP, 1985), *Sino-Soviet Relations After Mao* (IISS, 1985), *The Guide to the World Today* (Simon and Schuster, 1987, 1988), *Rethinking the Pacific* (OUP, 1990), *The Soviet Union and the Pacific* (Unwin/Hyman, 1990).

John A. Thompson is Lecturer in History at the University of Cambridge, and a Fellow of St. Catharine's College. His publications include *Progressivism* (British Association for American Studies, 1979) and *Reformers and War: American Progressive Publicists and the First World War* (Cambridge University Press, 1987). He is currently working on a study of the character of US foreign policy, and an essay, 'The Exaggeration of American Vulnerability: the Anatomy of a Tradition' will appear in *Diplomatic History* in 1991.

R.J. Vincent is Montague Burton Professor of International Relations at the London School of Economics, having previously been a Fellow of Nuffield College, Oxford. He is author of numerous books and articles on international relations, including *Human Rights in International Relations*, (1986).

Geoffrey Warner was formerly Professor of European Humanities at the Open University, having previously held the Chair of Modern History at Leicester University and the Chair of European Studies at the University of Hull. He has published widely on modern international history and is currently writing a book on the origins and early history of the cold war.

INDEX